WORKER:
Last of a Dying Breed

AN AUTOBIOGRAPHY
By: Brian Logan

Copyright © 2009 Brian Logan
All rights reserved.
ISBN: 1-4392-5996-8
ISBN-13: 9781439259962
Visit www.booksurge.com to order additional copies.

Worker: Last of a Dying Breed
Autobiography of Brian Logan

Chapter 1	Fight or Flee	1
Chapter 2	Rebirth	41
Chapter 3	Growing in the Business	57
Chapter 4	Wrestling, Weeping, and Women	71
Chapter 5	Hotlanta and WCW	93
Chapter 6	Intolerable Independents	115
Chapter 7	Puerto Rico	135
Chapter 8	The Big Push	169
Chapter 9	Blue Ridge Promotions	243
Chapter 10	A Shot in the Night	253
Chapter 11	Religion	285
Chapter 12	Jail Bird	287
Chapter 13	Reaching My Apex	297
Chapter 14	Conquering the World	305

For my son Dylan.
There is not a single moment of any day that you are not on my mind.
This book is so you will know who your father was.
I love you. I always have & will.

Forward

As you will learn from this book, Brian Logan had a rocky road towards carving out a career for himself in Professional wrestling. In my mind, many of his obstacles stemmed from two things—the place and date of his birth.

West Virginia is not a place noted for providing a variety of career opportunities, and pro wrestling is harder than most to break into. As well, the law enforcement community in the state has elements of an evil Mayberry, which Brian notes has caused him consternation from an early age.

The decade of the 90's was not an easy time to break into wrestling, not if you wanted to do it for a living. The territories were mostly gone. The independents often did not draw well. If Brian had been born 15 years earlier and broken in, in 1979, not 1994, with his size, talent and dedication, he would have worked steadily all over the country for those 15 years. But when Smoky Mountain Wrestling established itself in his area, he took the chance and leaped in. If I can say

I played a small part in helping him get established in our sport, I'm happy to do so.

Fifteen years later, Brian can truthfully say he's come farther than anyone would have predicted—He's wrestled for all the major organizations, all over the U.S., Canada, and Puerto Rico, branched out into booking and promoting, and became the traveling World Champion of the AWA. I will always appreciate his contribution to OVW. I hope you will enjoy his story as much as I did.

    Jim Cornette
    Louisville, KY
    September 2009

We are looking through the window of life.
Of which we peer in from the other side.
A world of success, a world of strife.
A world just waiting, but only for the taking.
By your rule only should they abide?
Should we sit and pay attention?
Should we start the opposition?
What do you see when you look through,
The window to the other side?

    Brian Kees
    February 3rd, 1992

After sixteen years, the night I had dreamt about was finally here. I found a secluded place, on the stage at the Memorial Building, where I could get dressed. Just on the other side of the curtain I could hear the fans cheer the match that was currently in the ring. Other wrestlers could be seen talking and joking around. I laced up my boots real tight. I found myself thinking back at the long journey that had placed me at this exact moment in time. I recalled the troubles I had experienced growing up, as well as my first breaks in the wrestling business. Most of all, my time I spent behind bars in prison. Tonight was my night. It was my turn. I stood and put my tights on. It was truly the biggest night of my entire life. In a few short moments I would be wrestling for the World's Heavyweight Championship. The little boy had grown up. He had truly become a man. I was afraid no longer. My life was about to change.

Fayetteville, WV April 18th, 2008

Chapter 1: Fight or Flee

Some stories are more easily told than others. Like the ones that parents tell when their children bring home their first girl or boyfriends to meet the family. These are usually light antidotes used to break the ice. Sometimes they can be embarrassing, but no real harm has been inflicted. Others are tales of sorrow or tragedy designed to warn others not to repeat things of the past. Most stories, however, are basically there to entertain. I feel that my story fits all of these examples. Parts of this book will be easy to write, while others will be an emotional roller coaster.

Oak Hill was the type of place that would be seen right at home in the movie frontiers of the old west. At the turn of the twentieth century it was considered as violent and corrupt as any town in the country. Saloons full of gambling coal miners and common working men led to great danger. Unrestricted firearm regulations and free flowing liquor was the forerunner to the shoot first and ask questions later attitude. On May 15th 1904, The Cincinnati Enquirer published an article that labeled Fayette County as the "County where they shoot a man everyday."

Vicky Trout was a thirteen year old pregnant girl in 1974. She was impregnated by an older man whose last name was Pennington. H er family, embarrassed by an unwed and pregnant teen, forced her to leave West Virginia for Michigan. Vicky moved to Flint to live with her Aunt. Before she left arrangements were made though her family to have a local West Virginia couple adopt the unborn child. On October 2nd, 1974, Brian Thomas Kees was born at one thirty seven a.m. The couple promptly adopted and brought the child back to West Virginia. My birth certificate has the names of the adopted parents, Kathryn Ann and William Thomas Kees. Kathy was twenty six. Bill was thirty.

The economy in West Virginia was, and still is, based on the coal mining industry. In the fall of 2003, it was reported that forty eight present of people employed in West Virginia worked at Wal-Mart. This is a good representation of the state of an economy that depends on coal mines as the top employer, when most of the residents work in a separate industry.

In 1974, my father was no different. Bill, as he was called, was the youngest of nine siblings. The men of the family were taught that you could do what you will at night, but be ready to work the next day. No exceptions. Along with his brothers Robert, Bannon, and half brother John, who was the child of his sister Veda, and was raised as a brother not a nephew, went to work, while the girls stayed at home. This was common place in those times. Bill worked in the coal mines, and several odd jobs, though the early years of his life.

Working in the mines is a tough way to make a living. Small places, long hours, and poor ventilation were combined with moderate to low pay to complicate the day. Work, as such, left my father wanting more. He was offered a job as a union rep for the U.M.W.A.(United Mine Workers of America) District seventeen. From the mid- seventies though the early eighties this was the happiest time of my father's life. He had a family, good job, and was moving up in life.

The job was for him to be an arbitrator between the miners and the coal companies. From the stories that are told, he was very good at labor relations. There were more rings on the ladder to climb. Bill wanted success. He longed to provide more material things for his family, and himself. This aggressive attitude would be the key to his success. It would also lead to his downfall later in life.

John Douglas Webb, my mother's father, was a WWII war hero. He raised his daughter in a Christian home. J.D., as he was called, was given an award by President Ronald Regan for serving in the Navy. He was a kind man, but was extremely strict, and disciplined her anytime physically when he thought it was needed. My mother's childhood was hard for her. It was buffered by her mother Gladys Bradshaw Webb. My grandmother was as close to a saint, as you will ever find, on God's earth.

Kathy worked as office personnel at Oak Hill Hospital for a few years, after it was first built. She quit the job after the adoption to be a mother. She would later return to work with several different jobs. They were all in the medical field, usually as an office manager.

I don't have too many memories of my early childhood. There was one that definitely stands out. The local wrestling company was based out of Oak Hill's WOAY television studio. Every Saturday night wrestling would be live on TV. This, like many other regional programming, was a mainstay for years. Everyone in town watched; because with the advent of television it was the only show on in the time slot. People made wrestling a way of life in Oak Hill. Whether or not you were a fan, you watched in the early days because they only had one channel. By the late seventies names like Dick "The Bruiser", The Madrid Brothers, and The Cuban Assassin were the main attraction. My parents were living in a friend's house on Summerlee road in Oak Hill. The Sport was a local bar located a mile from the house. It was a popular place to drink, gamble, play pool, and get just about anything you wished. My father, and his father, along with his brothers, had long been spending time there. This just happened to be the place that all the wrestlers went after the matches. My father became friends with some of the wrestlers. It was by total coincidence, as they never attended the live matches. Dick "The Bruiser" became good friends with my father and occasionally came by the house to drink. At age three, or so, I was being bounced on the knee of a wrestling legend. I can remember how big he was, and how strong he looked.

There is one memory that I received as folklore, but is well known in Oak Hill. Kim O'Neal was a local business owner. He had made a deal with the Madrid Brothers, Jean and Jan. They wanted to mainstream the angle, or storyline, to reach a larger fan base. Like when WCW used Dennis Roadman and Jay Leno in a series of matches. This was on a lot smaller scale though. They made a deal that a challenge would be made and accepted between Jan Madrid and O'Neal. They would promote three matches with O'Neal winning the first, and Madrid the next two. Kim owned a new bar called "Kim's Palace". They thought it would be great for the new bar's business, and draw a crowd for wrestling. Kim went around hyping the event, and talking trash. He bragged about what would happen in the first fight, and how he would be the winner. Keep in mind Kim O'Neal was not a wrestler or even "smart" to the wrestling business. All he knew was that he was going to beat one of the most feared men in West Virginia. The night came and the bar was sold out! The two men entered the arena and the ring. This was long before music entrances and all the pageantry you see today. American Independent Wrestling(AIW) was not a group that was affiliated with the National Wrestling Alliance, the sanctioning body that ruled wrestling with an iron fist. It was a low budget, or should I say no budget, wrestling company. The bell rings and the men meet in mid-ring. Madrid, aware of what had been said about the outcome, looks right in the eye of O'Neal and says, "Bet's off". Kim swallows a deep breath and replies, "What?" "The bet is off!" Returns Madrid. Then he proceeded to beat the ever living hell out of Kim O'Neal. It generated a sell out that night for wrestling, and I imagine a hefty pay off for Madrid. Needless to say the two other matches never occurred. The town of Oak Hill left the matches that night knowing that wrestling was real. At least for Kim O'Neal.

I have had the privilege to have become friends with the "most hated man in W.V. wrestling history" Jean Madrid. Who was the in-ring brother of Jan. Gypsy Joe, as he is known in other wrestling territories, is a true national treasure to our profession. He was inducted in to the West Virginia Pro Wrestling Hall of Fame in April of 2008. Back in 1994, when I first met him and wrestled him, he beat the hell out of me too. I, like the fans in Oak Hill that night, left the arena thinking wrestling was real! I am honored to have spent time with Jean. I have learned so much from him. He is a true legend!

All the memories from my childhood weren't as pleasurable as that one. One Christmas we had a family get together at my grandmother Kees's house. My grandfather, Homer Kees, died when I was little, so I don't have any memories of him. The entire Kees family was there for Christmas. There were like twenty or so people there. Everyone was talking telling stories, asking about relatives, and the children played together. One of my cousins, Eric, had a red fire engine. There were six or so of us trying to play with one toy. I didn't get as long of a turn with it as I would have liked, so as a small child I pouted. Instead of just having to deal with it, my father took me right on the spot to a local department store and bought me one. When I returned the other kids and parents were not happy about it at all. They saw it as my father showing off, and me being a spoiled brat. At the time I didn't think much about it. During high school, and when I first started in the wrestling business, I was best friends with my cousin Craig. He would remind me of this event several times over the years. That was the first time the family started looking at me different. I was a child at the time, and was found guilty from an act of love, and showing off on my parent's part. Not mine. I did not see myself as different or special, but I was beginning to be treated as if I did.

My generation was made up of latch key kids. When I started school it was just what occupied my day until I could get back in front of the television. My Grandmother Webb would keep me on weekends. She would read to me from encyclopedias. Most children learn to read from Dr. Seuss, but I learned to read from the Encyclopedia Britannica. So, when I started school I could already read and write on a higher level. I once took an IQ test and scored 171. They tell me this is the genius level, but with some of the decisions I would later make, that level is questionable. With all that early knowledge and extra learning I never could spell a bit. Spelling was just plain hard for me, but math I was good at. I have used it to count my paydays, or lack of paydays ever since.

In 1983, The Iron Sheik beat Bob Backland for the World Wrestling Federation Championship. About a month later, Hulk Hogan beat the Shiek in Madison Square Gardens. Hogan was the biggest thing that ever happened to wrestling, and wrestling was the biggest thing that ever happened to me.

West Virginia had no real territory of it's own in the eighties. It was a part of the Mid Atlantic territory, promoted by Jim Crocket Promotions. Georgia Championship Wrestling also promoted live events there. Located not far from Pittsburg, PA, it was just barely on the outskirts of the W.W.F.'s area. I.C.W. was promoted by the Poffos. They promoted in the southwest of West Virginia, but not often. After 1984, Randy Savage, whose father was Angelo Poffo, was off to wrestle for the Jarrett's office in Memphis. This led eventually to his arrival in the W.W.F. Being just dead center in the middle, thanks to the Mason Dixon Line, we would receive them all on television. I watched every second of it for the next six years. Watch does not do it justice, I absorbed every second of it.

In total around sixteen hours a week could be viewed. Fridays would be the American Wrestling Association with stars like Nick Bockwinkle and Curt Hennig. In fact, they would run syndicated shows on ESPN every weekday afternoons at four thirty. That would later turn into World Class Wrestling in that time slot. On Saturdays it would all start at eight a.m. with the National Wrestling Alliance. Followed by a different N.W.A. show at noon. Just before noon, World Class would air at eleven. At four o'clock Mid Atlantic would air for an hour. Then at six the big two hour N.W.A. on WTBS would air. This was the forerunner to W.C.W. Saturday Night. Later that night at ten, W.W.F. would air its Superstars program. If that was not enough to fill up a day, and it wasn't, once a month we could see Saturday Night's Main Event on NBC. Sundays were filled also. All American would air on USA at noon. Followed by the Monday night W.W.F. show. This was the time slot that led into what is now Monday Night Raw. Which is the longest running episodic show in the history of television. For a while we even had Tuesday Night Titans, W.W.F.'s version of The Johnny Carson Show. My week, for years, revolved around watching pro wrestling every single day.

A lot of guys write, or talk about, those days. How much traveling and work they had. All of the great times and experiences they shared. I love all of those great books and tales, but one of the reasons I am writing this book is for the generations of wrestlers and fans that were babies in that era and did not get to experience the times talked about by other writers.

The first live match that I attended was at the Raleigh County Armory in Beckley, WV. The main event was Ricky Morton and Robert Gibson, the Rock n' Roll Express, versus the Midnight Express, Bobby Eaton and Stan Lane. The Midnight Express would have Manager, Jim Cornette, in their corner. Little would I know at the time, but Jim Cornette would later have more influence in my life than anyone I have ever known. This combination was the hottest tag team angle in the history of the N.W.A. They had the sold out crowd, including myself, chanting "Rock n' Roll" all night.

At the matches that night my mother bought out the souvenir stand, or so it seemed. I had every single t-shirt with pictures of Jimmy Garvin, Nikita Koloff, Four Horsemen, and Dusty Rhodes. She also got me the magazines. I was a wrestling magazine fanatic. I would read about guys like Jerry Lawler, Lonnie Maine, and Mil Mascaras. Guys I would rarely see wrestling in my area. I wore the t-shirts everyday to school. In fact, I think she threw them out just so I would wear new clothes. As far as the magazines go, I flipped though them so many times they eventually fell apart.

It was not the first live event that would make history. It would be the second live event that would be famous in wrestling circles for many years. I returned the following month to Beckley to watch the tag team rematch from the month before. As Cornette and his bad guys (heels) were leaving the ring that night the crowd was extra riled up. They had just beaten the hell out of Ricky Morton and gotten away with it. The angry mob wanted to seek out revenge on the perpetrators, especially this one guy who was blocking the isle way. He hurled insults at the villains, then he spit on them. Stan Lane went to protect Cornette. He took a swing at the guy. The guy ducked. Stan connected anyway with the old man standing behind the insulter. Stan broke his jaw! The fans, seeing this poor old man get pummeled, rioted. Jimmy and the Express fought their way to the locker room. In the end, Cornette got sued. He settled out of court. The old man got paid. The jerk that started the whole thing got out of an ass kicking that he much deserved. I thought it was the greatest thing I had ever seen, at that time.

Jim Cornette had a bodyguard, Big Bubba Rodgers, who also went by Big Bossman in the W.W.F. He would wear a 1950's style hat to the ring. So, naturally I had to have one too. I would wear my t-shirts and this hat to school everyday. I would get picked on by the other kids for wearing them, but I didn't care. One day, however, was different. This kid started picking on me. You know the type. The ones that look like they are thirty in fifth grade. His name was Marty Treadway. He had dirty blonde hair. Oils stains poorly decorated his jeans. He always wore a black jacket that matched his oversized black combat boots. I was scared. He was short, but I took this as wiry and tough. Looking back now, I was so much bigger than him; I could have destroyed him if I had only stood up to him. I was afraid. If what happened next wouldn't have happened I would have probably been a different person today. He informed me that at lunch he was going to kick my ass. It was raining hard outside. When it rained they would have recess in the gym. So the entire fifth and six grade class was inside the gym. So, there I was in the hallway of the gym trying to figure out how to not let this thug kick my ass like a Mulkey Brother in a TV match. There was no avoiding it, there he was. I had two choices fight or flee. The kids were not allowed on the gym floor during recess, so they all sat in the bleachers talking and eating. For me it seemed like no one was absent that day. Faced with the possibility of getting my ass kicked, I ran for my life. I ran straight into the gym, with Marty on my tail as if he was the Roadrunner. How I stayed ahead of him I will never know. I finally ran out of room on the gym floor, so I slid like a baseball player going in for the score at home plate. He miss judged and over shot and ran right into the wall. The class all laughed, but not at him. At me for running. They did not understand that I had out smarted him, and that he looked like the fool. Instead they teased me for running away. Children are cruel. It is a proven fact. I realize now that being scared was natural, but I had never been in a fight. Everybody faces bullies. I just felt that my credibility as a non-scared cool guy was shot. I decided shortly after this, that I would never run or flee again. I would stay and fight for my ground. This is the fuel I used to motivate myself for my entire career.

The old saying, "You've got to stand for something or you will fall for anything" does not always apply. As I recalled this story to my good friend, Aaron Tippon, years later, he explained that sometimes discretion is a better part of valor. Shortly after the Marty Treadway race across the gym floor, a friend of mine talked me into asking a girl to go out with me. When the first one said no, he talked me into asking another. Then another. When I asked the first girl out I wasn't serious. When she said, "No", I got embarrassed. Not wanting to back down I continued to ask other girls out. One by one they all said, "No". It was brutal. They all turned me down, every single female on the playground that day. I was crushed. This time it was my own doing. My so called buddy thought this was hilarious. Time after time I would deliver my best line, and then make that long trek back to my friend. I repeated this process again and again, and oh yes, again. Word got around what I was doing. So, there I walked; this fat, obnoxious, dorky guy making a fool of his self. Some of the girls got a kick out of it. Some of them just kicked me. I can laugh at it now. It was pretty funny. Here is the funny part, what if they all would have said, "Yes"? That might have been worse right? Hell no! That would have been great. It did not happen so I was just humiliated. Why did I continue to ask them out? It clearly crushed me at the time. The fact was that fear fueled me into doing something extremely stupid; no matter how bad I looked.

Eighth grade came and it was a whole different outlook for me. I had just saw my first concert, Kiss's Crazy Knights tour. This was awesome! For some reason in life, when it gets so hard that you can't go on, a cool breeze blows though and makes things tolerable again. In this case the cool breeze was my first girlfriend. Her name was Carrie. Carrie was a tall blonde with Molly Ringwald type hair, which was in style back then. She was very smart and had slender build. Her dad, Tommy, was extremely strict on her. And, looking back at how things ended up for her I can see why. That can be discussed in her book not mine. I remember we went on our first date to see the movie, Over Board, with Kurt Russel and Goldie Hawn. My mom drove us, which was pretty cool considering that she was a mom. Her dad was going to pick us up. The movie was good, but my first kiss was even better. Defiantly for me, you will have to read her book to see how I did. She was the main event of first kisses, as far as I was concerned. After the movie Tommy picked us up. He asked if we liked the movie, which we did. Then he found out it was an "R" rated movie. This was way before PG13 (the rating not the tag team), or any thing else like that. Tommy was livid, a real jerk. He grounded her right there in front of me. No more movies for us. This started a long standing tradition, just recently broken, of my girlfriends' parents not liking me. Our social interaction was limited to a few ball games and dances. Carrie eventually broke up with me. Why? Because that's what kids do. It tore me up for a couple of years, but things prevailed I discovered that there are a lot, and I mean a lot, of women out there. I saw Carrie a few years after I graduated from high school. I was already in the wrestling business. She was working at a local restaurant while she was in college. I will talk more on the subject later of the "power of TV", but she had seen me on TV and talked as if we had never broken up. Nothing happened, but damn if she did grow up to be a hot looking lady. Almost as hot as the crowd that night in Beckley.

I discovered sports in High school. Even though I was overweight, I feel I was a natural athlete. I had been playing baseball ever since I was old enough for Little League. As a kid I always wanted to be a baseball player. My cousin Eric, I spoke about him before, had a good opportunity to play for the Cincinnati Reds. He had broken his arm when he was little, and by the time he got his shot, his arm wouldn't let him compete. I always saw myself playing baseball. It was a game I understood. To this day I am a huge lifelong Chicago Cubs fan.

My freshman year I was six foot one inches tall and weighed two hundred and forty one pounds. I weighed this the entire time I was in high school. In fact, my weight never changed until I became a pro wrestler. I was always bothered by my weight. Naturally, everyone thought I should play football. Everyone but me, that is. Football is a game of numbers and slots. Each slot has a number, and you match up numbers to find holes to run the ball through. I just never got into that whole thing. I played two seasons in high school, but it just wasn't my game.

During my freshman year in high school, my friend, Stephen Gravely, and I founded the Oak Hill High School wrestling program. Up until then Fayetteville, the neighboring town, was the only local school with a team. On the day of the first practice, forty three people tried out in the field house under the football stadium. Coach Aylor turned up the heat in the room to ninety degrees. This made the rank, stale smell of the football jerseys waft though the entire place. On the second day we had fifteen left. By the start of the season we had a team of nine. There were thirteen weight classes, we barely had enough for a team. We lost most meets by forfeit, before we ever got on the mat, because we gave up so many points.

What I am about to tell right now is extremely hard for me to admit. I feel I must come clean. I was not a great armature wrestler. There I said it! The charade is over! It was one of those things that was no one's fault. Our coach, Frank Aylor, was a decent wrestler, from what I gathered, at Virginia Tech. He was burdened with the large task of starting a wrestling program. Frank taught Masonry at the Vo-Tech center. Most of the team was his Masonry students. He also was the freshman and Junior Varsity football coach. Other than his time at Virginia Tech, some several odd years ago, he had no experience as a wrestling coach. Let me state this, Coach Aylor gave me something priceless, something that helped me more than anything when I started my wrestling career. He taught me the basics. I had a solid foundation that he instilled in me, that enabled me to learn the pro game faster. Too many times, now days, a kid starts out wrestling wanting to do power bombs and moonsaults. He has no concept of wrestling, only showmanship. I had a great base to build off of, for the pro that would later train me. The number one problem that held up my armature career was that we went half speed in practice. We never went full on. So, when we were at a meet, we were not prepared. It never caught on that this was war. Kill or be killed! If our team would have been more aggressive, we would have done a whole lot better.

I wrestled four seasons in high school. One season was cut short due to me catching Mono (the kissing disease, coincidence? Yeah, probably!) My first and only letter in high school was for wrestling. I was a letterman my freshman year. This was a huge deal, because wrestling was a varsity sport. The only other varsity sport you could letter in, as a freshman, was football. You had to be a junior to get one. I lettered as a freshman. Pretty cool!

A few years earlier my father was in an accident. This event changed my life completely. It was the winter of 1986. My grandfather had just passed away that August. That winter a terrible blizzard blew through the east coast. School had been canceled, and I spent the entire time at my grandmother's house. As usual, I was watching wrestling that Saturday. "Handsome" Jimmy Valiant, the "Boogie Woogie Man", was in full stride in his interview about Paul Jones's Army. "Brother this and Brother that; Alright, Alright!", he screamed, just as my grandmother walks into the room. She made me turn the TV off. She couldn't stand to hear the wrestlers scream and holler. What? Turn "Handsome" Jimmy off? No way! He might kill Paul Jones right there, and I would miss it. So I did what I had to do. I called my parents and told them I had to come home right away. I figured I could leave during a commercial, and be home before "Boogie Woogie" wrestled. The blizzard would be my Waterloo. My mom explained it would take time to get there, but at least she talked my grandmother into letting me continue to watch. When my father was cleaning the snow off the car, he slipped and fell. He hit his head on the top of the car door extremely hard. We would find out, a year later, that he had suffered a concussion. This is what began his health problems. Had I not called him to come to pick me up, he might not have hit his head.

His heath problems would later change everyone's lives that he was connected to. It took time, but the side effects would destroy our entire family. Dad had suffered from Post Concussion Syndrome. He would suffer a permanent migraine headache which led to seizures. He would be nearly totally confined to the house, even to this day.

Most children in the Eighties were "latch key kids". Kids would keep a key on their shoe lace to let themselves into their houses after school, because their parents were gone, still at work. In most cases this was unavoidable and safe. Kids would gain independence on their own. In some cases it allows the child to become the adult and do as he pleases.

I would arrive home, after school, at around three o' clock. I lived outside of town about two miles. There was no crime in my neighborhood. I would change clothes and grab a coke, my dad's favorite, a bag of chips, and head for the TV. I think one of the reasons I grew so much was the food I ate. I was constantly fed carbs like pizza and hamburgers. I think the overload of carbs led to the size I would later gain. The AWA would air on ESPN everyday at four thirty. I loved watching Nick Bockwinkle, Curt Hennig, and Larry Zybisco fight tooth and nail over the World's title. This would also be the first time I saw Jerry Lawler wrestle.

My good friend, Steven Gravely, would come by and we would watch the AWA and we would imitate the moves on each other. One day the phone rang, and it was a neighbor from down the road. Mr. Fox owned a farm just outside of Oak Hill. My dad had wrecked his truck into his fence. He explained that dad was having a seizure and didn't know what to do. I tried not to panic, and call the family for help. No one was home. I was helpless, feeling that my dad was dying less than a mile away and I could not do anything to help. My mom was late coming home from work. Once she got there, I told her what happened. She left, and it would be hours before anyone came and told me anything. Things like this would begin happening on a regular basis.

One time dad and I were at the mall and he had a seizure. He leaned up against the wall in the mall. I did not know what to do. They had not told me what was wrong with him, or what to do if he did get sick. He couldn't talk or move. He had a friend that worked at Baskin Robins. So, I went over and asked him if he knew my father. The man thought I was playing a joke on him. I told him he was my dad and that he was in trouble. The man looked up and saw my dad collapse to the floor. Dad finally came out of it. We called a relative, then went home like nothing had ever happened.

I started playing football my sophomore year. I never understood football. I wasn't very good at it, but I went out for the team anyway. I guess I thought I would get a date from being on the team. Maybe it was just to shut people up from telling me I should play because I was so big. I practiced for a couple of weeks, or two and I just didn't like it. I wasn't that good at it. My dad finally had my mom call the coach and she told him that I couldn't practice because I had to stay home to take care of him. I could go to the evening practices and remain on the team. The Coach took the entire team aside and told them that I would be on the team, but never play. That I had to stay home with my sick father, and I just wanted to be apart of the team. This did not do me any favors with the other boys on the team. This was about thirty of my only friends.

Half way through the sophomore year I started seeing Chris Anna. She had these long legs and strawberry blonde hair. The relationship was very serious. That is until her parents moved away to Conway, S.C. She lived with her grandmother, in the middle of town, until the school year was over. My cousin Craig was dating her cousin Susan. So, Craig and I would sneak in through a window after her grandmother passed out drunk. I began to realize the main motivation to what would later be named "The Player". Wrestling promoters would give me the name, but at age fifteen Chris Anna gave me an introduction to the desire.

I would later run in to her after I had been in the wrestling business. I was on my way to a concert on my day off. She was working a McDonalds. I hadn't seen her in years. We connected again that night after the concert. It was like we never missed a beat. That was the last time I saw her. I haven't talked to her since. Things like that would occur all the time to me.

One night, we hired a cab to pick up Chris Anna and Susan and drive them to my house. This was typical of the stupid stuff we got away with. The cab dropped them off at the Church above my house. We snuck the girls into my house. My parents were upstairs asleep. We had scored some Mad Dog 20/20 earlier, and served it up to the ladies as if it were Crystal. It was so bad that Craig and I wouldn't even drink this stuff. The girls drank the entire bottle. They got so drunk, and loud, we had to get them out of the house. We called the cab to get them to take them home. Craig and I helped the girls up the hill to the church and waited. And Waited. And then we waited some more! That no good cabbie just left us! So, we had to walk the girls two miles to their house. They were shit faced drunk. Singing, telling us they loved us. Craig practically carried Susan the whole way. When we finally got home dad was waiting on us. He told us that next time to wake him up and that he would drive us, instead of us walking drunk across town.

Another time, Craig and I, once again, snuck into Chris Anna's grandmother's house. Grandma was passed out on cooking cherry. Craig and Susan went into one room, and Chris Anna and I went into the other. Time had passed and it was time to leave. I put on a robe, and walked down the hall to tell Craig to wrap it up so we could go. The four of us talked for a little bit, and I went back to our room to change. One problem the door was locked. My clothes were in the room! There was no key! I was stuck like a naked rat. Craig and I hid in his room while the girls tried to get the door open. I was so scared. They made enough noise to wake the dead. They eventually pried the lock with a knife and I got my clothes. We didn't get caught! Imagine if that old drunk woman would have seen me in her house naked with her granddaughter.

Another time, dad dropped me off. I snuck in. By this time I was a pro at it. He was coming back to pick me up at a certain time. This was long before everyone had cell phones. I fell asleep. Dad was circling the block for hours. It was daylight by now. Granny could be awake at any minute. Dad was even trying to gently blow the horn. I woke and snuck out just in time. I never got caught. Her grandmother would pass away later that year. I liked granny! I always had a great time at her house!

I received my driver's license in the 1991. That, too, would be a situation. I had gotten my learners permit. I talked my parents into letting me take the car out. I asked a girl named Laura, whom I had wanted to date for a while, if she wanted to go for a ride. She did. There we were cruising through Oak Hill when I noticed it was getting warmer. The car fogged up. Not from any thing cool. I just didn't know you had to keep the air on, because even in the summer with the windows up and talking the windshield gets foggy. I didn't know how to turn the air on. I fumbled around and finally found it. I had swerved, however, when I leaned down to turn it on. We got pulled over by the Oak Hill City cops. It must have looked like Cheech and Chong had been in there, but it was only from lack of air. The cops arrested me and took her home. Her dad definitely did not appreciate that. They impounded the car. I didn't get into much trouble, after all my parents had let me take the car out.

I got my first job in summer of 1991. I became a lifeguard at the Fayette County 4-H camp. I was the youngest of five guys that worked there. Most of whom were in college and much older than me. We were all inseparable that summer. This was also a time for me that wrestling cycled out for me. I was a teenager, and had a job and license. This is the age group where most wrestling fans discover other things. Usually the business cycles in a ten year up, and five year down period. This is based on the economy, different

Presidents, and the folding of territories. However, the wrestling business looses the sixteen to a twenty one market due to boys and girls finally discovering life. The wrestling business will loose fans from around sixteen to twenty five years of age simply due to hormones. They all want to get drunk and laid.

The summer was so much fun for me. They older guys like Jeff Tanner, Jim Buck Jackson, Bryant Switzer, and Doug Fitzgerald taught me a lot in life. They taught me the basics. These basics were much different than what I had learner earlier, but just as important in my career. They taught me social skills. Not all of the skills were good ones, but skills none the less. People wanted to hang out with us. We were fun, the in- crowd. That was new for me. They helped me overcome my shyness and feelings of inadequacy. They did not care about the things that happened in school, or on a ball field. They were older and were also not petty. They did not know me when those things happened, so they accepted me for who I was. I can honestly say they were the only pals I every really had. They liked me for me. Doug " Fidge" Fitzgerald and I are still friends and hang out. I think that is why we all had so much fun. We were just ourselves, partying and having a good time. Nothing else got in the way.

We partied all summer. Like the time we had a blowout at Jeff's girlfriend's house and her parents came home. We all hid in the shower, keg and all. It was like you would see in the movies. They walked in, most people scattered like cockroaches when the lights come on. Jeff, myself, and the rest were caught red handed in the shower. No harm done.

Every time wasn't so laughable. I was dating a girl that was two years older than me. Her name was Tammy. I thought it was cool to be dating a girl who was eighteen. We all hung out and dated in a group. I liked her and things were going fine. We had had some small fight, and broke up for a week, but then got back together. The following week, not seven days later, her sister, April, came to the pool and was laying it on real strong. She was flirting and giving me compliments. Even though she was younger than me, she was attractive and I was flirting back. I informed her that I was dating her sister, and that it couldn't go much farther than flirting. She said she didn't care if I was dating her sister, she still wanted to be with me. She was rubbing my arm, complimenting me on them. I told her she should stop before someone accused me of taking advantage of her virtue. (Which sounds like me, huh?) She replied with, "You can't rape the willing!" At that point I should have taken off running for the hills, but I didn't. So, later that night, I snuck her out of her house and back to mine. I had the entire run of the downstairs of my house. My parents upstairs, I could come and go as I pleased. We spent the night together, and in the morning I took her home. Later I went to work.

That day was a cool day, and most people were waiting to see if the sun was going to come out before they came to the pool. The pool sat on top of a hill in the park. There was only one gate to the pool area. Once you were inside the pool area there was only one way out, back through that gate. To exit to the gate you either had to go through the maze of bath houses or directly though the guard shack to the gate.

Jeff and I were talking to the chlorine man who had just dropped off our weekly shipment. We looked up, and here comes Tammy cursing and screaming. She was a close friend with the girl who sold tickets at the gate, so she let Tammy in. However, when she realized what Tammy was doing she couldn't stop her. Jeff had no clue as to what was going on, but he immediately started working on "our" excuse. Right in the middle of working out an alibi, an announcement comes across the p.a. system, "She has a gun! I repeat she has a gun!" Much to our surprise, she actually did! We all took off like cockroaches again. That was sort of the theme to that summer. Lots of unclean fun, and me and Ol' Jeff running like hell at the end of it all. Tammy's friend, from the door, managed to stop her and talk her out of the homicide. The county's garage was inside the park and yards away. She was on state property with a weapon about to commit a crime of passion that she would surely go to jail on; not mention stopping an incredible wrestling career before it ever was dreamt of starting. She left. No shots were fired, the gun wasn't even loaded. We didn't find that out until after the fact. She just wanted to tell me we were done dating and scare me away from her sister. She accomplished it! I have not seen Tammy in over seventeen years, and I never spoke to her sister again.

After the summer I went back to school. Things would never be the same again. It was like listening to your favorite song, and then someone pulls the needle across the record. I was senior in high school in 1992. I had just come off the greatest summer of my life; I thought that being a senior would make the winter more exciting. It just wasn't that way. I didn't fit in again. This time it was for a different reason. The people I spent the summer with were all young adults. They were grown up and in the real world. Back in school they were all still kids. It just didn't click. It was like I skipped forward two years. I had always hung out with people older than me. Now I was the older one. All my friends had gone on to college; I needed to move on with my life too. I had grown up a bit over the summer. I still hung out with Craig and Steven, but they were caught up in being jocks. I was over all that armature sports stuff.

I was taking several college prep classes, even though I only need a few classes to graduate. Basically, I could pass two or three classes and fail four and still graduate. I realized quick that I didn't have to take college prep classes. So, I went to the principle and changed my schedule. I took easy classes, a lot of study hall, and planed to just bide my time till I graduated. I was instructed to just go to study hall until the paper work went through on the transfer of class by the principle. It would take a day or two to change the classes, and just go to study hall instead of the prep classes.

Mrs. Connie Taylor was known for her elitist attitude. Her class was considered the stepping stone to the upper class, only by her. Her family owned property and businesses in town. She thought that everyone had to take her Honors English class, or they would not make it in life. Her class just happened to be the one that I was dropping. I went to the study hall as told. Connie Taylor saw me in the hallways earlier in the day, but not in her class. She reported that I had skipped her class to the school's office. We had two assistant principles, Coach Ray and Mr. Coleman. Coach Ray was the Athletic Director. He handled all the athletes, while Mr. Coleman did all the real work. Coach Ray was the one that had changed my classes. However, Coleman was the one Connie Taylor went to. My schedule got changed, but I got suspended. I had a great schedule, but it was no wonder why they put a stop to it. I only had three classes in the morning, then lunch. Followed by four study halls before school was out. I really threw it to the system. That's why they made an example of me. The suspension was an in-school suspension. I had to do detention after school.

The detention teacher was Vikki Legos. She was the type of person that tried to overcome her lack of success in life by solving everyone's problems. She would act as an amateur psychologist to us poor degenerate kids. She would ask what terrible crime we had committed to get detention and tell us how to fix ourselves. She told me that mine was poor upbringing and bad parenting. I went home to inform my parents as to her diagnosis, and hoped that my parents would stand up for all of us.

My dad decided that my mom should go to the school and complain. Dad was being an armchair quarterback in this situation. He was mad, but didn't want to handle it himself. At this point in life he would just lay in bed, or in his recliner, and bark orders at everyone. The school did lift the detention once they found out what Vikki Legos had said. Mom had threatened to keep me home till the suspension was over. They caved in. Imagine if that would happen today. Imagine the lawsuits. It was a different time back then.

In 2002, I attended an amateur wrestling meet in Oak Hill with my girlfriend at the time. Her son was wrestling in the meet. I ran into Vikki, and her daughter Rachel. Rachel had gone to Harvard. She graduated and went for the lofty position of working for the local parks system. I had a huge crush on her in school. She was four years older than I was. Her sons were on Blake's team. They were the two worst wrestlers I have ever seen, but they had more fun out there than any of the others. That is what is important. Her youngest lost his match and just laid there on the mat. She had to drag him literally off the mat with one arm. He sold like Ricky Morton! I loved it. I cheered him on the whole way. My point to this story is that I began wrestling almost straight out of high school. I have wrestled around the world with the likes of Chris Jericho, John Cena, Randy Orton, Stone Cold, and the Rock. Her daughter went to Harvard and came back to the same town and got a job far below her capabilities. Vikki thought my upbringing was bad; her's was proper. It is all relevant to the desires inside the individual. Success is measured in happiness.

Every athlete in Oak Hill High school was pressured into being in the F.C.A. (Fellowship of Christian Athletes). It wasn't like we wouldn't play, or that we would be off the team, but every single athlete in the school was in the club. What are the odds of that? Hundreds of school teenagers finding religion all at the same time? It would have to be a miracle. Or was something a foot here? The F.C.A. would go to churches and give speeches. They had one issue. Most athletes at that age are not good public speakers. They would get in front of the crowd and choke. They approached me to get saved and speak publicly about it.

I took getting saved seriously at first. It was like a diamond shaped light that came from my heart. I would later understand this feeling as the Holy Spirit, but not in the beginning. I just knew it made me feel good. I was good at speaking in public. I enjoyed getting in front of people and talking. This would later help me on television in my interviews.

Rick Gage was the football coach at Liberty University in Virginia at the time. He came to our school to minister. The F.C.A. needed someone to open for his testimonial. Why do I say open? Because it was like show business. They wanted me to warm the crowd up for him. The kids in the F.C.A. could care less about this guy. They needed me to talk in a big crowd. The football coaches cared more about Gage than the kids. They were impressed by him being a college coach.

I saw an opportunity and made a deal with them. I would help them out. Get everyone I knew to attend. In return they would talk to Gage and get me a football scholarship. I wasn't good at football, but it would get me into a good school. They agreed, and I gave the speech of a lifetime that night. I spoke about partying the summer before and declared the stuff I had done wrong. People believed in what I was saying. They had seen me do all those wild things, and believed that if I could repent and change, then they could too. Days after the Rick Gage testimony I found out that there was no scholarship offer. They hade just promised it to me. They never even talked to him about it. Combined with the lies that caused the suspension and the let down of them completely lying about the scholarship, I vowed to not ever go back to school again.

After about a week of not going to school, dad, from his bed decided I should see a psychiatrist. This would be the second time they took me to a shrink. Once, at age five, they took me to see one. He told them that my issues were from a lack of independence. Lack of independence at age five? He told them to let me wake my own self up with an alarm clock, instead of them, and for me to pick out my own clothes. It was supposed to make me a better person. Yeah right! If it is brown, smells, and comes from a steer it can only be one thing. Bullshit!

For my lack of wanting to go to school they took me to see this lady shrink. She was over sensitive, burned incense, and talked more than I did about my problems. On the second visit she decided I should go to the root of the problem and confront it. I left the appointment and drove straight to Oak Hill High School. My mom was in her car, me in mine. We went to the school to confront my problem.

I arrived just moments before she did. All the emotions of a sixteen year old swelled inside me. My family treated me like shit. My dad would wake up everyday mad that he had not died in his sleep the night before. Everyone I knew lied to me. I had had enough! I was definitely not going to flee now. I was going to fight! The school was packed that night, because of a basketball game. Mom told me she would go in and talk to Coach Ray first. He refused to talk to her saying, "He did not want to hear anything she had to say." No wonder, he didn't want to face up to the lies he had told me.

Up until that point I had been in the lobby. Ray walked into the office. I followed. All I wanted was an explanation of why he lied. He told me he wasn't going to talk to me either. I responded that he was going to talk, one way or the other. My mom followed into the office. He asked me to wait in the hall while they spoke. Ray locked the door behind me. The gym started to empty for halftime. I could see a heated argument in the office between my mom and Coach Ray. They were screaming and pointing fingers. It could be seen by all walking by on their way to the bathroom. I had had enough. I was trying to get closure and that was just not happening. My mom was being abused right in front of me. I tried to get in, but the door was locked.

I punched a hole in the plate glass window by the door knob. It split my wrist to pieces. I still have scars today. As the blood started to pour from my wrist I opened the door from the inside. As I entered the room I asked, "Will you talk to me now?" He replied, "No!" I told him that he was going to talk one way or another. It would be his choice. Gary Ray was a large man of about three hundred pounds. He was nicknamed "Grimace" after the McDonald's character due to the resemblance in stature. I picked up a wooden lounge chair that was in the office and threw it at him. It grazed him slightly. Folklore will tell you that I hit him over the head. In actuality I barely hit him with the chair. Once again I asked him if he was going to talk to me. He still refused. I balled my fist up and hit him as hard as I could square in the middle of his face. By this time the football team rushed in, and pulled me away from the situation. My wrist was covered in blood. The office was a wreck. I was then taken to the hospital for stitches in my wrist.

As if all of this drama wasn't enough, things would really heat up from this point. I transferred to a different high school in the next town. Mt. Hope High School would be an entirely different experience. There were fewer students. The people in Mt. Hope were not caught up in playing the political games, which the people play in Oak Hill. I was only there for a short period of time, because the Board of Education decided to expel me. Coach Ray did not press charges on me. In the state of West Virginia the state has the right to pick up any case and prosecute it. I got home schooling while I waited for my case to come to trial. I basically taught myself one chapter at a time.

My Dad decided that I must have a chemical imbalance. It would explain why all these things happened. Remember what I said about if it is brown? The cause of all this was, besides teenage emotions, every authority figure had lied to me. My parents were nowhere to be found to help guide me or teach me about life. They were all sick; all the time. Illness came before anything. I felt alone. I had no support system. To top that everyone was telling me I was crazy.

I was sent to Raleigh General Hospital to have a sleep deprivation test to check my chemical imbalance. I would have a second one of this test in the 2000's to check my sleep apnea. They can not tell a chemical imbalance from a sleep deprivation test. So, why did they use it the first time to check? The test is, basically, you stay awake for twenty four hours and then they hook you up to this machine while you sleep. This test did not go like that. I stayed up for twenty four hours with nothing to eat or drink. Time came for the test and the doctor was not there. I stayed up twenty four more hours. Still no doctor, or food and water. I was completely delirious. Who wouldn't be after forty eight hours awake no food or water? My dad showed up to check and see what was going on. Mom told him what had happened and he sent her to talk to the nurse. Then he left and went home.

There I was out of my head, and all alone. It seemed like forever, but what did I know. I had no sense of time at that point. I had waited as long as I could, and I went looking for the nurse. When I staggered out the door into the hall a janitor was mopping. He wanted me to wait until he had stopped working before I walked down the hall. I could barely walk straight, and it was a long way from the bed to the hall it seemed. I told him something like, "Move out of my way". What I really said I have no idea because I was completely out of my head. Instead of helping me, he called security. He could have helped me. He could have called a nurse. Not this guy; his route of help was security. At the end of the hall I was met by security. The security officer told me he would take me to see my mom. This was a bold faced lie! He took me to a padded room and locked me in. I freaked out! I was sick, alone, and scared. I remember looking out the window, thinking I could break the glass and get out. Luckily, I realized I was on the third floor and didn't jump. I started hitting the Plexiglas in the door. Eventually it broke. I tore a piece of padding of the wall, and covered the jagged glass left in the door. I climbed through the window in the door into the hall way. This was not me being smart. It was clearly survival. I didn't know what sick and twisted things they would do to me, and I wasn't sticking around to find out. I went down each hallway of the hospital with nothing but a gown on looking for my mother. Once I found my mom she got my clothes. The hospital couldn't figure out how I got out of the room. I surly wasn't sticking around to explain. She took me home. No complaint against the hospital was ever filed. My parents would have had to do that. By the time I was eighteen and could do something about it, I was told the statute of limitations had run out. It turned out to be a lie also. By the time I found that out, the statute of limitations had actually expired.

As a result of being in that room, I began having flashbacks and panic attacks. Like the ones the Vietnam Vets have. I think I am still in the room. I still have the panic attacks every now and then. They would really affect me for years after that.

Instead of filing charges, my parents decided to throw me a party two days later. After I slept for a whole day and finally got some food, I was encouraged to have a keg party with my friends. I invited everyone I knew. My parents chaperoned from upstairs as we rocked out down stairs.

The first night I was in the hospital I was visited by a local youth minister. I can't recall his first name, but his last name was Estep. He and his wife decided to approach me to join his church. If I had had as many agents from WWE recruiting me, as well as these church people, there would have been no John Cena. I really don't know why these people were so interested in me, but the fact remained they were. I had attended the Oak Hill Church of the Nazarene once. I was spending time with two twins, Kara and

Tara. They attended the church. So they sent Estep to recruit me as a member.

Kara was my date for the party. The typical party things were going on. Drinking, dancing, and socializing. Compared to some of the other ones I had thrown, this one was actually mild when compared. Kara and I were sitting on the front porch talking when Estep pulled into the drive way. Of course, I was drinking a beer, and he saw it. He also saw Kara. He was totally offended, and left immediately. He went straight to her parents and stooged off the fact that their innocent daughter was being tempted by the devil's ways at the party. Her mom called my mom and started a huge argument. Needless to say the party was ruined. A few of my friends stayed, and we continued to drink. After a couple of cocktails I was drunk. I decided to call Estep and tell him off. It was just one of those drunken rants that were meant to be funnier than it was serious. It wasn't. During the rant I said that if he came back to my house again, either I or my dad would kill him. I wasn't serious. How many times do you hear some one say, "I was so mad I could kill him", or "I could just kill him". You are not serious. It is just an expression.

Estep went to the police with the answering machine message. I was arrested and was sent to court on attempted murder charges. That's right. There is a law in Fayette County that is referred to as "fighting words". It means that if your words incite someone to the point to where they think there might be violence, then it is a crime. I guess they don't believe in free speech. The key word here is "might". I was a drunken teenager. I had no intention of doing anything; I was mad he ran off my date. I was playing a joke. He just didn't think it was funny.

Dad hired Rod Jackson. A lawyer from Charleston that had handled the adoption. Jackson and my dad decided to send me to Radford, VA to a mental hospital to have me properly checked for my "chemical imbalance". They had doctors and classes to help in Radford. I was sent there for thirty days. I didn't have to take classes to better myself, just be observed. They wanted to see if I was crazy. I wasn't. The funny thing was I never took any tests. I also didn't speak to any doctors. I was basically just sent to a mental facility for no reason.

Rod Jackson was a short bald man who smoked a cigar bigger than he was. He spoke extremely fast. So fast I couldn't understand him. He and my dad just schemed like it was a huge coal contract. Dad liked anything that linked him to his former life. At the preliminary hearing Jackson came in muddered a few words and pled "not guilty" for me. It was literally that fast. I went home waiting for the trial.

Tension was high in the house from then on. The neighbors had a cook out, and the entire neighborhood got drunk. I was in bed later that night when I heard mom and dad arguing. I went to check on them and dad reassured me nothing was wrong. Mom ran down the hall. Dad followed her and began hitting her. I grabbed a ball bat and went to stop him. I couldn't. He took the ball bat away and hit her with it.

The next time was a little more serious. It would repeat itself nearly twelve years later. I was arguing with dad. He began punching my desk. He totally destroyed it. His hands were bleeding. I was terrified.

He left the room. Dad was paranoid, or should I say anti-paranoid. He wanted someone to try him; that was how he could get his manhood back from being sick. Two convicts had escaped from the regional jail and were reported to be in our area. So, dad began to duck tape pistols around the house. He had them taped in holster under the tables and various places. He was convinced that they were coming directly to our house. When he left the room I heard mom shout that he had a gun, and that I should run. I did. I ran down the stairs and out the door. As I went through the door he fired. It hit the wall by the door. I ran to the neighbor's house and literally beat their door in. They calmed me down, and I spent the night there. No police were called. I returned home the next day. It was as if nothing ever happened.

If you were to ask him today what happened. He would tell you that I was already out the door when he fired. That he knew he would miss; that he only wanted to scare me.

Mom treated the situation by giving me valium to calm my nerves. She said I was freaking out over nothing. It started at ten milligrams, and increased till she was giving me eighty milligrams at a time. One time I was high out of my gord on valium, and the police got called. I was arrested and taken from my house to the magistrate's office. There were no charges. I was told to be taken by the police back to the hospital. There was no way I was going back to that hospital. So, I got out of the ambulance. That was the first time the Oak Hill City police beat me up. They beat up a sixteen year old kid on eighty milligrams of valium right on Court Street in Fayetteville. I was taken home. They never filed charges. It was as nothing ever happened. See a pattern?

My trial finally came around. I got Judge Hatcher, "Hang'em High Hatcher". Jackson said something I couldn't understand because he was talking so fast. Judge Hatcher asked if the plea was still not guilty. Good ol' Rod said, "No your honor." My dad started snapping his fingers to get Jackson's attention, but he was being ignored. He snapped so much that Judge Hatcher told him to stop or he would go to jail. Dad stood and apologized. Jackson then pleaded me guilty. I actually said "What?" out loud. I was given thirty days in the Salem Home for Boys. The ironic thing was it was for "evaluation". Apparently I had not been evaluated enough by then. I was sent right then to Juvenile Jail for that damn test I had tried to get several times before. I don't know who told Jackson to change the plea. It was not me. My parents claim that it was not them. Someone made him change that plea. I was to return to court thirty days later for sentencing. I didn't understand this. I was on my way to jail for thirty days, and then I would return so I could be sentenced to go to jail. Remember I was only sixteen.

When I was little, all the adults would tell you to "straighten up, or you end up in Prunnytown." Salem Home for Boys was referred to as Prunnytown, because that is the name of the town it is located in. I was on my way there. I wasn't sure why. I just knew that bad people end up there.

Salem was an old school that they had built on extra rooms for cells. Inside the large fence was a huge yard that connected the cafeteria to the main building. It seemed like the sun was down for thirty days. I am probably being dramatic, but it seemed like it rained all month. They issued me a uniform, but it did not fit. I was six foot one, and weighed two hundred and forty pounds. I was basically the same size I am now. The uniform did not fit. It was for smaller children. I was a grown as a man.

Most kids attend school there. Unfortunately, most are illiterate. So, I didn't have to attend their school. Instead, I continued teaching myself. I did the entire second semester of the twelfth grade, by myself, in seven days. I graduated on my own with a 3.8 grade point average. I would have been an honor graduate had I remained in school. Not too bad for a vicious criminal. My diploma is from Mt. Hope High School, even though I wasn't there long enough for anyone to know who I was.

My parents came to visit me once a week. Strangely enough, this is how wrestling came back into my life. We were allowed certain things from home. So, they brought me every wrestling magazine on the stands. I spent all my time reading these magazines over and over.

At lunch one day in the cafeteria, two boys had a fight. It was rumored that something bad was going to happen to one of them later that night. Later that night I looked from my cell though the window to see an ambulance. They carried a boy out on a stretcher.

I had to see a psychiatrist at Salem. Of course, he asked me the famous shrink question, "How did you get here?" I am always tempted to answer, "In a car." The proper questions, which never get asked, "Why do you think you are here?", or "What do you think your issues are?" Those questions never get asked. I was sent back to Fayette County thirty days later.

When I returned to court, Judge Hatcher found that the evaluation was inconclusive. Can you believe that? If you can't, have you been reading this story? He sentenced me to ninety day on home confinement. I was allowed to return to work at the pool, but I had to be home at a certain time. I also could not leave without permission. They attached an ankle bracelet, with a GPS in it that hooked to a machine in the phone line. If the line is broken, or you wonder more than a hundred feet from the box, you are in violation. They think you're off committing another crime.

That summer I worked, but it was different. All my buddies were gone. I couldn't put things in the past; because of the ankle bracelet people kept asking questions. I would eventually tell them that it was a bee sting kit. The funny thing was that, when there was an actual sting, I couldn't do anything about it.

I got off home confinement and was put on probation for one year. Does this seem like several sentences for one crime? It did to me also. I was at Fayette County's mercy. What could I do? I had been suspended from school. Taken to shrinks repeatedly, locked up against my will, shot at, and sentenced to jail all by the age of sixteen. This all happened in less than a year's time. Remember I only threw one punch against a guy twice my size and twice my age. Thank God, I was going away to college. I had been accepted to Alderson Broaddus College in Philippi, WV. Guess what I was going to study? Law!

Chapter 2: Rebirth

What has been written, so far, is the birth and life of Brian Kees. I want to tell another story about a far different person. In some way the same, but in many ways the opposite. I'm talking about Brian Logan. Contrary to what many might think I am not schizophrenic. Brian Logan, the wrestler, is and will always be a totally different person than Brian Kees.

I was attending Alderson Broaddus College. I was studying Pre Law and Political Science, a double major. I was minoring in Religion. Is that heavy stuff or what? My plan was to fight the good fight. I was going to fight the system from within. I picked A-B because they were going to let me walk on to the baseball team. Coach Funk had talked with me earlier during my issues, and was open to the idea of me playing for him.

On the weekends at A-B most students would go home. One weekend I attended a wedding of a former teacher and friend Sam Calloway. Sam had a way with kids. I attended church with him regularly. I decided to skip the reception after the wedding and attend a live wrestling event in Beckley. I had to tell my probation officer everywhere I was going. So instead of asking him, while he thought I was at the wedding, I went to see the show.

I was late getting to the arena because of the wedding. I had missed the opening matches. Walking down the steps into the arena I literally bumped into a friend of mine. Joe Cochran. I asked him where he was going. He told me he was going to talk to a guy about becoming a wrestler. So I walked with him.

I would eventually end up training Joe Cochran, or Mighty Joe, as we would call him years later. He was a big, burly guy who felt no pain. I mean none. You could hit with a chair and he would head butt it back towards you. He was only a year older than me, though he worked his whole life. He took to wrestling naturally. I think he would have had a good career, but he was forced to quit. He had to take care of his ill father and the financial brunt fell on his large farm boy shoulders. His dad would attend the training session, even though he was ill. He was so nice to me. At times he would call me sir. I will never forget that.

The guy that Joe was going to talk to was "White Lightning" Tim Horner. Tim was known through out the south as a part of the N.W.A. His big break came with Watt's territory the U.W.F. (Universal Wrestling Federation). His biggest victory would come in 1984, when he pinned Road Warrior Hawk on national TV for Georgia Championship Wrestling. He was originally booked against Animal, but Animal would refuse to put him over. This plagued Tim his entire career. Tim also had a small run with the W.W.F. in the nineties. At that time he was opening a wrestling school for Smoky Mountain Wrestling.

I was asked to send an athletic resume to Horner. It consisted of my athletic achievements in amateur sports. One weekend, while I was at college, I received a call from him. He offered me a contract with Smoky Mountain Wrestling. He wanted me to be the first student they would train and produce. I, of course, had to pay the tuition. I had saved money from working at the pool. So, I paid him the two thousand dollars and signed the contract. The contact stated that I would be guaranteed twelve matches on TV after my training was done. It was a fair deal. Even if it wasn't, I would have taken it.

I had to finish the semester out, even though I never attended class while I was there. I concentrated on my wrestling career. I hit the gym and studied all the wrestling I could find.

I attended two wrestling conventions in 1993, to prepare me for the business. The first was in Philadelphia, PA where I attended Todd Gordon's W.W.A. event (W.W.A. was the precursor to E.C.W.). The main event was "Hot stuff" Eddie Gilbert versus "Terrible" Terry Funk. Funk was just off the I quit match with Flair, so they billed the match as an I quit match. It was a stellar and believable bout. Gilbert was just starting his series of matches with Cactus Jack. These matches led to the birth of hardcore wrestling. Eddie would die in Puerto Rico shortly after. The match that night would be one of the most talked about matches in hardcore history, and I was there to see it first hand.

The second convention was in Nashville, TN. Where I met several of the guys I would later work with. This convention would be the first time I ever stepped inside a ring. Al Costello, of the Fabulous Kangaroos, was holding a training seminar. The Kangaroos were famous for being the first team to compete in Australian rules tag team action. The seminar was taught by Al Snow. My very first lesson in the ring, and first lock up, would be with him.

I only had one obstacle before I could officially start my training. I had to be let off probation. In Fayette County when they have you they have you. If the probation officer wouldn't recommend me being let off probation, the court wouldn't let me go. My dad had actually planned to run off with me and hide if they had not allowed me to go. He wanted me to be a professional wrestler. They did let me off probation. On June 2nd, 1993, I moved to Morristown, Tennessee to start my career. My life was forever changed. In fact I have a tattoo now on my left arm that reads exactly that, "Forever Changed".

I woke early on June 2nd, 1993, and prepared to leave on a journey of a lifetime. I stepped into the bathroom to shower and I reflected over my life so far. I was asking myself if I really had what it took to be a star. I thought about all the rough times I had just gone through. Could I get over my overwhelming fear in life? I asked myself if I really knew what I was getting myself into. I reached up and turned on the radio. The song *Fancy* by Reba Macintyre was playing. Before I go any further, I know what the song is about. It is about a mother that sells her little girl into prostitution. There were parts of the song that rang in my head. The lyrics are "To thy own self be true", and "I might have been born plain white trash, but Fancy was my name". It spoke to me. I might have been a bastard son, with poor family values, and fresh out of jail; but I was going to be somebody. Just like in the song, I wasn't going to hold my head down in shame! Also like the song, I said to myself, "God forgive me for what I do, but I was going to make it!" I was going to prove that everybody, including myself, was wrong about how they judged me. I decided not to be scared. To embrace this opportunity, failing was not a option. I was going to fight for the right to live life the way I wanted to.

My dad and I arrived in Morristown that afternoon at Tim Horner's house. We all made small talk, and then dad said to Tim, "He is yours now. This is all he has ever wanted to do. He is your responsibility." It was done I was in the wrestling business now.

That night I made my first town. I went to Kentucky for a spot show with Tim and Sandy Scott. Sandy Scott was the General Manager for Smoky Mt. Wrestling. A position he held with Mid Atlantic wrestling for the Crocket family, and in Knoxville territory under Blackjack Mulligan. I moved into a small apartment that was shared by Sandy and another student Anthony Michaels.

Anthony was from Copiague, Long Island, New York. He had the thick Italian accent, and long curly black hair to accent his build. He had played in bands all his life. Copiague is located next to Amityville where the famous horror house. Which we visited on a trip up there. It was creepy.

Anthony had limited success in the business. He worked for E.C.W. for a short time. His most famous thing was being almost famous. He was the first Dudley Boy, Snot. The gimmick was created for him, because he looked like one of the Hansen Brothers from the movie *Slapshot*. It is ironic how he got the spot. I had sent a video to the office, and they saw him wrestling me. Tazz liked his look and he was hired. Due to a Jet Ski accident he retired from wrestling, and Bubba Ray, and the rest of the family, took over the gimmick. Anthony would later be immortalized in Chris Jericho's book. (Hey, Chris thanks for the picture, but would have a line about the Hornet killed ya?)

In Kentucky that night I met Ricky Morton and Robert Gibson for the first time. It was also the night that I had met Ron and Don Harris. I got along with them real well. I had done them a favor one night in Knoxville. They would carry a chain to the ring like Bruiser Brody did. They came though the crowd and some guy got pissed and grabbed the chain. He was going to really start trouble. I saw the whole thing coming, so I ran at him as hard as I could. I hit him and knocked him on his ass. I was worried that I would be in trouble, or even fired for getting involved. Instead, The Harris Boys officially accepted me as one of the boys. It was my first stripe in the wrestling business.

The next day I would start the toughest training on the face of the planet. The Marines, NFL, and MMA had nothing on this. In fact, I challenge any of them to last though a week of what I went through. We would work out on weights a hour to a hour and a half. Then go in the basement and train on the mats. The gym would have karate classes in the evening; we used the karate mats for wrestling. Anyone who knows, karate mats or aerobic mats are thin. I learned to take bumps on a thin mat on concrete. For three long months I was stretched in every way possible. Choked out to near death, and then revived again. I was beaten by grown men. They taught me how to fight. To wrestle, and to defend myself. It was like Jedi Knight training with giants. They taught me holds, and then after a week how to get out of them. Over and over we trained on the moves, till I could do it in my sleep.

Tim finally bought a training ring. He taught us spots. On the weekends we traveled to the towns where the show was, set up the ring and train. At first I did every little odd job I could. Fetching drinks, selling merchandise, or getting coats were the norm as I broke in to the business. I loved it! I was learning a craft.

I began to help with the lighting. I would drive to Atlanta and pick up the equipment the night before. I would then drive to towns like Jelico, TN, Barbourville, KY, Haysi, VA, Hazard, KY, and Hickory, NC. I would set up the ring, set up the lights, and then help with the gopher work. After watching the wrestling, I would take it all down and return it to Atlanta. For this I made the grand total of zero dollars. I was getting paid in a education in the business. So, for all you guys who say you have paid your dues, NO you have not, unless you trained like this.

Seven months into my training I went to Jefferson, NC. I had just finished putting up the lights, ring, ect. when I exhaustedly walk into the dressing room. There was a small meeting going on as I walked by. I passed by quickly with my eyes down and ears open, as I always did. "Killer" Kyle was booked for TV. However, he no showed to work for WCW. There was now a vacancy in the TV format. I overheard someone say, "What about him?" Then they asked me if I had my gear. I showered, ate, and slept with my gear. Of course I did! I was told to get dressed; I was working TV.

As I pulled my gear out of my bag I had two choices, white and blue or yellow and black, to go with my yellow boots. All the boys gathered around. This could be good or bad. Either way, they were going to rib me. Brian Lee and Jimmy Del Ray suggested the black and yellow. Chris Candido reached in his bag and pulled out a yellow mask. I dressed and they took me to see the booker. (A booker is the writer of the show and books the matches together). The boys suggested I be called the Green Hornet, as a rib on me because I was a green horn. Since I had no green on, it was dropped. The Hornet was born!

Later that night, The Hornet was booked against the Rock N Roll Express, Ricky Morton and Robert Gibson. My partner was Mike Collins. Who? I don't know either. That was the first and only time I have ever seen or heard of him. It might have been that he looked like a kid. He looked like he was twelve. We had five minutes of air time. It went something like this. I wrestled Ricky for about twelve seconds. Then Robert knocked me around like a ping pong ball. I tagged Mike. He got killed and tagged me in. They stretched my legs over my head. Then a punch to the gut, followed by the stiffest knee lift I have ever felt, even to this day. Then double dropkick! The move I had seen them beat everybody from Midnight Express to the Bulldogs with. One, Two, Three and The Hornet was a Pro Wrestler.

My first series of matches on house shows would be with Bobby Blaze. Bobby was trained by Dean Malenko. He was a exceptional wrestler. He could grapple and do high flying moves. A style that had not yet been popularized. Bobby thought of himself as a shooter. (A shooter is someone who is more legit as a wrestler than just a performer). He could hold his own in a fight. If I made a mistake he could easily hurt me. He never did, however he did inflict pain. Bobby liked to tie me up in pretzel holds. Then would give me the "office" to reverse out of the hold. I couldn't unless he let me. I would eventually learn to escape the holds. I loved working with Bobby. I learned so much from him. He could have easily just beaten me up to get himself over, but he took his time and taught me things. I am thankful to have worked with him.

I was booked on TV in Jelico, TN on February 7th, 1994. It was my second TV taping. I had only had five matches. That night I was told I would become the TV Champion. I couldn't believe it. I was already going to win a match. The match was between The Hornet seconded by Chris Candido against Robbie Eagle, who was the Maestro on WCW later in his career. Robbie had the gimmick of Gorgeous George III when he arrived at WCW, but sold the rights to that name to WCW so that Macho Man's girlfriend could use the name. It was his best character, and he can't even use it anymore. That's sound business. That night in Jellico he was seconded by Tracy Smothers. This match was a side venture in the Candido/ Smothers feud. The feud that led them to the finals of the N.W.A. tournament that crowned Chris the world's champion. Chris had a bet with Tracy who would win. Eagle or The Hornet. I came out the winner and the new Beat the Champ TV champion. My first title.

I had a long reign as champion. It lasted until the third hour of TV. Wait I'm getting a head of myself. On the second hour of taping I defended against the Dirty White Boy. This would be The Hornet's most famous bout. DWB and the Dirty White Girl were feuding with Brian Lee and his manager Tammy Fytch. Tammy would go on to become Sonny in the W.W.E. Brian Lee wrested Anthony on the first tape. Brian had Tammy pin Anthony. So, to hype the feud, the DWG got in the ring and knocked out the Hornet. I won by DQ. The match made the magazine, and that was the first press I had ever had. I finally got beaten by Killer Kyle on the third hour. What a run as champion! I was in the thick of things. I had no clue what I was doing, but I was surrounded by talent. Thanks guys for letting me get the rub!

I worked on the SMW house shows and TV for the next month working with either Bobby or Anthony. Then on March 7, 1994, something happened that would change the wrestling world forever. At the time we had no clue it would happen. It wasn't until years later I could look back and see that it changed the way our industry was. The wrestling business would officially begin to change from the old school to the new guard. The Thrillseekers would rock America. Anthony and I were paired as a team. Again I would don a mask as one of the Infernos. This was a direct rip off of the Blue Infernos from Memphis. Gypsy Joe was one of the original Blue Infernos. I spoke about Gypsy before; he worked as Jean Madrid in West Virginia. On March 7th the Infernos debuted, but it would be the debut of the other team of Chris Jericho and Lance Storm that would change wrestling a few years later.

The Seekers were nothing like we had ever seen before. In the match that night they pulled off moves that are common today, but then it was not even thought of, outside of Mexico. The locker room called them "flying squirrels" and said they would never get over. The boys always did get upset when they are out performed. A lot of people credit W.C.W. with bringing Rey Mesterio and Dean Malenko into style, or even credit E.C.W. with the innovation. Fact is, in 1994, Chris Jericho and Lance Storm had all them beat, just no one saw it except in the Smoky Mt. region.

This time can be documented in Jericho's book. Anthony moved in with Chris, and I got screwed. Brian Hildebrandt, Mark Curtis, suggested that Sandy move in with him to save the office money. That made my rent go up. So, I moved into my first apartment. So, Chris, Anthony, and I rode to the towns together most of the time. (Chris, would it have been so much trouble to ad the Hornet in the book?)

Lance was married and lived in Knoxville. So he traveled with Candido and Tammy. Tammy had a problem, all the boys made her a little randy, if you know what I mean. I have seen her hit on every single person in that locker room. Tammy and Chris lived in the same apartment complex as Lance and his wife. Chris went to Japan for Dory Funk Jr. This left Tammy to her own handling. From then on, Lance and she were real close. Rex King, of Well Dunn, was one of her conquests. Chris had returned from Japan, and in Hazard, KY, they almost came to blows over the issue. Bruiser Bedlam and the Armstrong Brothers egged it on. It was clear that she had, in fact, had relations with "Sexy" Rexy, but neither was willing to loose their job over it. All and all I liked Tammy, but then again who didn't.

The Thrillseekers tried every night to outdo the match from the night before. They accomplished it. It was wild. One TV they sat The Hornet on Chris's shoulders and Lance cross bodied him off the top rope. I fell five feet six inches to the mat holding Lance like a baby, with both of our weight crashing onto my lungs. Another match they catapulted Chris over Lance's head onto my shoulders driving me down head first into the mat.

I worked Lance in Morristown, TN, one night. He wanted to do a belly to belly suplex off the top rope, with both of us standing on the top rope. He was the veteran of the two of us, and that is what he wanted to do. So, that is what we did. He suplexed me. When we landed I hit first safely. Thank God! Then he landed, right on my left index finger. He bent it all the way backwards. This was the finish. Damn right it was the finish. Even if it was not the finish, it was now. I told the ref to count quickly because my finger was broken. I went back to the heel dressing room. Back then they had two dressing rooms separating the good guys from the bad. It hurt so badly I was sick, nauseous. Jim Cornette says, "You okay? You don't want to go to the hospital do you? You have to work next week. The doctor will take you off the shows next week. Just sit there and put some ice on it. You will be fine." Be fine? I can't feel my hand, just pain. I would have rather amputated the finger, than just sit there. I was about to pass out and they wanted me to just sit there. Cornette was right though. It hurt, but it healed. I taped it up the following week and worked. I have done that several times in my career, and I'm sure I will do it again. Wrestlers don't have insurance. If they get hurt they pay for it. If they miss work they don't get paid. So many times we work injured. That is just the nature of the game.

Jericho would leave the promotion in 1994. He was practicing the shooting star press and broke his arm. He had ridden on the ring truck with us all week and practiced everyday. He never got it. He was determined. At that time only a few people in the entire world could do it. This, of course, happened at the worst time, the "Night of Legends". Chris broke his arm around four and went to the hospital. Around seven he returned against doctors orders. He was pressured by the promotion to compete. He and Lance worked the Heavenly Bodies that night. Tom Pritchard and Jimmy Del Ray, along with Jim Cornette at ringside. Cornette would hit him with his tennis racquet. This lacerated Chris tremendously. He fought back in a incredible display of effort. After the match I carried him from ringside. He returned to the hospital and received stitches to go along with his broken arm.

Chris would work for E.C.W. Then go on to W.C.W. Ultimately ending up in the W.W.E. where he became the first Undisputed World's champion. He has also held the Intercontinental Title more times than anyone. Most recently returned to save us all.

Lance would follow Chris to E.C.W., where he would hold the tag team title with Chris Candido. He then moved on to W.C.W. where he won every singles title at the same time, except for the world's title. Finally ending up in the W.W.E., where he took I-C gold and the World's tag team title with William Regal. He now runs a wrestling school in Canada.

These guys are major players in the wrestling business. I can honestly say that I was there with them in the beginning, and have learned a lot from them. I consider myself part of what launched them to their fame. Thanks guys for letting a young kid work with you.

April 1st, 1994, in Pikeville, KY SMW's biggest match took place. It pitted Jim Cornette's Heavenly Bodies versus the Rock N' Roll Express. At stake, the company's richest prize, the Smoky Mt. tag team title. Also on the line was the looser of the fall must leave town. It would take place in the confines of a steel cage. Ricky Morton had said, on TV, that if they loose they would take their boots off and throw them to the crowd. Cornette vowed that this would finally be the end of the Rock N Roll. When I got to the building that night I wasn't on the line up. I knew that I had been booked. I had been booked to referee. Usually talent will get bummed out about going from full time talent to referee. The ref position would be a step down from wrestler, but not in this case. Several minutes into this grueling match. Mark Curtis gets knocked out. Here came junior referee Brian Kees. They used my real name. I opened the cage and stepped inside. At first I tried to revive Curtis. He wouldn't wake. So I did what I had to do, continue the match as the ref. In the finish Ricky Morton victory rolls Jimmy Del Ray, Curtis and I simultaneously count to three. The Bodies were gone from SMW. The sold out crowd was cheering on their feet as the house lights came up. This match is collected and traded by fans everywhere. It is the most historical bout in Smoky Mt. history. I was a part of that. I was so lucky to have played such a small part in such a huge thing. I appreciate all those veterans for letting me be a part of that moment. Not many eighteen year old kids, from West Virginia, get to do something like that.

I finally had grown my hair longer and was able to come from under the hoods I wore. I had gotten new gear. I am a tights fanatic. Presentation is everything in sports entertainment. That is why the W.W.E. spends so much time on look. It is the presentation of who you are that leads the crowd behind you. I am in Clinton, TN, and it is my first match without a mask on. I need a name. At first I wanted to call myself Brian Mavericks, a cowboy. It just didn't fit. So I suggested Brian Mavs. That sucked. One of the tech guys noticed I had a X-Men hat on when I came to the building. He asked who my favorite character was. I said Wolverine. He asked what his alter ego's name was. It is Logan. He got on his head set and said Brian Logan. My music played, and I was announced as Brian Logan for the first time. Some people might think I'm ripping off Hulk Hogan. Especially when I make my cheesy baby face comeback. While he influenced me, Hulk had nothing to do with my "Logan" name.

Between June 2nd, 1993, and April 4th, 1994, I was newly created and reborn. I was well on my way in journey that would stretch farther than I could ever imagine. I was so lucky already to have experienced so much, and this was just the first year.

Chapter 3: Growing in the Business

Every person is born, and then they have to grow up to be an adult through guidance of some sort. Imagine if all that guidance came from fifteen to twenty year experienced teachers, who were masters in their field. Every single night, for two years, I was being lead and instructed by guys like Jim Cornette, Tom Pritchard, Ricky Morton, Robert Gibson, Al Snow, Dirty White Boy and Tim Horner. Every single step of the way I learned from these guys. With all of their experience in hand, these guys took the time to teach me to be just as seasoned as they were. I have always thought of myself as a ring general with above average ring psychology. It is all because of what these men passed down to me. I soaked up all they showed me, as if I were a sponge.

Jim Cornette always told me that when talent gets fired be the first guy that the booker sees. I used this trick for years. When the booker fires someone he is usually pissed off. He wonders who will fill the spot, and how much of a hassle it will be. To make things simple, more times than not, he would hire the first person he sees. I made it a habit to be that guy. I got several spots on the card because of this.

I got to fill in for Brian Lee against the Rock N Roll Express, which was a Main event spot. Tim Horner was the original Kendo. He had a falling out with the office, and I took his place. One time, Jake Roberts fell off the wagon again, and I took his spot working in the Main with Dirty White Boy as Kendo the Samurai.

People ask what the true reason was for SMW shutting down. A lot of accusations have made their way around and I want to clear it up. It all started in Morristown, TN. Tim Horner was wrestling full time. Allison, his wife, had just given birth to their first child. Tim was in charge of the merchandise division of the company. Apparently Tim's checks did not reflect what he felt they should. In the middle of the live event, at East High School, everyone was out in the hall talking when Allison walked in. She was holding the baby in her arms. She instructed Tim that he had to go get his money right then. I swear she actually made him, as if he was a child. Tim began to argue with Cornette in front of all the boys. All this time Allison was standing next to him with a smug look on her face. What did he expect Cornette to do, just dig money out of his wallet right there? Cornette was the boss; there was no way he was backing down in front of the boys. Allison wouldn't let Tim concede either. Tim's small man complex kicked into high gear and said, "Don't yell in front of my baby!" The baby shouldn't have been there to begin with, Allison either, for that matter. Cornette responded with some colorful language, and Tim decided to "take some time off" after that.

The houses started to drop, due to the fact that the business was changing. The boys on top were getting lazy. They had the attitude that their run would last forever. Nothing lasts forever. Cornette had the opportunity to breathe life into the area by using W.W.F. talent. This drew some large houses in Knoxville. Cornette finally received a offer to work for Vince McMahon. The W.W.F. was a new market for him, and he took the job. Smoky Mt. wrestling had just run its course. No one killed it. Knoxville wrestling has always run in cycles, just like everywhere else.

I worked with DWB in No DQ matches around the horn. Tony Anthony was originally one of the Grapplers with Len Denton. They would later unmask and become The Dirty White Boys. Tony became a huge draw in the south. He would have a short run as T.L. Hopper in the W.W.F. Also, he was Uncle Cletus manger of the Godwin's for a short time. I learned a lot about how to pace my matches and really make things count from Tony. He is a true professional.

As a result of these breaks, I was asked to travel with Ricky Morton and Robert Gibson. They have always booked a young team to work with on Independent bookings. They asked Anthony and me to work with them on some Midwest dates. It was an experience of a lifetime. Deep down I was still that little boy chanting "Rock N Roll" at the Raleigh Co. Armory. There I was with two years under my belt, and I was wrestling them in the main events having that shouted towards me.

Robert, Hoot, as we call him, would drive hundred miles an hour non stop. Ricky, or Punky, would be complaining about something. Rock N Roll would wage their feud from West Virginia, to Kentucky, to

Indiana, on to St. Louis, down to Mississippi. Most car trips would be at least ten hours straight. We learned so much from them.

The first time we went to St. Louis was a trip I will never forget. I was told not to go to East St. Louis. My dad had done business there, and told me it was a bad part of town, stay away from there. We leave Glasgow, KY, and drive to Nashville to stay at Ricky Morton's dad's place. Paul Morton was a referee for the Jarretts, in Memphis, for years. We never got to see the ghost in Paul's basement, but most of the boys swear by it. Then next morning we were off to St. Louis with little sleep. We were full though, Punky's mom cooked us about an eleven coarse meal. It was the biggest lunch I have ever eaten. It made Thanksgiving look like a bag lunch. The plan was to drive straight through ten hours to the hotel, then get some sleep and wrestle that night.

About six hours into the ride we still had not stopped. Robert won't stop for anything when he drives, and he always drives. He also has a habit of smoking marijuana cigarettes, one after another, as he drives. At one point, we tried to explain that he could only get so high. That once that is achieved he was just wasting his stash. He continued to smoke at his own pace. Thank goodness he did. He got the munchies and finally stopped. Some where in Mississippi, he sees a small sign about the size of a shoe box, while going hundred miles an hour, and makes a strong hard right onto a dirt road. He made a ninety degree turn, at about eighty miles an hour, for barbecue. Thank God I could at least use the bathroom. So, we ate again, and then were on our way. It has been well documented that Punky tells the same jokes over and over again, so I won't re-tell that story. Just let me confirm that, after several long trips with him, it is all true. He thinks he is getting over by telling the jokes and being funny. Punky, you are funny. You are over. It is because you are Ricky Morton, not those damn jokes!

We finally cross the Missouri line in to St. Louis. Traveling straight for the hotel, right? Wrong! We went straight to where else? East St. Louis. We parked under a bridge in the oldest, worn out neighborhood I have ever seen. There were no street lights because they had all been shot out. The story that follows is not embellished one single bit. I can't believe to this day that it happened like this.

I locked my car door and slumped down in the seat partially for safety and mostly from fear. Ricky gets out of the car. Anthony, sounding just like Rocky Balboa, starts complaining. Robert reassures us this is okay and quite normal. Ricky starts yelling at the top of his lungs, "Ricky Morton, Rock N Roll Express, not 5-0, looking to hook up!" I covered my eyes and hid my wallet. After five minutes of this non stop, people started to gather around Punky. Robert then gets out and pops the trunk. Ricky, on one side of the car, purchases what ever paraphernalia they bought. Then asks them to shake Robert's hand, which was on the opposite side of the car. Robert then snapped a Polaroid picture with them and the tag belts. He then sold the picture to them for five dollars, eventually making their money back.

We make it to the Motel 6 at six o'clock a.m. Motel six does not usually have working clocks in them. A least this Motel 6 didn't. Ant and I were so happy to be out of the car, and also, out of the hood. All we wanted was to sleep. We fell asleep as soon as our heads hit the pillow. Then the phone rang. It was Robert. He was bitching at us. He said that we had over slept, and was going to be late for the autograph signing at the video store. We told him that it seemed like we had just fell asleep. He reassured us that we were wrong! He said that it was noon, and that we should get dressed and hurry; they would meet us next door at the diner. We jumped in the shower quickly. Packed our gear and headed straight over to the diner as fast as we could. The diner was full. Ricky would say that it was "sold out", and it was. We made our way to the back of the diner where they sat. I noticed the place smelled like bacon and eggs. I looked and every person was eating breakfast. Why? They were eating breakfast because it only seven fifteen in the morning. When we sat down Hoot and Punky laughed their asses off. Anthony and I went back to the room to sleep. Well, we had to stop at the front desk to get a second key. Hoot had told us to just leave the key in the room when we left. We did! I loved traveling with them. The shows were sold out. We got our receipt on Punky though. Anthony would suplex him every night. I had only seen Ric Flair suplex him. Punky would say, "I'm Ricky Morton, there ain't no need in suplexing me!" He was right. He is the best seller in the business, but he had it coming after the rib. I studied Ricky so much. A lot of what I do, as a baby face, is to try and emulate him. I am so thankful Ricky Morton is a part of my life.

Working in Smoky Mountain was the best beginning any one person could ever get, when starting his career. I was learning my craft, but also being worked to death. I was still driving to get the lights and driving to the towns where ever they were. I also had to set up the ring and take it down afterwards. Then wrestle, sometimes as much as four times a night, all as different characters. On top of this, Tim had stopped teaching the ever growing wrestling school and had put me in charge of running it also. So, I had to go to Atlanta twice every weekend there was TV, and find the town and work. Then teach two classes each day every Monday though Thursday. I was in the ring at least four to five hours every single day for a year non stop. I made good money. I made around five hundred dollars total per month for all this work. I was exhausted.

In this business you can't quit a job. It's like the mafia; you do it till you get whacked. If you quit, they will think you just aren't dedicated. If you have a problem, you just work though it. There are so many guys in the industry now that wouldn't have lasted five minutes in the REAL wrestling business. They complain now about job related issues and their children keeping them from having the needed time. Back then wrestling was your job and the craft was your baby. That was all that mattered. This is if you really wanted to be a wrestler. Back then if you quit they would replace you with one of a million guys. There was no going to another company. They were all connected. The one thing you could do is move on to work another territory.

I begged Tony Anthony to get me booked in Memphis. He got me a great spot. I would work Memphis territory Monday thru Thursday. Then the Smoky Mt. territory Friday thru Sunday. On June 6th, 1994, I debuted in the Mid South Coliseum in Memphis

TN. U.S.W.A. was the home to Jerry" The King" Lawler and Jarett promotions. I wrestled Mike Samples that night. It was also famous because that was the night O.J. Simpson was on the run from the cops. I worked with guys like Reggie B. Fine, Colorado Kid, Brian Christopher, The Spellbinder, and even Jerry Lawler. I found that all the Memphis stories about the pay was true. I got a pay check for a weeks loop four cities, and the check was for thirty four dollars and fifty cents. It was hard to eat there, but I enjoyed working the towns that have been worked since the inception of our business.

I stayed with a lady by the name of Anita. Anita was known though out wrestling as the place to stay. She was also famed for being the one who supplied Kerry Von Erich with his drugs. My first Memphis run would be short lived. Lawler had major heat with Anita and fired us for staying there. Lucky for us he hired us back. Anita would introduce me to Bert Prentice, who I would later work for. Once we moved to a hotel we were back on the regular rotation. Until one night in Nashville.

Pro wrestling had been in Nashville for as long as anyone could remember. Even Mea Young wrestled in Nashville as a young girl. So, that's a long time. We worked the fairgrounds Saturday nights. By this time I was working Memphis full time. That night the Hornet wrestled Anthony Michaels. They have had a very distinct style in Memphis for years. It is typically reversed everywhere else. In Memphis the heel out wrestles the baby and the baby out fights the heel. It was actually based on this style that I perfected my style of wrestling from. A combination of southern style and the Canadian Stampede style. I like to call it Southern Technical Brawling. On this night I had perfected nothing, I thought I had. Anthony and I wanted to do for Memphis what Jericho and Storm had done for Smoky. We were going to revolutionize the Memphis area. We couldn't have been more wrong. We came up with this huge fifteen stage spot that included dropdowns, leapfrog, back flips, arm drags, using a actual kitchen sink (no not really). We did it to perfection. The crowd who had literally had season tickets and sat there their whole life were completely silent. No noise at all. You could hear a pin drop. One single old man about ninety six shouted, "What the hell was that?" I replied, "Talent! Not like you have ever seen that here before!" As we finished the match quickly, they became more disdainful towards us. When my right foot crossed the threshold of the locker room door I was met by Eddie Marlin. "Boys we will no longer need your services," he said. Fired again. We would eventually be rehired and finish the summer there. After that I returned to work for SMW. This time only as a wrestler.

When I returned I was put on the road to take Rex King's place in Well Dunn on the house shows against The Thrill Seekers. Well Dunn was a great team. By the time he got a break, and made it to the W.W.F., they were past their prime as a team. Steve Doll (Dunn) would later be the booker for Bert Prentice's Music City wrestling. He treated me very well while I was there. I enjoyed working as a team, with him or against him. He was another one that helped bring me along. Steve Doll would pass away during the writing of this book.

Rex was a funny person. Sometimes somebody asks how you are doing and to be polite you just say fine. Not Rex. He is so miserable in life, but it is funny to listen to. If you ask him how he is, he will really tell you. Stuff like my wife just left me, my car exploded, I can't find work because I got so much heat for being miserable. Stuff like that. You could start him talking, leave for five minutes, then come back and he would still be complaining. I loved getting him started telling someone, then just walk away and never come back.

Jim Crockett reopened his territory in Chattanooga, TN, after he sold out to Ted Turner. The first match of the New N.W.A. would be "Nightmare" Ted Allen versus Brian Logan. Ted and I were good friends. We had traveled together several times. Ted had a love for the ladies. I did too. We had opposite tastes in women though. He liked to spend his time with the largest lady in the bar. That worked out good for me because the large ones always traveled with a hot friend. Ted was the perfect wingman. Keep on loving those large ladies "Terrible" Ted.

I got a great chance to wrestle top named talent with Crockett. I worked with Dory Funk Jr. in a six man tag. One of his partners was named Aries. He would later change his name to Moabi, before settling with the name Ahmed Johnson in the W.W.F. Dory beat the hell out of me with those forearm shots of his. I still loved every second of wrestling the former N.W.A. World's champion. Pictures of me wrestling him were published in Japan. Dory was impressed with me and got me booked on a tour of Japan. However, I was cancelled and replaced at the last minute due to the release of several W.W.F. stars. They were booked due to their drawing power. At that stage in my career I just wasn't ready.

I would finish up for SMW in late 1994. I would wrestle several matches as Chris Candido's partner. Brian Lee had left to the W.W.F. to do the "Faker Taker" angle. I took his bookings until Balls Mahoney would become Chris's new partner as Boo Bradley. The Gangstas also came into the area at this time. New Jack and Mastafa Sied were hot as new heels that were challenging the Rock N Roll. They needed polishing up. So I got the job. It was my spot to get them over on TV. I did. I later saw New Jack at an E.C.W. live event and he credited me with being the one who made him get over so he could have a job. He paid me back by making sure everyone in E.C.W. respected me. I had helped him get over so he could make money with Rock N Roll. That is how the business used to be. It was based on respect. We are still friends today. He gets a bad rap for his gimmick. That's his deal. There is only one New Jack.

In October of 1994, I wrestled my last match for SMW. That night I worked three times. First as Brian Logan versus my old partner Anthony, who was Inferno Brimstone. Next, with Shawn Casey, Brian Logan wrestled against the Gangstas. Finally, with The Inferno Brimstone against Brian Lee and Lance Storm. I would move on to other territories and SMW would close it's doors. A combination of issues and Cornette signing with the W.W.F. were among the cause. It was one of the greatest territories of all time. The little territory that could go. It was described as too big to be small, and too small to be big. It was just right. In my opinion it was the greatest place on earth to be.

Before I close the book on Smoky Mt. I want to talk about a family I have not mentioned much. The Armstrong Family is legendary in our business. They hold a special place in my heart. Bob, Steve, Scott, Brian, and Brad. I was only around Brad for a short time I really didn't get to be around him as much as I hoped. He is one of the best talents in the business. Brian started in SMW, but quickly moved to W.C.W. and later to W.W.F. as Road Dogg. He was a fine person and fun to be around. I spent most of my time with "Bullet" Bob, Steve, and Scott. We hit it off immediately. Bob was so down to earth, and loved to have fun. Steve was the same way. The brothers were super nice to me. I mostly wrestled Bob. Who's chops would curl your hair and drop your socks, brother. Anytime I was booked with any of the Armstrongs I would plant myself under the learning tree. They, however, taught me more about being a wrestler out of the ring than any other person.

We would all go out to the night clubs together. The Armstrongs were always looking for new "talent". Talented women that is to say. They have been described as amateur pharmacists. I would agree they always had the cure to what ailed you. They would teach me how to get by on little to no money. Which were the best places to go to like Nashville Sound in Johnson City, and Cotton Eyed Joes in Knoxville. How not to make a scene and get noticed as a trouble making wrestler.

In New Orleans, LA, one night, I wrestled Scott, Road Dogg, and the "Bullet" in a tag match. Ken Timbs and I were doing the Assassin gimmick. Road Dogg came out first and did his DX stuff. They loved it. The match started, and as Scott and Bob worked Ken and me, they shined. Then I hit the "Bullet". We started beating him down like we owned him, while Road Dogg rallied the crowd at ringside. They got to a fevered pitch. Then they rioted! There we were, Bob and I, both knocked down in the center of the ring, both of us starting to make a tag. The place erupted. The crowd just started fighting each other. Were finished the match, dropped kayfabe, and stood back to back and watched the police stop this chaos. We finally made it back to the dressing room unharmed. It was the wildest thing I have ever seen! I love the Big Easy.

Tim Horner had teamed with Brad. Tracy Smothers teamed with Steve. They were treated as illegitimate sons of Bob. I was trained by Tim so they took me in as one of their own too. I love the Armstrong family with all my heart. I will never forget how good they treated me.

My forefathers, people like Tony Anthony, Tracy Smothers, Ricky and Robert, the Armstrongs, and Tom Pritchard gave birth, so to speak, to Brian Logan. They raised him and did it the right way. I paid dues and learned lessons the right way. I benefited from all they taught. They raised me in a business that has forgotten it's responsibility. Now days a wrestler works one match and thinks he is a star. A promoter likes them and makes them the star of the town's promotion. They think he is a star because he can do back flips, front flips, and any other move. They forget the human elements of interaction with the fans. Fancy moves doesn't make a star, or even a good wrestler. I want to sincerely thank all of those men, superstars, who taught me the correct way. I am forever in debt to you men. Thank You!

Chapter 4: Wrestling, Women, and Weeping

    I had now spent one year solid on TV and traveled half the country. Not bad for a green horn, huh? I was now armed with enough experience to guide me on my chosen path. I was confident, and in better shape than I had ever been. I had lost forty pounds and put fifteen to twenty pounds of muscle on in its place.

    The power of TV can never be understated. People see you on TV and, immediately, you are a star. I returned home for a short visit. I looked completely different. I had long hair and was in great shape. Most of the people I knew didn't recognize me. Others only knew me from seeing me on the tube. I found out that a local bar where everyone I knew hung out, had been playing SMW's show every Saturday night. When I walked in there I was a smash hit. No one remembered what had happened just a few years earlier. Women who would have never wanted to be in the same room with me, now wanted to get to know me. It didn't take me long to realize I had only one thing I could do. Live it up!

In the towns I had wrestled in it was twice as crazy. I still lived in Morristown, TN. When Smoky shut down all the boys moved on. I hit the bars everywhere. In Johnson City I was one of the last real wrestlers to still come out to party. There were women all around. They wanted to be with a wrestler, even though the promotion was gone.

This is where I met one of my best friends of all time there, Crystal. She is now married to Glen Jacob, W.W.E.'s Kane. She would let me stay at her house in Elizabethton when I was in too bad of a shape to drive home. I would go out Honky Tonkin' all night and go sleep it off at her place. She always woke me up at the crack of dawn with a full breakfast. Bacon, ham, greasy eggs, and biscuits were all there on the table. I would get so sick. Her cooking was great. Those aren't the kind of foods to wake up to still drunk. She got a real kick from that. As I ate, and I had to eat, she would spend the next hour running down my behavior. I would eat to keep her happy then go back to sleep. She took good care of me. When she started seeing Glen, I slipped out of the picture. Private relationships are sacred in out industry. I admired Glen. He is one of the top draws of all time. It was something he did outside of the ring that impressed me most. He took care of Crystal's two daughters from her first marriage. He didn't have to, and some people wouldn't. He did. I respected that. The girls were good kids. They are grown now. I watched them grow up. They needed a father and Glen stepped in to help. Few of the boys would take that responsibility. I was glad to know both of them.

I continued for years to wrestle, party, and hook up with girls. I would go to the town and work the match.

Then I would hit the closest bar. I did that almost every where on the east coast. This is the problem with the wrestling lifestyle. We get caught up in fast living, and pretending we are something we are not. Before you know it, it is too late. This would be the beginning of that for me.

I was booked on a three day loop in Waynesboro, VA, for Doug Ward. He had booked Horner, "Killer" Kyle, Anthony, and myself. We had all appeared on TV in the area. Road Warrior Hawk was the big draw. The first night, Roger Anderson and I worked Doug and Hawk in the main. The match went well and Roger and I were billed as the Mid Atlantic tag team champions. The second night we worked with Tim and Hawk. This is where the trouble started.

Each night the house was worse than the previous. We were supposed to receive our money at the end of the loop. This was fairly common among real promotions. We were about to find out that this was not a real promotion. We dropped the belts to Hawk and Horner and, after the match, Hawk went to talk to Doug about the money. He feared, if Hawk feared anything, that he would get stiffed on his money. Doug reassured him he wouldn't. The two continued to talk. By the end of the conversation Hawk decided he was going home. He tells Doug to forget about his money. Here was Hawk's thought process. This is a classic by far. If Doug paid him he would not have enough to pay the rest of the boys. Then we would hurt him. If Doug paid the boys, then he couldn't pay Hawk. Hawk would kill him. So, Doug could continue to live life, Hawk decides to just go home and cut his loses and stay out of prison. He told Doug to just pay us. That was a great thing for Hawk to do. Most stars would just want their money and the rest of us were on our own. I really think the world of him doing that. Doug is off the hook right? Not yet. Hawk leaves, and Doug should now have enough money to pay the rest of us and still turn a profit. Right? Of course not, that would make sense, and we can't do any thing that makes sense in pro wrestling. Doug comes to us and tells us that Hawk took every dime of his money for the whole three days and left town. So he paid us early, but only half. What he ended up doing was getting rid of Hawk, paying us half of what he promised, and pocketing the other half. He got away with it at first. Then it caught up with him.

A few months later Doug would have a falling out with his business partner, Stacy Preston, who worked as Preston Michaels. Stacy called me with a stupid idea. I hated the idea, but I had my own reason for going along. Stacy rented a limo and paid me one hundred dollars to come to Virginia. He wanted me to dress in a suit and paid me to sit in the crowd at a show Doug was on. Stacy had hookers dressed up in prom dresses and champagne in the limo. I guess he was a Horseman mark. His idea was that this would promo his next show and steal away all the fans to his show. That is, if there were any fans there. This was the stupidest idea I had ever heard, it made me look like a mark. I had a plan though. I knew one of the guys booked on the show. I put it in his ear that Doug should start something with me when he came to the ring. Then I would hit the ring and Doug could put his finishing move on me and pin me right there in the middle. He thought I would double cross Stacy and actually promote him instead. Doug loved it, and it went down as planned, until we actually got into the ring. Some of the other boys filed out to work with Stacy and his goof cousin. They are going at it on the floor, and Doug and I are in the ring. Doug grabs me and I tell him to shoot me in and give me a back drop, which I would make him look like a million bucks. He fell for it, and Irish whipped me to the rope and bends over with his head down. I was wearing my snake skin cowboy boots. I kicked him right in the face, boot tip first, as hard as I could. His mouth was covered in blood as he fell over to the mat. I backed up and gave him a short kick to the ribs. I followed this up by taking the boot off and, with the wooden end; I hammered him till he cried. The crowd loved it, all twenty of them. Just before I exited the ring, I whispered in his ear, "Don't you wish you had paid me my three hundred dollars?" It wasn't over yet. I went back to my hotel room and dialed his number. His dad answered the phone, who had apparently been the mastermind behind stiffing us on our pay. I asked him if the hospital bill was worth it considering it would cost way more than three hundred dollars. I wasn't done there. I called Doug's girlfriend next. I had met her formally on the three day loop. I invited her back over to the hotel, and she became a "Playerette". I guess we all got screwed on the Doug Ward deal. He hasn't been seen since. Neither has his girlfriend.

Hawk loved this story. The first W.W.F. show I worked on, he went around telling everyone about it. He would tell it time and time again over the years. My friend, Road Warrior Hawk, passed away while I was writing this book. You will be missed my friend. Thanks for the laughs.

While I was working Virginia, I met another character that would go on to fame. David Cash. He is better known as Kid Kash. The first night I met him he was doing a crow gimmick. This was years and years prior to Sting ever thinking of doing that. It turned out that Dave's wife, at the time, was from Midland Trail, which is two towns over from Oak Hill. We knew a lot of the same people, so we became friends. Dave wrestled his first match and had not been trained. Not even a single move. So I invited him to Tim's school, which should have been my school. I did all the work. So, I began training him to work. He could do any flip imaginable, but couldn't wrestle a bit. Not even one hold. Today he is a top draw and a good performer, but he wouldn't know a wrist lock from a wrist watch. A real common misconception is that Ricky Morton trained Dave. That is simply not true. A lot surrounding Dave is not true. He is a bit of a habitual liar. That is just Dave; if you understand that about him, he is cool. If not, then he will take you for a ride.

The origins of the lie about Ricky training him got started this way. Dave was living in Johnson City, TN. Ricky's wife, Andrea, was an exotic dancer at the Mouse's Ear in Grey, just outside of J.C. Ricky takes Dave to the club and Andrea and Dave become friends. Then one thing leads to another and Dave sleeps with her. What does Ricky do? He takes him on the road with him. That makes sense doesn't it? Well, remember the "golden rule". If it makes sense, do the opposite, when you're in professional wrestling. So, Dave started telling everyone that Ricky trained him. Which got him booked a lot more than using my name at the time. I think Ricky's thinking was that if Dave was with him on the road, then he couldn't be with Annie Lou at home.

One of the first Independent promotions I started working for was Southern States Wrestling out of the Kingsport, TN, area. It was run by "Handsome" Beau James. What a character this guys is. He is around three hundred pounds and stands five foot six. He is a throw back to Jerry "The Crusher" Blackwell. Do not let his physique fool you; he is the real deal. He can wrestle an hour and shoot with the best of them. He would imitate his idol Jerry Lawler. He became the King of the Southern Independents. He copied the crown, Tarzan Butcher, and the wrestling style. We became as close as brothers.

SSW started out in Falls Branch, TN. The Sampson center only held about twenty to fifty people, but they were true die hard fans. They would see some of the best wrestling to ever be booked in the south, and some of the worst too. He had some of the biggest names in southern wrestling working there over the years. Ricky Morton, Tom Pritchard, Buddy Landel, Jimmy Golden, and Mark Curtis were regulars in the territory. He also had W.W.F. caliber talent. Edge and Christian both worked for Beau before they were stars. Edge immortalized Beau in his book, called him Mike. Beau has still got heat with Edge over that. Curt Hennig would be recognized for a short period as the World's Champion when he held the W.W.A. (World Wrestling All Stars) title. E.C.W. stars Sabu, Shane Douglas, and Tracy Smothers would compete in SSW as well.

I was brought in to SSW as the Hornet at first, then used as Logan. Beau and I formed a tag team called The Living Legends, the youngest old timers in the business. Looking back now it was brash for us to use that moniker, but it was true. We were booked all over the country as a team. We would later revisit our team in different incarnations over the years. The best business we did was the ten year feud that was on again and off again. We could always fall back on a Logan/HBJ feud to pop the attendance.

Beau always liked to joke around. One time, in Ashville, NC, we were on a show with the Hardy Boys. This was before they had even started working on Vince's TV. Matt, Jeff, Venom, who was Joey Abs, and Champagne were all very young. We started ribbing them immediately. We were going on and on about how pretty they were and what we would do to them. At one point, we had them all huddled up in the corner wondering what they would do.

Just before we go to the ring for our match, Beau tells me, "Those Hardy boys can go, so we got to out do them so we can come back here to work again." I understood and we went to the ring. I was quite a high flier at that point. *Pro Wrestling Illustrated* had credited me with being one of wrestling's perennial high fliers. So, the plan was I would fly and he would catch me. This was a bad idea. As planned, at some point, I spilled out to the floor, and Beau fought me up the bleachers. I was to knock him off to the floor then do a Moon Sault and he would catch me. I knocked him to the floor below, and did the best Moon Sault ever. I imagined it like the Japanese posters, or even a gazelle hopping through the air. As I am upside down falling, I looked around. I was wondering where Beau was? As I passed him I saw him step back and hold his arms up. I then fell the rest of the way to the floor. The bleachers were about ten feet high. Splat! I hit the floor. He had dropped me. To say that he had dropped me would infer that he attempted to catch me in the first place. I asked him later why he had done this to me. He replied simply, " It was so beautiful I had to see how it ended." I had just nearly killed myself and he wanted to see the ending. That's my friend. The Hardy's, as usual, stole the show. Beau and I fought each other the entire match. It was a disaster. In the end the crowd remembered one thing; the idiot that back flipped off the bleachers to the floor, then fist fought his opponent.

Beau was always doing stuff like that. We were driving through farm country in Nebraska. All you could see was corn on either side as far as the horizon. We had said all that we could say on that trip. There was dead silence in the car for about twenty minutes straight. Beau slides his hand over, grabs my knee, and squeezes. I jumped straight up, it scared me so bad. It was probably about ten feet, if I hadn't hit my head on the roof of the car. It nearly knocked me out. The car went out of control, and shot of the road. We went straight though the corn field. Shucks of corn were flying everywhere. I finally gained control of the car and forced it to stop. I looked over at Beau and he was horse laughing. He looks at me and said, "I'll teach you to stop talking to me!" I have been talking non stop to him on road trips for years now.

Another time we were in Charleston, WV. All the heels hit the ring and attacked me. What I didn't know was that the referee was actually slow in the head. I couldn't tell that he was before the match. It turned out he was. When it can time to knock out the ref he wouldn't go down. You know that retard strength. Beau finally knocks him down. At this point we still didn't know he was slow. When the heels attacked, one held each of my arms. Beau splits my wig wide open with a chair. He was so mad at the ref he didn't work with me, he took it out on me instead. If you watch the tape of the match, you can see my eyes cross and roll back into my head when he hits me with the chair. Then, all the color leaves my face as I was about to pass out. By the time Beau was done that night I was retarded.

    Beau had this valet that he claimed was his girlfriend. I got Dave Cash booked on a SSW show. Dave started flirting with the valet. I had told Beau to go easy with Dave because he was green and didn't know much. Beau had already saw him and her, and made up his mind. He put a real serious beating on Dave. Beau threw him to the floor. This is a simple move if you know how to do it, Dave didn't. Blam! He hits the floor almost knocking him out. At this point if Dave knew what was coming he would have wished he would have been knocked out. Beau follows him to the floor and levels him with a steel chair. I was at ringside, but couldn't help too much; I was supposed to be Beau's partner. I rolled Dave back in the ring. Dave was dead weight. Beau just pinned him. If you ask Dave his version of the story, it is the other way around. Dave is a habitual liar, so I expect that from him.

    Beau would also take his fair share too. He faced the Batten Twins, Bart and Brad in Lewisburg, WV.

The bell rings, and the first thing Beau does is belly to belly suplex onto the Battens. He dropped him uneven when he hit the mat. The twin, because in the ring I can't tell them apart, like out of the ring, grabs Beau and starts German suplexing his three hundred pound ass over and over. Beau crawled for a tag and said, "Save me Please." I worked the rest of the match by myself.

For years I would try to steal the crown from him in the locker room. He couldn't find it, have to go to the ring, then return to find it sitting where he left it. I stole his butcher one night and forgot to give it back to him. He had to wrestle with his belly hanging out. It was the only one that fit him. I finally remembered to return it to him. It was for the crowd's sake though.

Beau and I have had our differences and our share of memories. He married a beautiful young lady named Misty. He didn't invite me to the wedding. (I'm not bitter am I?) I returned to SSW and East Tennessee area Thanksgiving night 2007. I have been there ever since. I love Beau like he was my own flesh and blood. We are family, brothers. Misty is the best thing that ever happened to him. She is a wonderful wife and takes great care of him. He is one of my favorite opponents, and definitely my favorite partner. I love ya Brother! However, his own greediness and lies would overcome him finally as every one of his main talents would quit SSW. He now works as a carnival ride barker, and has very little to do with the real wrestling business. He never appreciated who his true friends were. It cost him his career in the end.

The year 1995, would be one of the worst years I would ever have. I started off the year working TV for W.C.W. against Harlem Heat. I would move on to work the Mississippi territory first, before I made the permanent move to Atlanta. I was plagued with a sort of flu or pneumonia that year. I tried to work though it, and did not seek a doctor's advice. I had no time to stop working. I could be just as sick at work as I could at home. As a result, I lost a lot of weight, about forty pounds. I weighed around two hundred and four pounds at my lightest. I lost a lot of muscle mass too, because I was too tired to work out.

In March of 1995, I was contacted by a promoter named John Horton. His plan was to reopen the Mid South area in Mississippi. I was recommended by Ricky Morton, and John and I hit it off from the start. The first shot for him was Port Gibson, Mississippi. Port Gibson is as far south as you can go and not be in the ocean. To get there you drive to the end of civilization, make a left, and drive about an hour and half farther. You can not miss it. If you get wet, you went too far. It was directly in the middle of swamp country. There would be pink painted shacks with stars and moons painted all over them every few hundred feet. They looked just like Kamala's belly paint. Once you arrive, there is a booming little town, right in the middle of nowhere, just like it should be connected to the real world.

I wrestled Abdullah the Butcher that night. Port Gibson is an all black community. Abdullah was a baby face if you can believe that. Anthony and I worked Abby, with a local worker, as his partner. John didn't want us to job to Abby on our first night in, so he booked us as the Infernos. Abby was such a pleasure to work with. It was so easy. We literally tore down the house. He threw me though tables. Hit me with the bell. He eventually pinned Anthony. Abby was so nice. It was almost scary. It was like he was being nice to butter us up for the beating the Butcher had prepared. Actually, it was not like that at all Abby is a great person and was just a class act. I always loved working with him.

We left Port Gibson on the trek of a lifetime back to St Louis to work for Henry Hubbard again. The ride was so long. Thirteen hours. Once we arrived, I was booked the entire loop with Ron Simmons. Henry had put Doink the Clown on the poster. Doink was Matt Bourne's gimmick in the W.W.F. at the time. He had not bothered to book Bourne. I said that I would do the gimmick if he provided a Doink suit. He had instructed me that he would have one, but just in case go to the costume store and rent a clown costume. Anyone who knows wrestling knows that Doink doesn't look like a typical clown. He insisted I bring the receipt and he would reimburse me for the expenses.

When I arrived in St. Louis, Henry did not have the Doink gear. Big surprise! Strike one. The clown out fit I had looked nothing like Doink. Strike two. I put four or five different items from my gear together to make a makeshift Doink. It consisted of blue tights, yellow boots, one yellow knee pad and one purple one, a yellow singlet, and red trunks. I painted my face like the original, and toped it all of with a green, red, and blue multi-colored wig. It was as far away from Doink as Port Gibson was from St. Louis. The show that night was sold out, Ricky Morton was on the show. When I walked down the isle, a kid snatched my wig off my head revealing my long hair. The real Doink didn't have long hair. I panicked and went running back to the dressing room. Ron was waiting at the door for me. I quickly explained what happened. He quickly told me to go to the ring or get my ass kicked. Foul tip. So I went to the ring. Ron was kind to me and didn't beat me up. I somehow managed to get some heat back and slide Ron over. Like he wasn't already over without my help. Then next night Ron grabbed that stupid wig off my head first thing and threw it to the crowd so we could work. Once the loop was over good ol' Henry didn't want to reimburse me the forty dollars for the clown suit. He said that I didn't use the clown suit, I used my own stuff and that he wasn't paying for it. Strike Three! In the words of Farooq, "Damn!"

Henry Hubbard would quit the business, but later resurface trying to undercut Thomas Reeder on the Army base tours. He called me several years later and said that he wanted to apologize to me. His son had murdered somebody and was getting life in prison. He had prayed to God that if he made good on all his mistakes, would God spare his son. Apparently, the death penalty was a sentencing option. I responded by saying just send me my money. He never did. His son was convicted of murder.

I traveled from St. Louis to Steubenville, OH, and then returned to Mississippi the following week for TV. John had the idea that our gimmick would be that of the guys from the movie *Billionaire's Boys club*. It ended up being a cross between the Midnight Express and the Thrill Seekers. Close enough for me. This was the first time we would wrestle without masks. Anthony kept his same name, but I was renamed Christian Devereaux. I am Brian Logan through and through, but Christian Deveraux is a cool name. Our team would be named The Lost Generation.

Our debut was on TV against good friend Tracy Smothers and Darkstorm (not to be confused with Eric Darkstorm), a local black worker from that town. We won our first match that night as a team. We won a lot. It was our first official push. We did several TV interviews and were the main focus of the TV's. That was a huge accomplishment considering the talent he had booked on a regular basis, Buddy Landell, Abdullah, Cactus Jack, Rock n Roll, and Tracy just to name a few. John took care of us too. He paid for everything. He put us up in nice hotels, paid our food expense, and also to wrestle. Looking back that is probably why the promotion went under. In my book, and this is, John Horton was a great promoter and treated us like kings. I will always be glad to work with him.

After the closing of Mid South, I moved on to Canada. I had met Scott D'Amoure in Atlanta working for W.C.W. He owned Border Cities Wrestling. It covered the Ontario province and also ran Detroit. He had heard about the Doink gimmick from Hubbard and had Bourne booked though the New York office all summer. Matt had gotten arrested on a domestic dispute with his girlfriend, or wife, and couldn't make the tour. Matt had been there before and the crowd knew it was the real Doink. Scott offered me real good money, so I had an identical Doink suit made. This is where the curse of Doink began for me.

I made more money in Canada than I had ever made up until that point. I got three hundred American, plus expenses. I also got all the money from my merchandise. This was a lot of sales in Polaroids. It was taking in around five hundred a night American. I started getting booked everywhere with that gimmick. The problem was that no one wanted Brian Logan. They wanted to book Doink. I had been doing the gimmick in Augusta, GA, for about a year. I tried to destroy the gear by letting them rip and not taking care of it, but the thing just wouldn't die. I finally sold the thing to the Augusta promoter so that Brian Logan's career could survive.

I was working in Canada when I was contacted by Bert Prentice. He was running Ozark Mt. Wrestling in Arkansas. He had seen the Lost Generation stuff and wanted us to come work his territory. I began driving from Morristown, TN, to Canada on the week ends. It is about twelve hours one way. Then, during the week, I would drive eight hours to Arkansas to work there. I traveled back and forth all summer long. I really liked working for Bert. A lot of the boys don't, but he always treated me fair and with respect. He always paid me, and always what he said he would. I respected him for that.

Rex King told me this story one time. Steve and Rex worked for Bert in Kansas City. Bert's promotion went under and some bills were left unpaid. Rex was one of the guys not paid. He wanted his money so he kidnaps Bert's dog. He held the dog for ransom. Bert was terrified about the safety of his pet, and the two arranged a meeting. Just like in the movies. Bert arrives at the pay phone. It rings, Rex is on the other end. Bert was instructed to walk across the street and dump the cash, then return to the pay phone. Bert did just that. The phone rings, Rex says, "Here is your dog." Then he let the poor puppy run across the street dodging cars to the safety of his master.

I worked in my first official story line while in Arkansas with Brickhouse Brown. He taught me a lot about converting what you do on TV on a house show match. He taught me how to tell a complex story. I had been taught how to tell the beginning. Now he showed me how to tell the ending of that same story.

I had moved my base of operations to Memphis, TN. I still had my place in Morristown, but was always on the other side of the state or the mid west. I moved in with Bull Pain and Samantha.

Bull had gotten me booked in Texas. I had grown up watching World Class wrestling from the most famous wrestling arena in the country, the Sportatorium, in downtown Dallas, TX. It had been reopened after the Von Erich tragedies. I feel so privileged to this day that I got to work there. I wrestled "Wild" Bill Irwin twice at the Sportatorium. I had watched Irwin wrestle my entire life. Unfortunately working with him would leave a lot to be desired. At one point in the match he tried to leap frog me and fell down. He would call an arm drag and just not take one, leaving me to fall flat on my back. I never liked Bill after I met him. He yelled at me in front of all the boys trying to make up for the mistakes he had made. I just thought more of him until I actually worked with him. He tried to cover up a mistake by embarrassing a young kid. That's low class. All his ribs on me backfired, just like the Goon did.

I liked Bull Pain and Sam, but it was like living in a war zone in their house. Bull Pain and Bill Dundee had gotten in to some legal trouble. It revolved around a bar and a fire; I'm not sure of those details. Bull took the rap for the whole thing. He was on probation. He had to turn down tours to Japan and other deals because of the probation. Sam had always had a crush on Bill ever since she was a little girl. Bull and Sam eventually divorced and Sam married Bill. I tried to stay out of every little bit I could, but it was hard. I really respected Bull, and would work with him several times over the years. He is still bitter about the whole deal with Sam and Bill. I would see Sam and Bill at OVW's Last Dance card in Louisville, Ky. She acted like she didn't even know me.

So far '95 sounds pretty good. There are always good points. It wasn't wrestling that made the year so bad, it was my private life that made me weep. I had been seeing a girl from Morristown. Her step mom introduced her to me. She brought Jennifer to a wrestling show and we hit it off from the start. Jennifer had two jobs at the time, and I was traveling a lot, as you have just read. It was hard to spend time together, but we managed. I was feeling better from my illness and started back to the gym. I was taken by the bodybuilding world at that time. I spent hundreds of dollars on supplements, and with rent, food, and travel things were tight. I managed it though. There was always enough money. Jennifer's actual mom was "old south". She was the kind of person who believed in the work till you drop theory of living life. She never approved of me, and certainly not my profession. I didn't matter how successful I was, or how good at it I was, it would never be a proper job. She thought I should get up at dawn and be a tobacco farmer. It was none of her business; she wasn't paying the bills. I was.

I was ready for a commitment, so I asked Jennifer to marry me. She accepted, and I brought her home for Easter that year to meet my friends and family. The night before Easter we all went out on the town. Craig, Steven, their dates, Jennifer and I. Even Mom came out with us. I wanted them to all approve of her. We had dinner and drinks and the girls all went dancing. It was fun. The next day Dad threw a fit. He was mad at Mom for going out without him. The night before it had been okay, now it wasn't. We were all going to have Easter dinner at my Aunt's house. The entire family was going to be there to meet Jennifer. Mom and Dad argued all day in front of us. We never went to the Easter dinner. I was so embarrassed. Jennifer went home to Tennessee and I returned to the road.

Later that year we went back to West Virginia for a wedding shower. My Aunt and Mom had planned the shower to make up for the Easter incident. This time my Mom was overbearing and clingy. The exact opposite as she was before. I didn't realize it at the time, but Jennifer was getting frustrated.

The wedding was scheduled for June 2nd, 1995. It was also my anniversary of entering into the wrestling business. Everything was set. We had the church, cake, flowers, tuxes, everything for a huge wedding. Craig and Steven were to be in the wedding, and my entire family was coming to Tennessee for the wedding. Even Tim Horner was going to sing at it. On June first, Jennifer calls the wedding off. I tried to get in contact with my family to tell them, but they had already left. Jennifer left our house and went to her mother's place. My family arrived, and I explained what had happened. No one asked how I was, if I was okay, or that they were sorry it happened. I spent the next day canceling everything. Craig and Steven went home. They never said a word to me about it.

Once everything was canceled, I had the great pleasure of entertaining my family. I had to take them to sightsee. My Dad, Mom, Aunt Glad, Cousin Tammy, and her boys Larry and Joey, along with my Uncle Paul all wanted to go to Pigeon Forge. Once we were back they acted like that I was the one that wanted to go sightseeing. I lived there; I'd seen it. All I wanted to do was figure out what happened between Jennifer and me. I wouldn't find out for a long time to come though.

A few days later I talked to Jennifer. I had paid for the honeymoon already and she told me that she wanted to stay together, just not get married. So, we went on our honeymoon even though we never got married. I took her to Panama City, FL. Everything went well there, so we decided to still live together. We tried to put all this behind us.

Towards the end of the year Mom phoned with bad news. She was divorcing my Dad. It didn't surprise me, but it still hurt me. Just as things brightened up, someone was always turning out the lights. My whole life was like that. Even to this day things are great in my life. I still wait for someone to pull the rug out from under me. It is a major flaw I have. My Mom had moved out and took a job in Charleston. She would eventually move into my Grandmother's house. She was sick and Mom had to put her into a nursing home.

I remember when my Grandfather Webb had died. My Grandmother and I took a bus trip to Florida. I and my Grandmother piled onto a bus with several old people, and rode down to Florida seeing the sights. We stopped at PTL, Jim Baker's Christian retreat. We ended up in Coral Springs and she took me to NASA. We were going to see the Space Shuttle launch. It took two days, and there were several delays on the launch. Then, the next day, they finally launched. All you could see from where I was at was a bright light. Then, all of a sudden, a lot of smoke. A noise could be heard followed by another light. This turned out to be the day the Space Shuttle Challenger blew up. I was right there to see it.

So, I now had to deal with my personal problems, my enormous travel schedule, and my parent's divorce. My biggest worry was for my Dad, believe it or not. He had been waiting to die for about ten years now, I guess his sickness and mental abuse just took its toll on her.

One of the cool things that did happen was a trip my Dad and I took to Columbus, OH, to the Arnold Classic bodybuilding competition. I was still in my bodybuilding phase. I got to meet Arnold. He had the biggest arms I have ever seen. Arnold was great. He only had a minute to talk, but was one of the nicest people I had ever met. I also met Gregory Hines, the movie star, who was doing a personal appearance for an exercise company. Lou Farigno, The Incredible Hulk, was also on hand. I was so excited to meet him, I was a huge Hulk fan as a kid. I talked with him and we shook hands. He wasn't overly friendly. I think he cared more about selling his book. Dad and I had a blast meeting all those stars.

The worst thing about the divorce was that even though I was an adult they were about to put me in the middle. They still treated me like a kid. They would constantly want me to spy on the other one. Mom was terrible for doing stuff and asking me not to tell Dad about it. It wasn't my place to do either.

I had decided to take of a few months from December of 1995 to March of 1996, and train to get myself in top shape and make a run at a major company. I trained with a couple of bodybuilders who were training for Mr. Knoxville competition. While I never got into bodybuilder shape, I was still in phenomenal shape as a wrestler. I was 255lbs. with 8% body fat. I was intense and religious with my workouts. I sometimes wonder back if I over trained, because I can't keep up that kind of regiment today. I guess I got older, but my workouts were never as intense as they were then.

Jennifer and I were spending quality time one night in the throws of passion when she starts laying this news on me. She tells me, "I don't want to be with you, and you will never amount to anything! You are a Failure at your job!" She actually said this as we were making love. Keep in mind that this girl said these things to me as I was penetrating her. What a blow. I was destroyed. I was in love with her, and this is what she thinks of me. Her timing was the worst of all time. Why say that right then? Needless to say I, we, did not finish the session. She got up and left the room. I cried my eyes out right there, all night and early into the next morning. Up until that moment I was fighting. Always fighting something. Fighting to get away from my past. Fighting to get ahead in my profession. Sometimes, fighting literally not to loose my love ones. Then I just gave up.

Chapter 5: Hotlanta and World Championship Wrestling

The Power Plant was advertised as "The Harvard of Professional Wrestling". It was actually like the Ten Buck Two Community College. I was confident in the shape I had gotten myself in. I decided to call the offices of World Championship Wrestling. They put me in contact with Jody Hamilton. Jody was the man behind the mask of N.W.A. legend The Assassin. He informed me that it was W.C.W. policy that all new talent had to go through the Power Plant training center.

The Power Plant was designed to physically break anyone who entered, and it did. Their workouts consisted of unrealistic calisthenics, and very little ring time. The ring time had total supervision, and zero ring psychology to it. Everything that I had already been taught and experienced, they threw it out the window. I saw people intentionally hurt for no reason. I also saw careers being made, and also broken, for no reason. Instructors like Buddy Lee Parker, Mike Winters, and Pez Whatley just didn't care about the business anymore. They were bitter at their own failure.

They were washed up midcarders, and never had beens that were now forced to teach to get a paycheck.

My Grandmother had passed away and left me ten thousand dollars. Jennifer had moved out, and back in with her mother. So I was ready for a new start. In March of 1996, I moved to Atlanta, Ga., to work for W.C.W.

I had to actually tryout for the Power Plant. It took place over three days. The physical calisthenics were unbelievable. We did thousands of free standing squats. All morning in fact. They wanted all of us to do them in unison, while counting them off. If one person missed the cadence we started over at one again. This went on until we reached one thousand. We never did. We performed the exercise from nine o' clock in the morning until noon. Non stop. Well, every two hundred we would hit the deck and do two hundred pushups, then start over. I watched as football players, baseball players, military men, bodybuilders, and MMA fighters all fell and quit before me as I went on. We started on day one with thirty guys. By the end of day three there were only me and two others left. We would take a break and lunch for an hour at noon. Then, after lunch, we ran wind sprints till four thirty. This was an endurance test; it had nothing to do with wrestling. That was just how W.C.W. handled talent. The only way I survived until the end was pure determination. I suffered through ten thousand squats in three days. I just wanted it so bad, I did not care how much pain I was in. I was accepted into W.C.W.

I had to fill a few dates as I moved my things to Georgia. One of the commitments was a shoot, or legit, wrestling tournament company promoted by

Tim Horner in Morristown. This Street Wrestling tournament was a combination of an amateur wrestling meet and the Tough Man contest. This was when the UFC had only had a few events. Shoot fighting was a lost art in the states. Tim and I were talking about the line up of entries in the tournament. Tim bragged about how much of a shoot it was going to be. I told him that nothing with money on the line is always a straight up shoot. So I entered.

The tournament was sold out, and Ricky Morton wasn't even there. Every redneck tough guy, beer drinker, ex-athlete, bodybuilder, and wrestler signed up for this thing. All of the entries wore sweats or jeans. Not me. I had a point to prove, so I wore pro tights, a different color for each round. I also wore my white patent leather jacket I wore to ringside every night. I definitely stood out.

In the first two rounds I drew two drunken hillbillies. I was in top shape, they were not, especially not ring shape. I toyed with them till they about puked. I even strutted around the ring as I taunted the crowd. When I had run them in circles enough I cross faced them with the front sugar. Out they went.

In the semi-finals I told the referee, 8-ball Jones, that this was it. I had trained with 8-ball several times and wrestled him as well. Tim had asked him to ref the event. One of the basic rules of a total shoot is have the ref on your side. N.W.A. champions for years had kept their legit titles by having the ref in their pocket. When it came time for me to lock up with my opponent, I backed up and taunted the crowd. It was just like I was a heel on TV. My opponent in the semi-finals was a local football hero. His entire high school team was at ringside cheering him on. It was a perfect set up. Over and over I kept refusing to lock up. He would attempt to tie up and I would either back into a corner or strut around the ring. My opponent didn't know what to think. Finally 8-ball came over to the corner and asked what I wanted to do. I told him to DQ me. We started arguing. He told me several times to lock up. Then he told me if I didn't fight he would disqualify me. So I pushed him. He pushed back, and I soared through the air and took a bump. He called for the bell and I got disqualified. The crowd was furious. They had just spent every bit of fifteen minutes waiting to see me get mine from this guy, and I had yanked it from them. On top of all this, it looked just like pro styled wrestling.

It didn't stop there. I quickly changed and hung around to see the finals. It came down to the footballer I had put in the finals, and a local tough guy bodybuilder who was the ex-stud of the high school. At one point, the two hit each other and fell out of the ring. While on the floor the bodybuilder, who had wrestled in high school, takes the footballer over backwards, sort of a belly to back suplex type throw. When the footballer landed he hit his head hard on the floor. He was carted out by stretcher and taken to the hospital in an ambulance. The bodybuilder was declared the winner of the tournament. The crowd was hot. The last two matches that they had waited to see all night had ended suspiciously. They felt ripped off. So they decided to riot!

At one point in the riot one of the football player's teammates decided to hit Tim. He knocked four teeth loose. I stood in the middle of the whole thing laughing my ass off. I took fourth place that night, they even gave me a trophy. The best thing was that I had taken a real event and turned it into a work. I had proved my point to ol' mush mouth Tim.

8-Ball Jones was a black man from Detroit, MI. He was a part time truck driver, and part time wrestler. This guy had "IT". His gimmick was half pimp and half black militant, a cross between "Badnews" Brown and Flash Funk. He could wrestle as well as talk. He could have made money in the sport, especially as a manager. His only set back was that he was thirty eight when began to train. He never stood a chance to make it. He was one of my favorite people to be around and a favorite opponent.

I had been at the Power Plant four days when Terry Taylor came in to workout. We had a practice match, at the end of it I made a little come back and he stopped me. He asked me what next. I told him to shoot me off and hit me with his finish. He asked what that was, to see if I knew what his move was. As he was whipping me into the ropes I said, "Five arm, because it is one star better than a forearm." After he hit me with it he asked me why they were not using me on the TV. I told him I wanted a spot, and he booked me on TV the following week.

I made Greenville, but they did not put me in the ring. I was an extra, or enhancement talent as Terry Taylor liked to call the jobbers. I was used in a brawl between Chris Benoit and Kevin Sullivan. I had the task of trying to separate the two. The feud between Sullivan and Benoit was very violent. At the time, they were feuding over Nancy, who was Woman. Benoit eventually married Nancy and had a classic feud with

Sullivan. The scene went like this. Benoit and Sullivan were to be in the dressing room arguing, and then the fight breaks out. I would come in and Benoit would hit me, then they would resume fighting each other. I entered the room and get leveled by a stiff punch. If you watch the tape you can see my blonde hair enter the screen for a millisecond and then I go flying the opposite way. I was paid one hundred fifty dollars for that episode, not too bad of a pay ratio for work done, huh?

Chris Benoit would later murder Nancy and his son while I was writing this book. I was so saddened when I heard the news. I won't say a bad thing about Chris or Nancy. I respected Chris and Nancy both. They were always nice to me. I would go out to clubs with Chris socially over the years and I thought the world of him. I would rather remember him for how he treated me, not for what he did.

Earlier that day in Greensboro, I almost made a huge mistake. I was walking back stage, trying to politic a little with the boys when I saw this little boy. He appeared to be about nine years old. He was just wondering around lost. I almost said aloud, "Who is this kid just running around loose back stage." Thank God I didn't. It turned out that it was no little boy. He was Rey Mysterio. I had never seen him before, I had only heard of him, plus he wasn't wearing his mask. He worked with Dean Malenko for the first of many of their legendary match. This one was their debut on Saturday night show. People for years would talk about what an awesome match this one was over the years. It was. I was lucky enough to see it live and in person.

W.C.W. did business very strangely. I worked that TV and it would be months before I would be booked again. They continued to pay me, but not use my talent. This was just one of the many times they missed used talent. I was stuck training in the Power Plant. It was so hard to adjust to the politics. No one there wanted to work. They all just wanted to get paid to sit on their asses.

High Voltage, Robbie Rage, and Kenny Kaos got booked in Chattanooga, TN. By Pez Whatley. These guys were the shining starts of the Power Plant. They got a huge push to the bottom of the card by selling steroids to the entire mid card boys. Sgt. Buddy Lee Parker was their main man. They were booked against two friends of mine Eddie Golden and Stan Lee. Eddie and Stan have been around forever. They are damn good athletes and wrestlers. Eddie is one of my favorite people to be in a locker room with. He was good friends with Kid Kash. We would talk and laugh about all the tall tales he would spin. The only problem Eddie and Stan ever had was too much Southern wrestling style and too little of bodies. Still they were top talent in my book. The four are about to go to the ring. Eddie comes over and asks Kenny and Rob what spots they wanted to do. Kenny says to him, "We don't do spots, we just react!" Eddie replied, "Well I'm from Tennessee and we work here." I guess that is why High Voltage sucked, they were just reacting. They eventually quit the business. They should have never gotten started in it.

Pez Whatley passed away while I was writing this book. Pez was the only one at the Power Plant who had a clue. By that point he knew he was just a token black man. He was only there so he could receive his pay check. Pez was a huge star, a classic. I will miss him.

I hated the Power Plant. It just wasn't about wrestling. One time I came in real early and started doing my squats by myself. Buddy Lee Parker came by and asked what I was doing. I told him I wanted to get them out of the way so that when the stars came in I could sit and do nothing. He got hot at me. He made me do what seemed like a million extra. I did them also, he was really pissed then.

After lunch every day we could workout in the rings, but we had no supervision. The instructors were Mike Winners, Pez, and Buddy Lee. They all had their way of doing things and the other two were flat wrong. If two guys were working out in the ring Pez would teach them one way. His was Southern style and mostly correct. Then Mike Winners would come by and tell them his version, followed by Buddy Lee yelling and screaming that they were all wrong and only do it his way.

Mike Winners had made a small name for himself in Portland working for Don Owens. This was towards the end of the promotions run. They were on their last leg as a territory by then. So was some of the talent. Mike was one of those talents.

Buddy Lee Parker was a great wrestler, but no one cared about him. He was boring to watch, and every character he did was lack luster also. Buddy Lee's personality made Lance Storm look like the Rock's in comparison. Sarge would actually yell so much that he would turn purple in the face. He would get mad at the students then take them in the ring and beat them up, instead of teaching them how to do it. Buddy Lee has the worst Napoleon complex I have ever seen.

He would try that stuff with me, but I would fire back at him. I hated him so much that I would rather have dinner with the Devil than to spend one single second around him. Every time you would get in a good rhythm of a work out and actually make progress they would all come along, led by Sarge, and destroy all you had worked on. No one ever got anything done because of them. It showed in the new talent that W.C.W. would produce. Where are any of them now? Exactly, not in the business. Right where they should be, selling roses on the side of the road in downtown Atlanta. I would leave practice at the Power Plant feeling like a sixteen year old virgin who just spent the entire night entertaining all of Tijuana, donkey and all.

Atlanta is a huge place, a booming major city. The night life there was tremendous. There are so many things to do, restaurants to eat at and hot spot night clubs that can be found every night of the week. I started going out to bars every night, drinking and carousing for women.

I was brought into Jody Hamilton's office one day. He told me to get off what ever supplements I was on. He said that they drug tested there. He was implying steroids. I never saw one single drug test while I was in W.C.W. Everybody was on the gas. I was so confused from the meeting. Much like the girl in Tijuana who had just woke up and wondered what had happened the night before. Keep in mind that Sgt. Buddy, High Voltage, Lodi, and the rest were on so much stuff that they were ready to pop. I had a similar meeting about a year later with Jody. He told me that if I wanted to be on TV full time, and be marketable that I had to get on the gas. He actually told me that I had to go out and use steroids to be in the business, or I did not stand a chance to work for W.C.W.

W.C.W. wasn't all bad. I got to work with some real great talent. I wrestled Vader several times, and even got a count out victory over him. I worked with Harlem Heat, Bobby Eaton, NWO member VK Walstreet, and Disco Inferno. Even though I was there two years I only wrestled on TV twenty times. I worked several matches, but they just wouldn't air them. People like Konnan and William Regal would let me have most of the offence, and the office just wouldn't show it on air.

There was a buzz around the Power Plant that Kevin Nash and Scott Hall would be leaving the W.W.F. and joining W.C.W. This is what would eventually lead to the Monday Night Wars. Their arrival would change the power struggle in wrestling for over eighty straight weeks. How did this affect me? It flat out didn't. I was lied to constantly by the office. We were told that with the adding of the Thursday Night Thunder show that there would be three crews and that all the Power Plant students would be used. The first crew would be on Nitro, the b crew on Thunder, and a third c crew would be used on the Saturday Night show as a developmental system. It never happened. The NWO took all the slots and there was no room for advancement. This was in spite of the fact that three hundred of us were being paid to not wrestle.

Sarge had a meeting with the "non stars", and explained to us that all we could hope for was to be "beat meat". This was a term I had never heard before, or since. He told the entire Power Plant that none of us would ever make it in W.C.W. and that all we could hope for is just to be beaten up on TV every week. That was W.C.W.'s version of positive reinforcement. Sarge did, however, live up to what he described, as his career hit new lows.

The biggest lie I was ever told was told to me in Charleston, WV, at a Nitro. After the show the boys always go to one of two places, Joey's Bar and Grill, or the bar in the Marriott Hotel. This particular night I went to the Marriott. Several of the boys were there. Flair, Big Show, who was The Giant at the time, Booker T, Jericho, and Malenko and I were all drinking and eating steaks. Arn Anderson and my buddy, Terry Taylor, were also there. I started a conversation with Taylor and reminded him of the workout we had had. I also stooged off what was going on at the Power Plant. He called Arn over to join the conversation. They both told me how I looked like Barry Windham. At the time I had long blonde hair and was lanky. They expressed how good Barry could work, and wondered if I was any good. Keep in mind I had worked with Taylor months prior. I told them that Tim Horner had trained me and that I had worked for Smoky Mountain for quite some time. They told me about a gimmick that would be similar to Barry's. I loved it. I was going to be a cowboy. They told me to call Terry at the office Monday in Atlanta. I did call, but never talked to Terry Taylor. No gimmick, no push, or return call was ever given. I heard Arn give this same line to Lance Cade years later in OVW. Cade was being told word for word what I had been told. I sat right next to them having the conversation. I thought to myself, "Don't count your money before you earn it, kid." When he debuted on Raw they had cut his hair, changed his tights, and he looked totally different, so much for the Windham gimmick. Just think I was that close to being one of the West Texas Rednecks. That is where they went with the idea that started in a conversation in Charleston with me.

W.C.W. booked me in Florida. They would tape the Saturday Night shows over fourteen day periods. I worked most of my W.C.W. matches on this loop. I had a blast in Orlando. We filmed at MGM studios. It was at Disney, we were considered crew, and we all got crew passes. So, we would all go into the park and ride the rides when we were not working. Scott and Steve Armstrong spent hours riding those rides, either after we had wrestled or on the days we were off. At night we would all go to Pleasure Island. The clubs were packed. Everybody always wanted to party with the wrestlers and Orlando was no different. Meeting women down there was like shooting fish in a barrel.

I was at the Baja Beach Club one night. I got there late that night. They were all wound up by the time I got to the club. I walked in and the first thing I saw was Rey Mysterio on his knees, hands hand cuffed behind his back doing body shots from a girl in a thong bikini. Then the bikini came off. That was okay, because Billy Kidman had his clothes off too, and was running around the bar naked. I went over to talk to some of the boys. Chavo Guererro came over to the table and demanded that we all leave right then. He was all shook up, and we asked why. It seems that he was at the bar helping bartend when Bill DeMott, Hugh Morris, came over and wanted to help him. Bill was blitzed and began spinning bottles like in the movie *Cocktail*. He dropped a few and got all the wrestlers kicked out that night. I can't imagine why. We were all choir boys.

Everything finally came to a head one day at the Power Plant. We were all doing some drills, when Sarge comes over. He begins to explain, "This business isn't a dance! All your moves should be choppy, make them look like they hurt! Because they do!" That could not have been a more wrong; an ignorant statement. I was always taught that this industry was to be used in a way to make as much money as possible, with the fewest injuries. It is a dance, but not ballet. Two partners helping one another to a common goal. The goal is a pay off. The more you could work gracefully the more money you could earn. It's physical, the injuries are for sure real, and sometimes unavoidable. You do try to avoid them though. I have never went in the ring and tried to hurt someone on purpose. If you did that the boys would see that you didn't have a very long career. (Sgt. Buddy who?) I stopped and questioned his statements. He knew he was wrong, but his job was to make us quit. Hard Body Harrison, a former tough man winner, who is in prison for life now on a kidnapping and a prostitution ring charge, stepped in and said that he would teach me how to break all those bad habits I had picked up working for Cornette and all those other Southern Indy guys. Hard Body actually named these guys by name as bad examples, and Sarge agreed. It was like being in the Twilight Zone, or Bizzaro World! These people, The Harvard of Professional Wrestling, were all idiots! I was more talented than these guys and had more experience than over half of them, but I was still wrong and they were still right. I almost broke down and cried.

I left that day and did something extremely stupid. I don't ever recommend anyone ever doing this. My Mom had been visiting for a couple of days with me in Atlanta. I had hurt my knee earlier. It was the simplest thing that caused the injury. I was in Arkansas one night and fell a sleep in my car between towns. While I was a sleep my arm hit the electric seat adjustment and moved the seat closer to the dashboard. I must have jammed my knee between the seat and the dashboard. When I woke it hurt so bad I could not walk on it. I had to crawl across a parking lot into a Hardees restaurant and sit there till I could get feeling back. The injury continued to bother me. I transgressed all my emotions from that day at the Power Plant into this injury. Mom found a doctor in Knoxville, TN, that would see me. So we both drove to Knoxville, it was on her way home from Atlanta to W. Virginia.

I saw the doctor, he ran some test and declared nothing was wrong. I was pissed off. I realize now that the doctor was right, I was just taking out my anger on this injury. I had suffered from Osgood Slaughters disease as a child. This is a common affliction where bones grow faster than the tissue surrounding the bone. It leaves calcium deposits and is extremely sore until it sits up in the tissue. I had basically just aggravated the old wound. I tore out of the doctor's office, got in my car, and drove as fast as I could to Morristown, TN. I was driving so fast and reckless that it took me about fifteen minutes to get from Knoxville to Morristown in rush hour traffic. That in itself was stupid. I, of course, stopped at Jennifer's work long enough to have an argument with her. The real reason I was so upset. All this time Mom was following me as best as she could. Next I went across the street and checked into a hotel. This is where I did one of the most stupid things I could ever do. I took forty, ten milligram, valiums. Next I chugged a six pack of beer. That should have killed me right there. Thank God it didn't!

I wasn't trying to kill myself. I just wanted to zone out from these problems. I just had to do it on a large level. Everything in my life, at that time, made absolutely no sense to me. Mom and Jennifer finally made it to the hotel. By this time I had totally trashed the hotel room. Mom saw that she could do nothing and left, so she could be back to work the next day. Jennifer stayed to try to talk, but she and I could not settle anything. Probably because I was wasted, she left and I have never seen her again.

Jennifer called me one night after that in Atlanta. She wanted to tell me the real version of why she left. While I was on the road in Arkansas she had started seeing the delivery man that supplied her store. In a sense I lost her to the milk man. She went on to tell me that she was pregnant by him, but there was a catch. He was married. Eventually he got a divorce and they got married. They had a couple of children and then he left her. Nobody could see that happening, right?

I was taken to the hospital to get my stomach pumped for the forty valiums. (Bet you couldn't have guessed that one either.) I ended up ripping the IV out of my arm and leaving the hospital. I had just made it back to the hotel when the cops showed up. I had not committed a crime and wasn't wasted anymore, but I had left the hospital without permission. So they retuned me back. The hospital posted a guard at the door so I wouldn't leave. He was a wrestling fan, and had seen me wrestle. He asked me to stay for his sake, because if I wanted to leave he couldn't stop me. I was tired and I felt bad for dragging this poor guy into this mess, so I stayed the night.

The Universe is a funny thing. I believe in karma. I think it comes from God, but exists. I did something real stupid. Nature in return paid me back. I shit charcoal for three days after having my stomach pumped. I felt so sick from that that I never tried a stunt like that again. I learned a lesson the hard way.

I was sick, but I continued to drink. Crystal came by to tell me how dumb I was and to lecture me. I would talk and she would listen, then tell me that I was stupid. She was right. I was being stupid. I just didn't realize it at the time. Crystal really helped me get through that tough time. I couldn't have made it without her. I really appreciate her being my friend.

After this I decided to ask for leave from W.C.W. They were not using me so I produced a death certificate that there was a relative who died and took time off. I was having a nervous breakdown. I came back to West Virginia.

I went back to working for Beau without W.C.W. knowing. We had done so much there we wanted to put a new twist on things. Beau along with Alan Berrie, The Duke of New York, came up with "The Player" gimmick. The gimmick had nothing to do with hip hop or any thing like that. My catch phrase on the t-shirts was "Always be the best Player in The Game". This was long before Triple H was The Game.

I met Triple H in W.C.W. One of my first TVs was one of his last there. He was John Paul Lévesque and Tera Rising, at that time a so-so performer. He is now our generation's Ric Flair. Vince really knew how to use his talent. He is now the measuring stick inside and outside the ring. He is completely professional in the locker room, and nothing he does in the ring can be questioned. He genuinely cares about this industry as a whole, not just himself, like so many top draws before him.

I wasn't ever trying to copy him, especially since I was called "The Player" first. The nickname came from my hard work in the ring and my hard work out of the ring as well. That is the hard work I was famous for at night with the fairer sex. This eventually became more legend than truth. I did have wild times, but it seemed that the boys' version of my conquests were always wilder than the actual events. In that situation you print the myth. I just liked to have fun, and was always around girls. The name fit and we stuck with it for years.

I continued to work Tennessee and Kentucky areas. I also started doing TV for N.W.F. (National Wrestling Federation) out of Columbus, GA. They ran the old Macon territory. I was brought in as a singles. Anthony was brought in as well. We pitched the tag team idea, but they did not like it. Anthony quit, of course. They tried to team me with Joey Mags; it just didn't mesh. Joey was so lazy and milked a knee injury. He wasn't there long either. They eventually teamed me with David Young. I loved being around David. Our personalities were similar. We complemented each other in the ring as well as outside the ring. He, at one time, was one of the most talented, underrated highfliers in our industry. He is slower and a complete wrestler now.

We teamed in Anniston, Al. We wrestled Ted Allan and this guy named Festus. They worked as the Nightmares that night. The match was your typical grab a hold, do a move, walk and talk affair. They put the heat on David and I swear they just wiped the mat with him. They were not fighting him, they were working. They just showed him how it was done. They worked him over, and did it through wrestling. I looked down at David and he said, "Tag they are killing me". I responded with, "I dare you to get blown up in an old school match!" I refused the tag for twenty minutes. He was screaming that he couldn't breathe. David was so worn out at the end of the match. We both to this day still laugh at how two in shape kids in their prime, were showed up and schooled by the grizzled old veterans. Remember, though, he was way more blown up than me.

While working in the N.W.F. I met the "Ragin' Bull" Manny Fernandez. He was quite a character. He was basically a crook and a bully, but we had respect for each other. On Indy shows no one wanted to wrestle Manny. They were scared of him. I was too, but if he beat me up at least I could say I had been beaten up by Manny Fernandez. He never did though. They were some of my roughest matches, but they were good bouts. He never took liberties with me. Manny was trained by the great Lou Thesz. So Manny could definitely go. On top of that he wrestled in the Olympics and played football in the NFL. He was a tough cookie. He would grab me and put me in some impossible hold, but I would counter into something. It flowed well. He would grab me in some stiff hold, I would tell him that he was just playing with me, and he would hurt my feelings if he didn't just let go. Manny liked the fact that I was a competitor and that I didn't mind to get rough out there.

Manny liked to go to the ring with young guys and not give them the finish. More than half of the time Manny would try and put them over him in the end. He just didn't want them to know until it was time. This made a lot of young boys nervous. They would never make it to the time to get put over. They would panic and Manny would beat them up.

Roger Anderson, another former partner of mine, wrestled Manny in Kingsport, TN, one time. I had already worked him that night, but the promotion needed one more Manny match. No one volunteered. Roger was asked if he would do it. Roger kept asking Manny what the finish was, over and over again. Manny wouldn't tell him. Finally Manny answered, "We will see." He had full intentions of putting Roger over. Roger just wouldn't stop bugging him. As they went to the ring I followed. One of the boys asked me where I was going. I told him to watch Roger get his ass handed to him. He did! Manny hit him with everything he could find in that armory. If it wasn't nailed down he hit him with it, if it was, he threw Roger through it.

I finally had to return to W.C.W. My vacation was over. I was there for around eight weeks. These weeks revolved around one guy, an ex-football player who was being groomed for the top spot. To me, at the time, I wasn't impressed. He was just another so called "real athlete" that they were trying to exploit to make money off of. They didn't even try to teach him much. That guy was Bill Goldberg.

I entered the Power Plant for the final time. I was unaware of what was about to happen. I mean they could have kissed me first. Sarge asked me what I was doing there. I told him the same thing I had been doing for the previous two years. He took me into Jody's office and the two pretended that they had never seen me there before, ever! They told me that I was not an employee and that I needed to pay to attend the Power Plant. Not an employee? I had been there for two years! The secretary for the Power Plant was a black woman named Brenda. She was the first one to sue W.C.W. for discrimination of blacks. Brenda said she had no evidence of my employment. I drove twenty minutes home, twenty minutes back, and walked right in Jody's office. I threw the copies of all my pay stubs from the past two years on his desk. I told him to go to hell and that I quit! I walked out to never see W.C.W. again. They folded three years later when Vince bought the company.

The way W.C.W. handled business was pathetic. They could have made better decisions if they would have put ideas on a wall and threw darts at them. All of the top money stars were lazy. It wasn't their fault. Remember the rule, make as much money as possible with littlest of effort. It was the office's fault for not making them earn their paycheck.

Two perfect examples of this is Lex Luger and Buff Bagwell. Neither of them could wrestle worth a damn, but were top draws. Both drew money, both made money, and both were crybabies!

Brian Knobbs got in to Lex's bag at TV on time. He took his trunks out, put them on, and walked around mimicking Lex. Lex got mad and went to Arn. Lex told him that it was his only pair of trunks and that he wasn't going to put them on after Knobbs had been wearing them. He made Arn scratch his match that night over a silly rib. A funny rib, but silly none the less.

They put Buff in singles matches for a while after the Patriot, Buff's partner, suffered an injury. He had three matches scheduled for TV that night. This was standard. First he worked with Flair. Second against Arn and Flair in a tag match. Finally, he was to face Tim Horner and get a win. Buff was so blown up at the end of the tag he publicly begged to have the Horner match scratched. It was. Only DDP stood up and said, "As much as this company is paying you, you should work every TV match!" Needless to say the Horner/Bagwell match never happened. I have wrestled Buff several times, beating him every time, and we have become good friends over the years. He will admit that W.C.W. was messed up. He will also admit his own faults.

W.C.W. was the worst company that I have ever worked for. They were selfish, unprofessional, and at times cruel for no reason. People had egos that shouldn't have. They wasted money. They turned me bitter towards the business. It would be a long while before I would regain my love for the "Big Business" side of pro wrestling.

Chapter 6: Intolerable Independents

The year that followed W.C.W. I needed to make way for a change. In true fighter fashion, I staged a comeback. It seems that I was making a comeback my whole life. I had only wrestled a handful of times since I moved to Atlanta. I showed up for a booking once. With the combination of me hardly being seen on W.C.W. TV and the stunt that I had pulled in the hotel, it had been rumored that I had died. When I showed up, you should have seen their faces. It was as if they had seen a ghost.

Up until now I had worked Independent shows, but had never wrestled for any outlaw promotions. Everyone I had worked for had some roots in the legit wrestling business. Either they had been raised in the sport, or were an ex-wrestler turned promoter. In some cases they had just been around enough to pick up on how the business was suppose to be ran. I had never worked for somebody who had a "real" job by day, and played wrestler on the weekend. I was about to meet them all. The industry had changed.

My buddy, Steven, was getting married. I was going to be in his wedding. I felt extremely uncomfortable in it, because of my own wedding experience. I dealt with all that and supported my friend. The wedding was held in Alabama. I was in West Virginia wrestling when I began this classic journey. My plan was to leave the West Virginia show and drive back to Atlanta to rest and change my clothes. Then drive to Tuscaloosa for the wedding. When I got on I 77 towards Charlotte, I made wrong turn where it meets I 26. I drove and drove, daydreaming I guess, never noticing I was going the wrong direction. Once I realized, I stopped to wet my whistle at a bar I saw on the side of the road. I was only going to have one beer. Well, a six pack later I met this stripper. She was the feature act at this club, and had been featured in a couple of adult movies also. Her stage name was Bodacious Babbitt. We started talking and she was familiar with Atlanta and the Gold Club. After a while of sharing conversation, she asked me to follow her. I told her that I wasn't going to spend money on dances, that I just came in for a drink. She let me know that she wasn't going to dance, and did not want any of my money. We went into a room in the back of the club. You could say that I auditioned with her for her next film.

Newly refreshed I started back on my journey to Alabama. After gathering some new clothes and sleeping it off, I managed to make it to Steven's house. His whole family was there. Here is where it gets seedy. His cousin Tina had been having and affair with Steven's brother's friend. Tina's husband was on to the whole scheme. I had known Tina ever since I was a teen. So, Tina decides to use me as a diversion to throw her husband off course. She stated aloud that she wanted to hang out with me because she had not seen me for so many years. The guy she was sleeping with decides that he was not going to get any further into this drama and leaves. She never got to spend time with him. In order to keep her story going, she had to continue to spend time with me. We have the rehearsal diner and I went back to shower at my hotel. Tina decides to come along. It was only about an hour difference between the rehearsal and where they were gathering afterwards. I showered changed and she watched TV. I was thinking nothing about the possibilities at this point. As we walked to the car she says, "I've spent two days around two hot guys, and still have not gotten any yet!" We turned right around and headed straight back to my hotel room. Three hours later everyone was looking for us. Her husband especially! To this day I swear it wasn't three hours, but it sure was a long time. I spent the rest of the trip tiring to convince the husband that nothing had happened so he wouldn't divorce his wife. It worked too, until about six months later.

I started going to Tina's house on a regular basis. Her brother had a girlfriend that was best friends with Craig's sister. This sounds just like a soap opera, and it was just as exciting. After one visit, the girlfriend had been watching Tina's kids while we visited. She need a ride home. So innocently I volunteered. On the ride home we decided to hook up. (Big surprise, Huh?) It got so bad that Tina and the other girl would ride to see me in the same car! Then they would come up with reasons to talk to me separately. Tina actually had no clue about the other girl. When she found out it all hit the fan. Tina told her brother, who told his mom. His mom told Steven's mom, who yelled at Steven. Steven told the husband. Janie, his wife, blamed me for running her wedding. I thought it was a lovely ceremony though. In the end everyone was mad at me. I guess that is the way life is if you are going to be called "The Player".

On May 19th 1997, in Mobil, Al, I wrestled my first ever match for the W.W.F. I faced old friend Al Snow. He was doing the Lief Cassidy bit at the time. He loved being a Rocker! The match was taped for Shotgun Saturday night. It was an important night for Al; because it was the first night he started losing it. The first signs of what would later bring Al a little head. Later that night he was beaten by Scott Taylor on Raw is War show. Taylor is known now as Scottie 2 Hottie. This match sent Al to E.C.W., where he got head. I mean received head. I mean had the doll's head given to him.

The match was great. He tied me up like a pretzel and then suplexed the hell out of me. I fought back, and the match was actually an even bout. Al took real good care of me. When we returned though the curtain, we got a standing ovation. I'm not sure if was a rib. I don't think it was. Either way I was very proud of the match that night. Not a bad first impression.

I would have great matches with top notch stars, but then have to return back to work with less talented people on outlaw shows just to make ends meet. I was getting frustrated. Things at home were not making it any easier. Between Christmas and New Years of 1997/98 my relationship with my father fell apart even more. He had been real sick over these three days, more than usual. I had gone out, but came back shortly. I had had a couple of beers, but was far from being drunk. He threw a fit. This was unusual, because he had been a drinker in his day too. He refused to let me leave again. I had my keys in my hand, and he tried to take them away. He hit me. It was the first time he had ever done that. It was a good blow, it staggered me to the wall. He charged at me, but I hit him back before I realize what I was doing. I called my uncle for help. I didn't want to fight my father, but I sure as hell wasn't going to let no man hit me. I was blamed for the whole ordeal, even though I didn't throw the first punch. He would try to hit me several more times over the years. Sometimes I would block them, but others I would just let him hit me. It was the only thing that made him feel alive. Any time I would try to talk to him about it, he would just blame it on me. He would say it was my chemical imbalance. The one that they tested for and never found. Why would an elderly sick man try to fight a pro wrestler, no one ever believed me. They still don't.

I started dating this girl from West Virginia. Her name was Jennifer Blevins. I met Jennifer II on night after a match while me and Craig were out partying. She was actually out on a date with another guy. In true Player fashion I just sat right down at their table in the restaurant and picked her up. The poor guy never stood a chance. She actually left her date sitting right there and came out dancing with me. We had such a good time that night, so we started dating.

The first Jennifer was short and had black hair with a great figure. Jennifer II looked a lot like her. Now I know they were different people, I am just saying that they had similar characteristics. Jennifer II was taller, but not real tall. She had a great figure; most importantly she wanted to be with me. That is one characteristic the first Jennifer never had.

My thoughts at the time was that I couldn't be with the one I wanted, so I created and loved the one I was with. By created I mean, I tried to mold her and shape her into the girl I wanted. So she would not leave me. That is sad, but that was how I was feeling then.

Jennifer's parents were okay, I guess. Tension was very evident in her house. Her sister Vicky and her husband could do no wrong. Jennifer II was left feeling inferior. All my baggage did not help matters either. I never referred to her as number two; I am just using the number here to keep you, the reader, straight on who I am talking about. I knew I was hurt, but I thought I knew what I wanted. I was determined to get it no matter the cost.

Jennifer II and I decided to get married. I was still seeking that perfect family dream. We were married in 1998. I was feverously working to support us. Her family had promised to pay for the wedding. They never repaid me for everything that I had put on my credit cards at their request. We started off in debt. She had a good job, but Atlanta's cost of living was sky high. I had to make a certain amount of money from every show each night just to make ends meet. My parents gave money to help, but it just wasn't enough. The cost of the wedding, the Georgia economy, and my expenses on the road were all adding up. It was killing me.

By working full time in wrestling, this meant I would be gone a lot. Jennifer II was young, just twenty.

She had never been on her own. We had met when she was nineteen. That whole first year of dating we spent together, but being alone was hard on her. It is hard for any wife of an entertainer.

I was wrestling everywhere. Georgia, Carolinas, Tennessee, W. Virginia, Virginia, and Alabama were all common stops in one month. I would average being in three to five different states per week. This was the hay day of Beau James and I as the "Living Legends". On top of this we were having all kinds of different matches, anything from Pole Matches, First Blood, Texas Death Matches, to Chain Matches. And, of course, a lot of tag team matches.

My body was starting to take a pounding. I wrestled Beau in a Texas Death Match. This is a falls count anywhere, no disqualification, no count out, last man standing contest. Beau decides to throw me into a wooden panel wall. I went elbow first through it. I ended up chipping my elbow, and it gathered water on it. I had to wrestle around that injury. It was very tender. It was hard because it was my right elbow, and I am right handed. It still bothers me today.

We faced the team of Death and Destruction several times. Roger Anderson, my former partner, and Frank "The Tank" Parker. These guys seemed to be booked on every event we were. If we weren't wrestling them, then we hung out in the locker room with them. They are definitely on the top of the list as one of my favorite opponents. I have wrestled Frank several times. I think some of those matches were my best. His also. We faced each other hundreds of times. Frank is in my top two favorite people to work with. Scotty Mckeever is the other. I have wrestled, and beaten, almost every top name in our industry, but I prefer to work with these two guys. They are the greatest pure wrestlers, or the biggest named stars, but something just clicked when I was in the ring with these two guys. I have had a lot bigger money matches, from a lot more famous stars, but if I could only wrestle one person for the rest of my career, it would be one of these guys. Frank is dear to my heart. The business we have done together is one of my fondest memories.

It was during this time that I met Troy Strimel. He worked as "Bad Boy" Eddie Edmunds. He and I had a definite common goal on how to promote West Virginia. There had never been a real territory here in West Virginia. There has been plenty of shows, but never a real territory. Along with a lawyer from Clarksburg, WV, Jim Hawkins, we laid the idea for a foundation of a territory. They promoted live events, while I was on top as the big star. The problem, like with all promoters, was that they were cheap bastards. My original deal was one dollar per person. For the time, it was more than fair. I would be paid for the amount of people I drew. I was getting about half of what I should. Which was nothing new, history is well documented that every wrestler expected more money. On top of that, they would make me wrestle twice a night. Once under a hood in the opener, usually as the Panther, then in the Main Event as myself.

I worked Eddie Edmunds for the company title. Troy was a good performer. I worked with him a lot, with the same finish every time. He would hit me with a foreign object, and then get DQed, and then I would challenge for next months match. This was not a bad formula, except that I had to win his title every now and then for it to really draw. If I did win the belt they would strip me of it the very next show. The top star in the company was promoted around nothing. The fans lost faith in me, and interest, once they caught on to the formula.

Troy had a tag team partner Mike Morgan. Mike was a good hand. He was a former minor league baseball player with the Pirates organization. He had a dropkick that would rival Jimmy Golden's or Hardcore Holly's. Mike was attached to Troy. That was his only set back. They shared a mind together. Split the two up and Mike was as dumb as they come.

We would travel to Florida to work for the newly revived Florida Championship Wrestling (not to be confused with the current WWE developmental territory). I would work with my old friend Anthony some, or Gangrel who was working then as Vampire Warrior. I had a few matches with E.C.W. star Hack Myers. Anthony wanted to try to get his job back, so he got us a tryout with E.C.W. while they were down in Florida taping TV. I first worked with Justin Credible, who was the only person that has every really blew me up in the ring. He was without a doubt the fastest competitor I have ever faced. He took care of me and I made it though the match. I met with Paul Haymon and Lance Storm. They offered me a spot. The problem was that they wanted me to travel across the country with no guaranteed pay. I just simply couldn't afford not to make money and still meet expenses. So I turned down their offer.

1-800-Collect sponsored a USO tour of all the Army bases in America. I got booked on the tour. The tour was promoted by Thomas Reeder. The tour stopped in Ft. Gordon, Ft. Bragg, Ft. Stuart, and Ft.Campbell to name a few. Those crowds were great. The troops would finish up training on "Hell Week" and literally come out of the woods to watch us wrestle; as they received pizza and chocolate for the first time in seven days. These poor souls would be out in the woods being shot at, starving, and were so glad to be done with that that they popped on everything we did.

The tour featured ex W.W.F. talent such as The Headshrinkers, Brian Lee, Honkytonk Man, Patriot, Tatanka, Greg Valentine, and Jake "The Snake". I got to know Sammy the Headshrinker, known more as Samu, because our merchandise table was always side by side. The Samoans are known as good, respectful, talented people. Sammy was no different. I liked him a lot. We hung out afterwards in the hotel drinking Canadian Mist every night. We even shaved, well attempted to, but only got half, the head of a young rookie who was on his first ever road trip. The Samoans were known pranksters.

I was sitting in the locker room talking to K.C. Thunder when Jake Roberts started preaching to K.C. He began giving his full testimony with fire and brimstone vigor. He had just done the Bennie Hind show. He was explaining how God had saved him from a terrible life. Greg Valentine walked in and took a seat next to Jake. Jake in mid-testimonial, without hesitating or breaking stride, looked at Greg and asked if he had any pain killers. He was hard up he explained, and then without taking a breath continued to preach on how his life had changed. He even went as far as to say that he was off drugs thanks to the Lord. That was just how Jake was. He performed great that night, and eventually Vince brought him back up to the New York territory.

We did the tour for three years in a row. Eventually a t-shirt deal would stop the whole thing. Brian Knobbs of the Nasty Boys started complaining that he never received a royalty check from the merchandise. 1-800 Collect put their name on everything on the tour. They had shirts made with all the boys' pictures on them. They gave them away each night to the soldiers as a promotional item. They, in return, paid the guys around a hundred dollars each for the use of their likeness. They boys thought they would receive more, and the checks were passed out towards the end of the tour. The boys had wrestled at every base in the country and saw thousands of shirts being worn. They thought they should be paid for each shirt. Knobbs was hot and began screaming at one of the bigwigs from 1-800 Collect, he even made her cry. This led Tom Reader to step in. He was caught in the middle. He offered to pay Knobbs himself just to get him to shut up. Knobbs wasn't having it. Eventually MCI, the parent company, pulled the sponsorship and the Tours were ruined. Tom tried to do the tours on his own without sponsors, but lack of talent and advertising just didn't help the cause. Henry Hubbard would eventually take over the tour and rape the government for more money in a scam that did not deliver.

After the tours I formed a tag team with Ken Timbs. Ken was a former Mexican Champion. He was a southern boy that worked several of the N.W.A. western territories. He had suggested that we go to Mexico. I was all for it. We contacted Paco Alonzo in Mexico and he gave us our dates. We were scheduled to fly out from Atlanta on a Tuesday and work all week. We would return seven days later, then return for a full tour. I was booked the weekend before in West Virginia. I was going to drive back to Atlanta on Monday and leave Tuesday for Mexico. I worked my three days and called Ken as soon as I got back to see which terminal to meet him at. Ken was aware of my three days and was cool with it. His wife Juanita answered the phone when I called. She told me Ken had already left. She said that the promotion called and added an extra day to the tour that he had just left that morning. This was before everyone had cell phones. It would not have mattered; Ken never tried to call me. He could have easily reached me at my parent's house. He had actually cashed in my ticket for the money. This was pre-9/11 so you could get away with things like that.

The tour would back fire on Ken. It was terrible from what I was told. The room was not fit to stay in. He only made three hundred dollars for four days. He could have made more working in Georgia. Finally he was canceled off the longer trip. What goes around comes around. Things like this seem to work out in the long run.

I liked Ken and we had great time teaming. Sadly my friend and partner Ken Timbs would pass away while I was writing this book.

I was making that long trip to work for Hawkins and Troy way too often, for way to less. I decided to call Steve Doll who was booking for Bert Prentice. Bert and Bill Behrens were running Music City Wrestling. They had two promotions working together. M.C.W. Nashville and Bill promoted M.C.W. Georgia, which would later turn into N.W.A. Wild side. Steve booked me for TV in Nashville.

I competed in a few matches at TV. Bert, of course changed my name to Lance Erickson. I mostly worked for Behrens in Georgia where he booked me as Logan. It was odd business, because I was Erickson on TV and Logan in the arenas.

Bert booked me on a larger show in Louisville, KY, at the Gardens. I was to work with Chris Michaels. It was a weird little event. For starters it was upstairs in a convention hall instead of on the main floor. Al Snow wrestled Brickhouse Brown in the main. It was definitely sold out, even though it only held about a hundred people. Alan Berrie, The Duke of New York, was the TV announcer at the time and he was in charge of the show. At the end of the show Bert instructed The Duke not to pay anyone. He explained that everyone would get paid at TV Wednesday in their weekly check. I didn't get a check, I got cash, and I was not booked on TV Wednesday. I knew Bert would pay me, he always did. I had a bigger problem. I was driving from Louisville to Kingwood, WV, about a four and half hour drive. I wasn't sure I had enough money to make it to the next show. Duke couldn't help, he had his orders. I tried to call Bert and of course he didn't answer. I then called Behrens and left a real harsh message on his machine. It was rough, but I did make it to Kingwood to wrestle.

I was booked the following weekend in Eaton, GA, for Bill. Bill loves this story. He tells it anytime I am around. When I arrived Bill met me at the car. He apologized for the mix up in Louisville, and paid me the money I was owed. We went into the building and there was no ring. Something had happened and the ring never made it there. Shannon Moore was explaining the whole deal to me as Bill walks over. "Before you say anything, let me give you this", Bill told me. It was half my pay for that night. He gave me half, because there was no show and I was the only one that he had not called. Shannon was staying the weekend at his house riding jet skis on his lake. The fans were showing up, because they had no idea the show had been canceled. Bill planned to stick around and give them free tickets to next weeks show. Shannon and I stayed there to keep him company. I decided to set up my merchandise stand. Shannon would meet and greet the fans, Bill would give them tickets, and I would sell them something. (Thanks Robert for showing me the way.) Everyone had brought money with them to spend, but there was no show. They spent the money on my pictures. By the end of the night I had sold a couple of hundred dollars worth of pictures. I thanked Bill for letting me do it. He laughed it off. For once one of the boys capitalized on an opportunity instead of getting screwed by a promoter. Bill did the right thing by paying what he owed me. Besides if he was too pissed off why is it one of his favorite stories.

Over the next few months I got to see several of my friends like Bull Buckhannon, Wolfie D, Flash Flannigan, and The Colorado Kid while I was working for M.C.W. It was a good experience. Bert is still promoting Nashville, and Bill is involved in T.N.A. I made some money there, as much as could be expected. I enjoyed working there, but had to turn in my notice. I could make more money in West Virginia. There were less travel costs, and I could stay at my parent's house instead of a hotel.

As many times as I tried to leave the West Virginia area I was always drawn back, for one reason or another. I had several ideas for the promotion of the area, but the promoters never seemed to want to do them. Hawkins promoted the northern part of the state. Morgantown, Clarksburg, and Kingwood were run there every month. Shinnston, Buckhannon, and Elkins were run often as possible. Troy ran the middle half of the state. Towns like Clay, Beckley, Oak Hill, and Spencer. He would also run Mann, WV occasionally. This is where I met the third part of the W. Virginia promoter's triangle, JD Rottenbery. He would eventually run the southern half of the state in places like Princeton, Bluefield, Matoka, Pineville, and Coal City. These guys covered the entire state. They could have ran four day loops and cleaned up. They could have done all of this without TV, which was unheard of. The problem was that they all wanted to do their own thing and not cooperate with any other promoter. Which translates to they did not want to put in the time and effort, or share the profits. They all wanted to use different talent, and run separate story lines recognizing different titles. This would eventually lead to the cluster fuck of all cluster fucks that is now West Virginia wrestling. One could drive from Bluefield located in the bottom of the state, to Morgantown located at the top in around four hours. It was just too confusing for fans, lots of times they over lapped. They would see faces be heels on separate shows, and partners feuding with each other on another. The only common thing they all had was me as the top baby face.

JD was your typical conniving crook promoter. I liked him immediately. JD did, and still does, things I don't agree with, but I have always made money with him. Sometimes we just agree to disagree. He, at the time, had more of a clue than the others. He always knew who to keep happy and who not to care about. He knew how to keep me happy, which was paid. He had a good formula. I would chase a heel champion for six months, and then beat him. Next he would send me a barrage of heel challengers I would work in a series of four matches with. Once I was done with them, I would drop the belt, and begin the chase all over again. JD also always tried to keep a strong under card angle or two.

Troy, on the other hand, put me on top with him. He kept no under card talent that would amount to anything. If we had an off night in our match, the show sucked. It was literally on my shoulders to carry the entire promotion single handed. I was stressed the entire time. If the show tanked, I made less money. It was unfair for me to have all that trust on my plate, but I wasn't the first one in the business to live like this.

Hawkins had me work with different heels, but I never beat them. I worked for him for years and I never pinned anyone. I always won the match by DQ. He understood the need to book under card talent, but he always booked guys that could never pull it off. He would constantly have two idiots, that were barely trained, trying to pull off a complicated angle. It just didn't work either.

Hawkins's biggest angle involved a kid named Punchy McGee. He turned out to be one of the better talents that I have worked with. He started out as a referee. He then became involved with me, eventually wrestling me. He first caused me to loose my chance at a title match. Then the next week he was in the main event with me. Talk about a hot shot! It had no credibility. How do you pull off a match where your opponent was a ref one week and a main eventer the next? I should have mopped up the ring with him, instead I had to make him seem like he could hang with me. Stuff like this went on constantly. I wrestled Punchy about a hundred times and hardly ever beat him clean. Hell, with a push like that he should have been champion of the universe. Punchy now only works a handful of shows a year and works for the 911 center. All that talent, such a huge push, I wonder why it never took him anywhere?

As I look back there were a lot of unforgettable characters in West Virginia wrestling over the years.

"Play Boy" Buddy Rose. He actually thinks he was an original member of the Fabulous Freebirds. First of all it was Buddy Roberts, not Buddy Rose. Buddy Rose was a large fat worker from Portland. Who is this guy fooling, he was neither. He strutted around the ring acting just like Michael Hayes. I seriously don't like Buddy as a human being, but as a wrestler you could have a match with him. That is all that matters when you are trying to make money.

Scotty Blaze from up around Morgantown (not to be confused with the other WV wrestler Scotty Blaze from Virginia) is the cheapest man alive. I once saw him pass on eating an entire weekend, because a store wanted thirty-eight cents for a doughnut. He was a big and bulky bodybuilder that looked thick, instead of cut. He always thought that he was small so he constantly pumped up. He would always bring weights and cables to the locker room and workout before his match. By the time the bell rang, he was done. You could get a good match out of him, if you could do it in about three minutes.

Chuck Jones. Old good time Charlie himself. Probably the best over all performers in the state. He was a cross between Gorgeous George and Freddie Blassie. He was great and a true friend of mine. He is super intelligent, but at the same time awkward. Wrestling him was a night off; he always knew what he was doing. He only weighted about two hundred pounds and that being generous. His skin was pasty pale, which looked hideous when he put on his purple Tarzan like gear. This guy was a heat magnet. I wrestled him in a looser leave town match in Bluefield, WV. When he lost he left the business for good. I guess you could say that I was the man that gave Good Time Charlie the blues. Chuck will always be "over like the Tokyo Dome" with me. He is married to Nicole Starr now. His second wife and a former student of mine.

When Chuck married his first wife, Melissa, he took her to Vegas. She was only seventeen. Her birthday was only a couple of months off, but they couldn't wait. So, off to Vegas they went. Her parents freaked out. They called the police and filed a missing person's report. While in Vegas, the police saw them walk by a camera that was filming something for the news that night. They broke down the door and took them both back to West Virginia that night. It all made the local news. Chuck just took this in stride as always.

He lives out on a farm raising chickens. He doesn't keep a phone, because he says he doesn't need to talk to anyone. He sleeps on the floor instead of the bed. This guy was a true one of a kind. Chuck never drank. He always said that there was no sense in putting something in his body that could alter him. One night he went to the bar with a student of mine. He had had a bad day. So, when he was offered a beer he took it. He hasn't stopped drinking yet. He drinks constantly. Maybe it wasn't me; the ol' fire water gave Charlie the blues.

If I were asked who my favorite Independent wrestler was I would say the Cuban Assassin. Ritchie Acevedo is the son of the Original Cuban I mentioned earlier. He looks and wrestles just like his father. He is a good solid heel, whether it is at the top, middle, or bottom of the show. He could draw money in the main, or lead a greenhorn in the opener. Simply, you just have to have him on the show. The following are not the reasons why, though. He repeats everything he says three times. So a five minute conversation takes fifteen minutes. The funniest thing is his use of the English language. You know the old saying, lets eighty six this. Meaning, let's get rid of this. Cuban would say, "Let's ninety six the whole thing!" He is so funny to watch. His gimmick, other than being Cuban, is that he smells really bad. Some people think this is a shoot, but I know it is a work. He smells sometimes, and other times he doesn't. It works like this. His catch phrase is, "Shut your stinkin' mouth". The crowd, who can smell him, chant back, "Wash your stinkin' ass!" It is classic.

I had a student Ron Ray, who went on to polish up at the Dungeon in Calgary, Alberta, Canada, with the Hart family. Cuban would always talk about what a big star his dad was, sometimes too much. He would continue on to tell what good friends his family and the Harts were. Most people just thought he was nuts. I knew he was telling the truth, because I knew his father. Most people didn't have that pleasure. So, Ron goes to dinner at the Hart house one Sunday afternoon. When he walked in the door there sat the Cuban! Ritchie was up there wrestling and Ron didn't even know about it. The Harts loved Cuban and his dad; they put them both over all day. Ron told me later that he went all the way to Calgary to have dinner with someone that lived five minutes from his house in West Virginia. Ron also respected Cuban more that day. More people should too. He and his family are definitely legends in this business.

I continued to wrestle several dates around the country. I wrestled in every flea market, bingo hall, coliseum, and tent revival there was. Independents are for recognission, in most cases just for fun, unfortunately. I was trying to make a living in a changing industry, not have fun. If I made a name for myself along the way so be it. There wasn't much money to be made due to poor promoting and inexperience. I was lucky; I would say I made more money than most. I was lucky! It just wasn't enough to live on. These Indy shows were definitely not easy, and at times intolerable.

Chapter 7: Puerto Rico

My relationship with Jennifer II was struggling. I was traveling several thousand miles a week. I had gone through several cars in just one month. The bills were piling up. My parents were helping, but it was still hard to make ends meet.

Jennifer II had moved in with a friend of her's from work, Emily. Emily came from an abusive house and needed a sanctuary. They were close friends, and I thought she could keep Jennifer II company while I was gone. It would later backfire as their relationship grew physical, but the thought of two women with me at nights sounded good, at the time.

It was the beginning of 1999. While at the gym in West Virginia I got a call from my Mother for me to come home right away. I thought something was wrong at first. Then I was pleasantly surprised when it was Jim Cornette calling from the W.W.F. offices. Five minutes later, and a return phone call, and I had a tryout for the W.W.F. in Birmingham, AL. The best thing about this was I was not extra talent anymore. They were considering me for a job!

On February 15th, 1999, I wrestled Billy Black in a dark match before Monday Night Raw. I had known Billy, and wrestled him before. He had worked for Bill Behrens as well as in Smoky Mt. Billy was famous for teaming with Joel Deaton as part of the Wild Bunch. They did very well in Japan, where Billy had many tours under his belt. He was not as big of a star in the states. I think because he didn't travel that much, wanted too much money, and promoters just wouldn't use him. I think he falls under the case of, "It doesn't matter how bright of a star you are, if no one sees you shinning."

Tony Garea was the agent in charge of our dark match. Tony had a formula for the opening dark match. It was done this way in every town. The baby face would be announced from the town they were in and he would beat the heel. Billy did not like that plan at all. He thought he was a star and couldn't put me over. He claimed no one knew me, even though we had both wrestled all over Alabama for years. Tony wanted the baby over, that was me, and that was that. My first W.W.F. victory!

Tony played a little rib on me though. I'm sure he does that with the new boys a lot. He took me aside around two o'clock in the afternoon. He told me to go ahead and get my gear on. He continued to explain how the office likes to see the boys ready. I got dressed. I was in that gear several hours before my match. All the boys kept ribbing me. They would say things like, "You sure are ready for tonight!" While the office does like to see the boys ready, they don't need to see you dressed at two o'clock for a eight o'clock start. It was a funny rib!

I went down the isle to the ring. I could see myself on the large titan tron which was very cool. Billy and I wrestled a good match that night. At one point, however, Billy went for a Moon Sault onto the floor. He got stuck on the second rope. He was not used to the real ropes that W.W.F. uses instead of cables. I had to cut him off and get on him a little. This was good for me. It pissed Billy off. He was embarrassed. He was mad at me because he missed his own move. He didn't flip, so I couldn't just stand there forever, I took over. I eventually climbed to the top rope and did my best Ricky Steamboat like cross body and pinned him. Billy told all his Georgia buddies that he was going to beat me up for missing that move. Should he have to beat me up for messing up the match, not his Moon Sault? It was a stupid claim. That's the business for you. I'm still waiting for him to beat me up, but he was not asked back to the W.W.F. They told him they would be in touch. He is still waiting to be called.

I had wrestled the week before the W.W.F. tryout with my good friend Cuban in Beckley. He had given me Carlos Colon's number and address in Puerto Rico. I had Fed Exed him my promo package just before the W.W.F. match. I wrestled Cuban once again in the only sold out show ever at this little flea market called "Bargain Park" in West Virginia. There was a tremendous sixty eight people there. A sell out is a sell out! They were wall to wall as there had only been about thirty prior to this afternoon. They were all excited because Cuban and I went to a local bar and got into a fight with each other to drum up attendance. They bought tickets to see us kill each other in the ring. Suspension of disbelief is the key thing in making our industry work. Without it, it just won't draw money! The fans must believe that the main event is real. The angle must be perceived as legit. Over the years I would become a master at this. There was a old adage in early Pro Wrestling. This was brought around by legit champions. "Pro wrestling is fake; but the Main Event for the N.W.A. World's title was real." People would sit though what they thought was hoakie to get to see what they thought was real. This is what wrestling, especially independents, over look today. Don't insult the people by telling them that it is real when it isn't. Make them believe it is real, when they know for sure it isn't. That is a true work!

The next day after fighting Cuban tooth and nail, I got a call to go to Puerto Rico to wrestle for Carlos Colon's World Wrestling Council. It was that quick. I sent a package, worked a few matches, next thing I know I was landing in Puerto Rico. I think that the office had to put a word in for me. It happened too quickly from the tryout with W.W.F., that I had a job in W.W.C. Carlos had connections with Vince for years. His sons, who were real young when I was there, Carlitos and Primo now wrestle for Vince.

Puerto Rico was the last real territory. It has been in business non stop since the seventies. It had their top stars like Abdullah the Butcher, Ric Flair, Roddy Piper, Andre the Giant, Dutch Mantel, Val Venus, Bruiser Brody, and, of course, Carlos Colon to compete there. You work a five day schedule there, four shots and interviews on Wednesday. This would leave two days a week to enjoy the island. Which is what got most of the boys who would go there in trouble. The wrestling style is very old school there. Coliseums are full to compacity every night with dedicated fans. This could be dangerous. Not just as a heel, but because of the crime and drug problems that cover the island in the same towns they would promote. Both of which plagued the American boys for years there.

I walked off the plane into the airport, and it was a third world country down there. Puerto Rico is a territory of the United States and receives over eleven million dollars a year from the United States to help it survive. In reality it is a small Latin community. I walked outside and looked for my ride. Native Puerto Ricans were not allowed in the airport unless catching a flight and this was pre-9/11. A man named Victor picked me up and drove me to my hotel. On a side note, everyone in Puerto Rico is named Victor.

He took me to the Dalia 15. This is the hotel where all the boys have stayed at for years. This place was the biggest dump ever. Remember the room from *Scarface* after the guy used the chainsaw; it was nicer than my room. It was located on the beach and I was going to make due with it. I had my new friends with me, lizards and cockroaches were seen everywhere. They would watch over me, and I could ride them down to the pool sometimes instead of taking the elevator. My room was far from nice, but it had all I needed to survive my new odyssey.

My roommates were a kid named Shawn Hill, who was trained by the Bushwhackers and Mexican Legend Peiroth. I had met the Bushwackers on the 1-800 Collect tours and thought they were hilarious. They were not known for their fabulous ring skills as technicians. It showed in Shawn. He was terrible, and thought he was the second coming of Lou Thesz or Ric

Flair. He was an elitist punk, who knew nothing and thought he was above everyone else. It didn't sit well with me at all. He was built and claimed to be a former male stripper. He reminded me of Shawn Casey with no hair and no talent.

Pieroth, who wore a yellow and black mask in Mexico, was the exact opposite from Shawn. I liked him right of the bat and it made it easier to put up with Shawn. He was a maniac, but our maniac. His gimmick was the Latin equivalent of the Joker from *Batman*. He always used a menacing laugh when he did promos, or talked, and when he drank. He worked hardcore, lived hardcore and, according to him, was hardcore. He would get hit with everything in the arena, and bleed like a stuck pig. Although he never drank, each night he would talk me into having one drink with him, because it would be his last. He spoke broken English, and I broken Spanish, but we talked happily as he explained the world of Lucha Libre to me. He was a "Crazy Mexican" and fun to be around. Even though he scared the hell out of me, I think the crazy Mexican was a gimmick, however, he was hardcore.

The booker of the territory was "Dirty" Dutch Mantel. They really broke the mold when God created Dutch. Dutch plays a tough Texan in the ring, in real life he is a wimpy instigator. He never wants to fight, but always seems to start one. He was one of the islands first stars and has been touring there since the seventies. I originally met Dutch in SMW where he competed and announced. He did not seem to remember me. I spent a lot of time with Dutch. Mostly cause he made me. So much time that all my stories start with, "One time me and Dutch were…" He would tell me about the Memphis territory, or any place else he had been. He was another ridiculously cheap guy. All I ever saw him eat was toast and coffee in the mornings. He would then eat the left overs that Pieroth wouldn't eat when he would cook dinner that night. I am all for saving money, but one thing I always did was eat. I saved by cutting corners elsewhere.

Dutch told me a story once about Jerry Jarrett calling a meeting in the Memphis territory. He announced that they would be doing business with Vince and the W.W.F. He went on to tell them to get off steroids if they were on them. Dutch stood up and said, "Steroids, hell, they ain't even on food!"

Dutch had a simple philosophy to booking. There are only five true finishes in wrestling. So he stuck with them. The five being strait pin, disqualification, count out, reverse decision, and no contest. One of these would end every match. This is one of the reasons the people down there believed so much. Dutch never educated them to anything else.

On long car rides I would get Dutch started telling stories or complaining. You could wind him up and just let him go. He was so funny. He would also get bored and instigate fights between the passengers of the car. He started one once between Shawn and I was about to kick Shawn's ass. Then I smartened up to what Dutch was doing. Then I wanted to kick Dutch's ass. Thank God for Dutch's sake Lloyd wouldn't stop the car. I loved being around Dutch. He is a paradox of the wrestling business. Either you love him or you hate him. He is fun to be around and you can always learn something.

The final character I met to round out the cast of misfits was Lloyd Anoita. The Tahitian Warrior, or LA Smooth, son of Papa Affa of the Wild Samoans, he is brother to Samu of the Headshrinkers, and the Rock's cousin. What a family. We were best of buddies from the get go. He had wrestled in Puerto Rico for years, so he taught me the ropes. He was on a W.W.F. developmental deal and was making a killing. He received a check from Vince, and got paid from Carlos. Ultimately, the W.W.F. released him years later and went with Three Minute Warning, and now his brother Afa Jr. Lloyd was a great person. A true brother in arms. I would do anything for him or his family.

I debuted in Puerto Rico on February 27th 1999, in the Main Event in Kahunnas. Brian Logan and the Tahitian Warrior faced Ricky Santana and Glamour Boy Shane for the W.W.C. tag team titles. Ricky Santana wrestled most of his career in Florida and Puerto Rico. He was a larger star in Florida, than when he was a mid carder later in his career working for the Crockets. He had several tours of Japan under his belt. Glamour Boy Shane was Val Venis's former partner. He was a cross between Ric Flair and Austin Idol. He looked like Flair and worked like Idol. I wrestled these two numerous times while I was down there. They were all great matches. Shane made his T.N.A. debut as Shane Sewell, the wrestling referee.

We were traveling home from Kahuannas that evening after the show. The highways are very dark at night. Only the actual towns had lights; it was all that was affordable. Lloyd pulls over the car abruptly to the side of the road. He instructs me harshly to get out. I panicked! He kept insisting I get out. I get out of the car and the road is pitch black except for two headlights. I was standing on the side of the road, with total strangers, in a foreign country. I knew this was it, the last moments I would ever know. Rumors about the dangers of the island cascaded though my mind. Just then a second car pulled over and three men got out. I thought to myself, they are just going to kill me right here! My last place on earth was going to be a ditch on the side of the road on some third world island. It was the baby faces! Thank God, it was the boys!

Puerto Rico is old, old school. You do not even see your opponent except inside the ring. They all wanted to stop so we could all meet. Scaring the hell out of me was just icing on the cake. We talked a bit. Well, they did. My nerves were still shaken from the whole rib.

Black Boy was a perfect example of kayfabe being alive and well in Puerto Rico. I worked with him in my first feud there. He wore black and gold tights and a black mask. Sometimes we would run into the baby faces as we finished up our interviews for TV. Black Boy was never there. I never saw him, except in the ring. He was on the other side in his dressing room prior to the match. I never saw him without his mask on. I have no idea what he looks like or who he is. We had exceptional matches together, but he remains a mystery.

The air down there is very humid. It is close to the equator. It stays hot all the time. Day or night breathing is harder. So, to get my wind right, I started having broadways, time limit draws, every night. Over and over I wrestled Ricky Santana for twenty or thirty minutes in the hot thin air. That is an exceptionally long time for a match down there.

I started loosing weight. How could I not? I was sweating it all off. The best thing was that the water on my elbow had finally evaporated. Nature healed my wound. Far more than what medical science could ever do for me. I was working out hard and in the sauna everyday, with Dutch's encouragement.

Dutch would come to my room every day at noon. He would start over to eat breakfast at seven o'clock, then knock on my door every ten minutes until I would get up. This was around noon. I am and have always been a night person. I think it was from all those nights driving home or to the next town. Working out with Dutch was more like him coaching. He didn't work out he just told me how to do it. I had trained for years. Sometimes it showed on my body, other times it didn't. It wasn't my first time in the gym; I did have a clue. I was respectful to Dutch and never said a word. I was just happy to spend time around him learning.

Dutch told me this story several times. I asked him about it every chance I got. The Invader killed Bruiser Brody. Everybody knows that, it is common knowledge. The Invader got away with it because no one testified against him. Tony Atlas saw the whole thing, but refused to say anything. Dutch was the booker at the time this story took place. This was a few years after Brody's death. The hallway at the old office had a hallway with a coke machine on one end and a stairway at the other. The only door to the outside was on the other side of the stairs. Dutch goes into the hallway to get him a coke. The Invader follows. Dutch puts his money in and get him his coke, opens it and turns around. There is Invader standing right there behind him. Jose, Invader's real name, says, "Amigo, we must talk!" Dutch described his voice as high pitch and twangy.

"My people won't buy what is happening to me. You make me stronger, so people make happy." He said in broken English.

Dutch responded by saying, "Okay we make you stronger!" He was scared to death.

Invader has been Superman ever since in Puerto Rico. Dutch thought he would end up like Brody if he didn't make him a world beater. He took no chances and went to great lengths to avoid repeating the incident.

I was a quite taken by the night life of the island. There were two tourist bars located three blocks from my hotel. All the Americans who did not enjoy the casinos hung out there. Although heel and baby face interaction was forbidden. The company had very strict rules in public. Like staying out of trouble, and still remaining tough guys. The casinos were cool, but I didn't gamble. I figure my life is a big enough gamble, why waste my money. I did, however, scope out the women from time to time that were in the casinos.

I snuck into the pool area at the El San Juan Hotel and Casino a lot during the day. The pool and scenery were much nicer than at the Dalia. Felix Trinidad was fighting on the island one weekend. I got to sit poolside with Don King and Felix Trinidad while they handled their business.

It got even better than that. I had many heroes growing up. Most in the wrestling business. I loved heavy metal music as a teen. Kiss was my favorite band. Kiss played Roberto Clamente Stadium while I was down there. I would go over to the Ritz Carlton hotel a lot to use their pay phones to call home. I went to the concert and, afterwards, I called home to tell Jennifer II about the concert; when I hung up I decided to walk though the Casino. There they were, Kiss members hanging out in various parts of the casino. I walked over to Ace who was playing slots and introduced myself. Paul Stanly was at the bar and Gene was sitting at the Poker table. I chit chatted to Paul and Ace waiting to talk to the man, Gene Simmons. I finally shook his hand and we talked for a while. He was so nice and personable. When he found out I was a wrestler all he wanted to talk about was wrestling. I would find out over the years that stars are as big of marks for the wrestling business as we are for their work. I wanted to tell Gene how much I loved their act, and he wanted to tell me about wrestling. He asked me about W.C.W. and I told him good things, which was hard but I didn't want to be negative. After about a half hour he and his date went upstairs. It wasn't long after that that Kiss performed on Nitro and Dale Torberg, a fellow Power Plant student, became the Demon. Just think if I would have been negative, maybe Dale would have been out of a spot. (Oh, that's right he is out of a spot, that deal lasted about long enough for a cup of coffee.)

I wrestled Kevin Quinn in Guynabo on April 17th, 1999. This was booked to be a big match to help move me higher in the card. I was asked to attack Quinn and give him the pile driver on the floor. This was going to lead to a series of gimmick matches between us. Kevin had been partners with Chris Daniels in Chicago. I originally met Chris on the 1-800 Collect tours. Chris did the Curry Man gimmick in Japan and the states, and went on to be a star for T.N.A. At the time Kevin thought he was in line for a developmental deal with Vince. He was being considered for a part in the Too Cool angle which eventually partnered Brian Christopher and Scotty Taylor. They didn't need him, but somehow he though he could be called up any day.

The plan was that I was going to run his head in to the ring pole, and he would bleed. He would then do a run in on me in my match with a chain and set up for the chain match the following week. Kevin began complaining to Dutch that no one bleeds anymore. For God's sake this was Puerto Rico, everyone bleeds! Kevin went on to tell Dutch that Bruce Pritchard had expressly told him not to bleed. In fact, if he did the office wouldn't consider him anymore. He was too much of a prick to do this. It was all horse shit. Dutch came to me and put the entire thing into my hands. He told me to get over, and that not to worry about Kevin, that he was about to be fired.

We stumbled out to the floor and Kevin and I exchanged blows. Then I grabbed him by his long black hair and rammed his head as hard as I could into the post. He ended up bleeding after all. Not by his way, but the hard way! Then I gave him the pile driver onto the hard concrete floor. I left his head sticking out just a little at the bottom. His head made an evil thud onto the floor. The crowd went nuts. They threw rocks, paper, and anything else they could get their hands on. Kevin was on a stretcher out. He was sent home the next day. I had broken his neck. Now, I know that I am supposed to take care of my dance partner, and that Bret Hart would frown upon hearing this tale. Kevin had a choice, he made the wrong one. I had to get myself over, and protect my possible earnings. Sometimes in this crazy business people forget how the rules make it possible to advance. They do it at their own expense. I'm not sure if Kevin ever wrestled again, but I bet that if he did he did exactly what the booker asked him to do.

Kevin was not my least favorite opponent in Puerto Rico. Sangria Taiania was. The national symbol for Puerto Rico was a long haired, boriqua, which wore a straw hat. This symbolized the brothers of the island that were farmers. This was his gimmick. His name translates to Native Blood. He was a jobber, a straight out jobber, and he hated it. He also spoke no English at all. Every time we wrestled he would forget the finish. That finish was me pinning him, so every time I had to shoot the finish on him. He would then play dumb with the office and say it was a lack of communication. He understood, he just didn't want to lay down.

There were a lot of great people down there though. Chickie Starr, who is a legend, was one of the nicest people I have ever known. He always carried beer with him. Puerto Ricans drink from the time they get out of bed, until the time they go to sleep, no matter who it is, bankers, business men, students, and, of course, wrestlers. He always wanted me to sit and drink a beer with him.

There was Rico Suave, who was my interpreter on TV. He also doubled as my manager and tag team partner occasionally. I would say something like, "Saturday in Cobo Rojo you will be mine!" Then he would talk for five minutes in Spanish translating what I had said. He is the son of W.W.F. hall of Famer Johnny Rodz, and brother to Hurricane Castillo of the

Boriquas. It was along side him I got to work with old friend Abdullah the Butcher. This is one of the highest honors in Puerto Rico.

The biggest thing that took place in Puerto Rico was the Te Ammo angle that connected me and Brandi Alexander.

About three months before I left for Puerto Rico I had a nightmare. I had been having them ever since I got out of that room in the hospital. I had problem sleeping my entire career. I dreamt that I was wrestling in a huge coliseum, in a ring that was higher from the ground than usual. A female wrestler with long black hair ran into the ring and slapped me, then body slammed me. I woke up saying the name Brandy. It was very strange. The ring had a red canvas, which no promotion had at the time. I only knew one Brandy at the time, Brandy Wine. She was a blonde. A week later I woke suddenly and looked down the hallway. Jennifer II did also. We saw a black haired girl walking down the hallway holding a little boy's hand. We were both obviously dreaming, but we had had the same dream at the exact same time. Keep this in mind as the story continues.

The promotion brought in Brandi Alexander for a week. She was a replacement for Sweet Destiny. Destiny worked later on for W.C.W. as little Jeanie. She would later date several of the boys who would ultimately meet their demise prematurely, either by suicide or other health problems. Destiny couldn't make the trip, so she got Brandi to fill in for her.

I was walking back from the gym when Lloyd pulled up and introduced her to me. He had somewhere he had to be, so he left her with me to entertain. I showed her where everything was located on the island. Everything was within walking distance.

Brandi wrestled Tygressa. The Te Ammo angle, which is Spanish for I love you, went like this. We taped several weeks of TV in one night. On week number one I came out and watched her match. The second week I came out and I had an interview live in the ring. The ring that night in Guyunabo was elevated so that everyone in the stadium could see. The canvas was, of course, red. See where this is going? I called out Brandi and told her that I had a huge crush on her. The storyline stated that we had known each other from the states, even though we didn't. Rico translated in Spanish everything I said. It was unusual for an American to do a live interview in the ring. I told Brandi how much I loved her and then asked her to marry me. She milked the crowd, and then finally slapped me, and as I spun around from the slap she body slammed me. Just like in the dream. How strange is that? Then Tygressa jumped her from behind. I didn't realize it until the next day that it was my dream coming to life. Brandi and I were out getting a bite to eat and it hit me like dejavu, only I knew where I had seen it before. I have had dreams that parts of it come to life several times. It just happens. The angle set up mix tag team match for the week with various partners and Brandi versus Tygressa and me. It also gave me my new manager/valet. I enjoyed working the angle; it was a lot of fun. Brandi and I spent a lot of time with each other, but it never got physical between us. She left after the week and went back to the states. We continued to talk a lot on the phone.

Back in Atlanta, Jennifer II and Emily were becoming very close. Their relationship was becoming physical. Every man brags about wanting two girls at the same time. What I didn't realize was that with the realization of that dream, I would be starting to create a monster that would come back to bite me in the end. I would call home and listen to the two of them on the phone in the throws of passion. Jennifer would begin to start acting funny also. She would have fits of crying and rage. It was all very strange. At one point, it was joked about that a group of local Wiccans had cast a spell upon Flex and I. It was all in fun, and a joke. Still strange things would result from then on. I would continue to work in Puerto Rico. In my off time I would spend it on the telephone either listening to them, or talking with Brandi in a real conversation before going out to the bar.

WORKER: LAST OF A DYING BREED

1000th match

BRIAN LOGAN

AWA World Champion

WORKER: LAST OF A DYING BREED

Logan with country music super star Aaron Tippin

BRIAN LOGAN

In 1995 during my bodybuilding phase

At a personal appearance

Bloody after a street fight with Scotty McKeever

WORKER: LAST OF A DYING BREED

Cornette tells me what he really thinks of my career

BRIAN LOGAN

Apex Champion with manager Babydoll

WORKER: LAST OF A DYING BREED

In Puerto Rico with Tygressa

U.S. Champion

WORKER: LAST OF A DYING BREED

Logan Vs. Mr. Black

Logan Vs. Chase Owens

Flex, Logan, and Waylon

WORKER: LAST OF A DYING BREED

90's Promo Picture

Disciples of Synn (Damien & Slash a.k.a. Wolfie D)

WORKER: LAST OF A DYING BREED

Damien corners Lita

Logan Vs. Tommy Rich

The circus had came to the island. In the Dahlia you were a wrestler, stripper, prostitute, or a carnie. In some cases all the above. By this time the business had consumed me. Roddy Piper talks about it in his book, *In the Pit with Piper,* as the sickness. I had it. I was tired and lonely, but living my dream. The business is funny, the more you work, the more time you want to be home. The longer you are home, the more you need to work. It consumes people who can't handle it. It was beginning to do just that to me.

I had been on the island for six months. I was up partying one night, when I made a huge mistake. One that nearly cost me my life. I had went to see a guy in the hotel for party favors. He had told me to come back in twenty minutes. When I returned I received a funny answer when I knocked on the door. A stranger opened the door, and I saw my guy sitting on the corner of the bed. He was shaking his head. I should have left, but I thought nothing of it. I entered the room. There were always different carnies hanging out, so I thought nothing of it. The door shut behind me and the guy, along with his friend that was hiding behind the door, pulled knives on me. My connection owed money and these two were there to collect it. I was now involved, and they had the guy and his girlfriend tied up. I could have easily took these two thugs, I was shaken, and had never faced a situation like this. They took my watch, a five hundred dollar Seiko Kinetic, and my wallet. I never carried money on me, I never did, only my ID and some spending cash. They instructed me to lie on the floor. Then put the guy in the floor behind the bed. Thoughts raced, as Jennifer II, Brandi, and my parents ran through my mind. They told the girl to take her clothes off, they were going to rape her right there in front of my eyes. I couldn't let that happen. It wouldn't be good for her, and if I got out alive somehow, it would forever be in my memory. I stood up. They were startled, I made four of them. I told them that I had friend that was coming to look for me, and that if they didn't let me tell him where I was, he would be in the room at any minute. If he got suspicious he might call the police. They made me lay back down, then they quietly left the room. They bought it. My story had scared them off. Truth be told there was no friend, no one. We were all at their mercy. I out smarted them. I untied the girl and the guy and went to my room. I was so freaked out by the experience. The police came the next day to collaborate the guy's story. He was unable to pay his rent because of the robbery, so the land lady called the police. I was the only credible witness. After I explained to the police, I went to straight to Carlos and turned in my notice. At four o'clock that same evening I was on a plane back to the states, headed for Atlanta once again. I didn't know who to trust, Carlos, the guy, the police, myself? I just wanted to go home, so I did.

Chapter 8: The Big Push

I was met at the airport by Jennifer II and Emily. We had had a nice dinner and then home for the festivities. It was nice for a change to be involved instead of only being able to hear it on the phone. It was apparent that the two of them were much closer than Jennifer and I. That was to be expected because I had not been around, and Emily had. The two of them would later begin to spend time with each other, leaving me to watch TV, not join in. This was not quite the idea I had imagined, but that was life. I made what I could out of the situation. I had only been back in the states for less than a week. I was headed back on the road for the West Virginia independents.

Nothing had changed in my absence. Nothing ever does in West Virginia wrestling. My friend Jeremy was ready for the road, and that brought a breath of fresh air. Flex, as he was called, had grown up with me in near by Fayetteville. He was a former teen dead lift record holder, and an avid bodybuilder. We always seemed to date girls that were close friends, while we were in high school. All we could talk about for as long as I could remember was wrestling. He had attempted to join the SMW in 1994, but I had moved on to Memphis and it wasn't realistic for him. Over the years our friendship would grow as I would tell him the tales of my experiences on the road and he would explain his Hunter S. Thompson like philosophies.

I started out with three students of my own. The first class of what would later be known as the Disciple Dojo was Ron Ray, Eric Lester, and Flex. They were all close friends or acquaintances. We worked out a monetary deal, so that it would be business. I was concerned that they would get mad when I yelled at them to try harder. This way it would not affect our friendship.

Flex was a natural athlete. He was great at football, and had the looks of a model. He regularly conditioned himself by running and lifting weights. Inside the squared circle things are different. Wrestling is performed in a circle. This will sometimes throw your equilibrium off. Athletes would play other sports in a straight line. The contrast would separate the king of sports from all others. Flex would have a long road to learn endurance. To make things worse he was regularly hung over, or still drunk from the night before. The thing that made him survive in the end was his determination and heart. The desire to make him into a star was present.

The entire time I trained them I was on the road. Flex was perfect to travel with. He is totally reckless in his life; however, he is extremely careful in a car. He could be in the bar drunk and tackling people. Which I have seen him do several times. Then he would get in the car and buckle everything he could find, and hold on for dear life.

He was notorious for crazy stuff. One night a female friend of ours gave him a ride home. They made small talk as the car warmed up. It was winter and freezing. As she pulled out of the parking lot Flex says, "I'm getting naked". He rode the entire way home in the nude. This poor girl didn't know what to do. It was not sexual; he just likes to be naked. Apparently in the freezing cold. They arrive at his house. He thanks her and gathers his clothes. Then he walks into his mother's house naked.

Flex and I were becoming inseparable. Our self medicating practices had also become a habit. We made humorous references to being Hunter S. Thompson and his lawyer Dr. Gonzo from the novel *Fear and Loathing in Las Vegas*. It was never quite that bad. However, it was bad enough for Craig to vow never to associate with either of us again.

Flex is such a character that entire books should be written about his exploits. We worked a shot one time at the University of Georgia for Bobby Fulton. I brought Flex's cousin Scott McComas and Rocky Blankenship with us to work also. After several beers we arrived at the hotel after the show. I took all my things and gear and stowed them high off the ground on the bathroom counters. We moved the mattresses immediately into the floor to create four beds and Flex passed out dead immediately. The others questioned why my gear was being moved to higher ground. I responded with, "You will see." About five minutes later Flex begins sleepwalking. As he is getting naked he knocks off a lamp from the stand. I just looked at the boys and shook my head. Flex then pissed all over everything. The mattresses, the floor, their gear. I said, "Now you see why I moved my gear!"

Another time we were at a promoter's house partying after the show. I was talking with the promoter when, in the kitchen, my tag partner at the time received oral pleasure from a girl. Flex goes over and sits right next to the girl, who was kneeling on the floor. He sits there for a second and watches the action. Then looks up at the guy and says, "My God, what a cock you've got!" Then he goes back to what he was doing before that all began. It wasn't sexual; he just did stuff like that. The promoter and I cracked up laughing.

One time Flex found a cover to a gay prono magazine. The guy on the cover resembled him in looks, but clearly was not him. You would have to really look at it to tell, and at a glance you would believe it was him. Flex cuts the picture out and carried it in his wallet. At certain times, just when it was right, he would tell this elaborate and outrageous story about being a porn star. Then climaxing the yarn, by pulling out the picture and showing it around. The people hearing the story just wouldn't know what to think. Flex would then laugh his ass off.

J.D. had been running quite often. Between him and Jim Hawkins it was almost a full schedule, and I returned occasionally to Tennessee to fill in the gaps. I decided I needed to live in West Virginia instead of Georgia. My expenses would be cut down, as well as the traveling time. Jennifer II refused to move back sighting that it would be a step backwards for her. She explained that she knew way too many people that had moved away and then return because they had failed. She refused to be one of those people. In a way she was one hundred percent right. Sometimes people settle for less to be comfortable, instead of sticking it out though the hard parts to make it. In lots of those cases, you don't realize that until it is too late.

In the summer of 1999, Jennifer and I called it quits. After less than only nine months my marriage had failed. Emily and she moved into a house in Alpharetta, Georgia. I moved back to West Virginia. Looking back now, I did not treat Jennifer II right anyway. I had confusing emotions inside of me, and expressed them even more awkwardly. I take full responsibility for her pain and baggage. No one should attempt to make another human into something they are not. I should have worked more on my marriage, or not gotten married at all. I failed her, but learned a lesson in the long run. I am only sorry it was at her expense. I have not talked to her since I left Atlanta. My wish is that she experiences and lives life to the fullest; happy with herself and her relationships. Jenni, I am truly sorry!

During the writing of this book, Jennifer remarried. This time to a doctor. She always understood the concept of upward mobility.

I continued to talk to Brandi, whose real name is Jeri Lynn Sarafin. She came down from Connecticut to visit me in West Virginia. We talked a lot and decided to try a relationship. She would eventually move to Fayetteville. We moved into my Mom's house. She had recently moved back in with my father.

Mom suffered a hurt back in a car accident. At least that is what she told me. She and her boss, at the time, were on a trip in the Carolina's when she was in the accident. I don't know why or what they were doing, just that the wreck had occurred. Mom moved back in with Dad so that he could take care of her. This is the same man that has been waiting to die since 1987. Mom would later get cancer. Although, I seemed to be the only one she told about that. Both the car accident and her cancer had the entire family in chaos, with my Dad in the center of it.

Brandi got me booked on a couple of cards with her, before she moved in. I teamed with Mantaur in Pierce, NB. Mantaur was the former W.W.F. wrestler that was half man, half bull. We wrestled the Rock N Roll Express. It was sold out! It was fun to see them again. It started raining profusely during the match. I couldn't do anything because of the rain, so I just grabbed Ricky's ankles and spun him around through the puddles that had formed in the ring. He was shouting, "Whee!" the entire time, until he got water in his mouth and began to choke. I thought for a minute I would be famous as the man that choked out Ricky Morton with no hands.

The second booking was far from fun as the first on was. It was a two day loop in Plymouth, Mass. The promoter was Mike Sparta. What a piece of work this guy was. Mike's brother was Freddie Sparta, a ref in the W.W.F. during the expansion years. Freddie was immortalized as being the ref Bret Hart talks about on his RF video shoot tape for being the shits. Freddie lived next door to Pat Patterson. So what did all this make Mike? NOTHING! He thought, however, that it put him one step from Pat in the New York office. Which would make him two steps away from being Vince's next right hand man? He was an idiot. From my understanding no one in the W.W.F. ever liked him, which is if they even knew him at all. He was classic for showing up to work at the W.W.F. events telling people that Pat or Vince had told him to show up to work there. He even threw Killer Kowalski's name around too. These two nights he advertised "The Man from the Dark Side" along side a picture of the Undertaker. He had booked Brian Lee to wrestle, not Taker. Mike had talked Brian into doing his "Faker Taker" gimmick. So I was booked in the main event against The Man from the Dark Side both nights.

Mike's big plan was to dim the lights as Taker's music played. Brian would make his long slow entrance. Then I would attack him. Once the house lights raised we would be moving and no one would know it wasn't Taker. We were to fight all over the building and finally back into the ring for the pin. It happened just like that. Except, the people knew it was Brian and was shouting out his name during the match. The match was good and eventually we won the crowd over. Mike had done the one thing you can never do in the business. Lie to the fans. You can cheat them, yank them, but never ever flat out lie to them. If I didn't have to deal with Mike Sparta, then it would have been all the better. But I made due, as usual.

As all things in wrestling, the fun stopped, and business took over. The trip was booked as a three day loop. The second day got canceled. To make up for it Mike had all the boys over for dinner. Brandi and I were staying at Mike's house. Mike was married to Brittany Brown, a ladies wrestler from Providence, Rhode Island. Brittany Brown, or Patty Sculli, was Brandi's best friend. When the "stars" arrived Mike paid them for the lost day. He gave them half their original nights pay.

Brandi had always done private video tapings before the matches when working for Brittany. These are usually empty arena matches with two girls or a girl and a guy to be taped and sold to private collectors. The matches a scripted very strictly. These were basically high quality apartment wrestling videos. Male fans buy them to do what ever they do with them, and are viewed as a fetish film. It is supposed to be their own private match. Get the picture? Brandi and I did one of these on the first day of the loop. It was a straight wrestling match, nothing different from an intergender match that would be on Raw. These buyers just turn them into something they are not.

This taping was extra money for us. Mike had nothing to do with it. When it came time to pay me for my lost day, Mike claimed I had already made my money on the video taping. That is how promoters think. I explained that I was in the main event, and had traveled just as far, if not further, that the rest of the talent. For Brandi's sake I broke my strictest rule in the business. I let it go. Brittany told me that she would pay me the money. I never saw a penny of it. I did nothing at the time to get it, because Brandi assured me that I would receive it.

My stock had risen in West Virginia with my tour of Puerto Rico. I was still getting screwed by the promoters there. I wanted to move up in the promotions and help with the booking. I thought that this would eventually lead to more money. I had more experience at the time than anyone in the wrestling business in the state of West Virginia. I should be a natural for this spot, but the promoters had ideas of their own and did not care about my experience. They wanted me to work and be seen, not heard. All I wanted was to help the houses draw more, and in return make more money.

Brandi started to work some in West Virginia after the move, mostly she didn't. Girls, lady wrestlers, are a novelty in our industry. They are used to dress up a bigger event. Promoters would bring them in right before summer, while using the capacity in the same composites just before fall. It was all designed to help the economy of the show, by using raging hormones of children to help increase attendance. School would let out and the raging hormones of summer would be attractive for teens to purchase tickets to see the women fight. While at the end of summer, just before school, starts to attract the younger kids to see the comedy of the midgets. In early 1900's to 1970's the N.W.A. World's champion could not appear on a card with either lady wrestlers or midgets as it would be seen as a secondary draw to the World's champion. Thus women had been banned for several years from Madison Square Garden events in New York City. With all this in mind it paved a way for the women to make more money to appear, since they were booked less often as the men. This made the modern girls fickle about their worth, and their pay scale. They assumed that they were a special draw so they demanded more money each time. This was true and still is the rule, except the new talent of women performers have forgotten the times and their role as they are needed only sparingly. If they were used in a local territory every night they would not be special any longer. They would be apart of the regular roster and not special draw talent. They would receive less money for more work. Brandi never understood this, or how to do business at all in fact. She felt that she was too much of a talent to work for the Indies for little pay. She also began to understand what it was like to not work either, as a result.

Brandi and I went to work in Muncie, IN, for the newly reopened A.W.A. Verne Gagne had nothing to do with this version of the promotion. Dale Gagner was the new owner. I did not meet him on any of these shows, but he would later play a huge role in my career. The American Wrestling Alliance took some time to get up and running, but they treated me good as they started their promotion. They featured me as their TV champion. I was beginning to be paid as a top talent and rewarded financially as well. West Virginia was the last place to get behind me. Brandi was a great help at getting my name out to promoters that were located outside of the south.

On the car ride to Muncie, IN, Brandi and I fought the entire way. We argued for hours. I was given a gift that night. One that I would not see for some time to come. It was the greatest thing I had ever seen. The best gift God, or any person, could have ever given me. My son was conceived that night just outside of Muncie, IN.

I promoted my first show on October 13th, 1999. It was at a little bar in Beckley West Virginia called The Outer Limits. That night the attendance was around twenty or so people. After I paid the boys, I made a grand total of forty four dollars. It was a success. It was not even close to the greatest house in the history of the business, but it wasn't a loss either.

J.D. had quit promoting, and Hawkins was slowing his pace down. This left a huge opening for a new promotion. I was contacted by two men, Leonard Simms and Ward Wilson. They wanted to open a promotion and promote the southern West Virginia area. All of the current problems in West Virginia wrestling can be traced back to this very moment. It was the beginning of the end of our state's rich wrestling heritage.

Leonard Simms was a school teacher by day and life long wrestling fan by night. He masqueraded as a photographer, taking pictures for the boys. He had no real experience in the wrestling business, except buying a ticket. His looks would remind you of the typical promoter with his short stature, fat body, and toupee. He claimed to be a born again Christian, which I have no reason not to believe. However, he was blatantly homosexual. At the time he was in his late thirties to forties, and lived with his mother. He did so until she passed away leaving him a huge amount of money. I'm getting ahead of myself. While I have no first hand knowledge of his sexual persuasions, his actions and mannerisms were that of a gay man. His private life was not his downfall, his total lack of business sense was.

Ward Wilson was your typical average fan, total mark. He had been attending the local cards promoted in Beckley by J.D. One day he decides he was a wrestling promoter. Despite his limited knowledge of the sport, he claimed to be a life long follower. His only reference point did not exceed the early nineties. He was the money man, as it was rumored that he had just received some type of settlement. (Ward Wilson died of a heart attack in Princeton, WV in the arms of Frank Parker after refereeing a match as I was writing this book) Where any of the money came from between the two of them was suspect to me. I wanted to do something right in West Virginia. I thought the end would justify the means.

The three of us had a meeting at a local restaurant. I was the original idea man. I should have known something was up when they didn't even pay for my lunch. The meeting was their idea, but they couldn't pay for a lousy eight dollar buffet? We discussed their overall plans for the company. Which towns to run and what talent to use. They listed thirty towns that day. Over the next three years they only attempted to run five or so of those suggested. They asked me to be the booker. I accepted. I was considered by the real wrestling business as the only one who could be responsible, at the time, for the area. The time of God Fathers and Lieutenants were gone, but there was still order. Cornett passed the torch from the Smoky Mountain territory to me to watch over this area. The problem was the old guard forgot to smarten the new kids up to this fact.

November 2nd, 1999, Appalachian Pro Wrestling debuted. A.P.W. was a name I created, even though they took credit for it. The plan was to run a weekly town out of the Bradley Prosperity Fire Dept. I had been injured in a car accident and suffered from a stiff shot, by a kendo stick, giving me a concussion. The concussion caused me to pass out while driving. I only wanted to do an interview on the first show to set up for the following week. That was when they informed me I would receive two pay days, one for wrestling and one for booking. I had asked for a percentage of the house, but they were not comfortable with that. With that they ushered in the era of guarantee pay for West Virginia independent workers, which eventually led to war.

I have always had a philosophy with my booking that I am running a marathon, not a sprint. They had me do the interview and set up the match for that night. Eddie Gilbert would have been proud of how fast they hot shotted that one. If a show didn't draw that night I couldn't do anything about it. It either drew, or it didn't. I was worried about four shows from that night. I wanted to make sure it drew, and so on down the line. I was concerned with the payoffs of the major angles. If they didn't draw, I needed to change up the talent so that I could. They didn't care about drawing. That's why they wanted to give guaranteed money, not a percentage of the house. Every night was Wrestlemania to them. They didn't care, and still don't, if it draws. It was all to be fun, not necessarily make money. After a year of my system, you could track the trend in talent, time of year, and area so that you could make a model to go by on how to promote. With this model you could adjust the cards accordingly and show a profit from every show.

One trend I noticed in West Virginia was the opposite of most of every other area I had been in. Most promotions build their angles with the big pay off occurring at the beginning of the month. It didn't work like that here. I discovered this through trial and error. Your typical southern independent/outlaw wrestling fan does not have much money to spend, especially if they have a large family. They would usually go out as a group once or twice a month. This excludes the die hard fans that will come out to see wrestling hell or high water. Typically they will go out when they receive their checks, which in most places is around the first of the month. People will spend their money while they have it. Most people here in West Virginia receive miner's checks, retirement benefits, or compensation from the mine that come between the third and last week of the month. If we ran a house show on the first Friday of the month to wind up the angle the house would be significantly down. However, in contrast, the houses would drastically improve on the third and fourth weeks. When I first started booking people would see the start of the storyline, but miss the big ending until I figured out the market trend. I studied the numbers and switched the formula to fit, and received increased business by doing so. In some cases it increased two hundred and a half percent. It was also easier on those up weeks to bring in "big named" talent. Most promoters book talent on the first two weeks of the month, and the talent find it hard to get booked on the last two. I was able to bring in "names" at a cheaper rate because of their availability. This formula worked for my market. It took me years to figure out the formula. It doesn't work in every area the same. You have to spot the trends. This is something most promoters don't think about, or care.

My opponent on the first A.P.W. show was Jensai Rohnin. Jack Miller was under a hood doing a luchador gimmick, billed from Japan. Jack had started as a ref for J.D. Ward and Leonard; both wanted him to be a huge part of the new company. Huge mistake! He wasn't ready. Ward's wife, June, was in love with him, so they made him a star, or at least tried. He had barely been trained, but they pushed him as a top talent. Their big plan was to leave him under a hood until he learned to work, and then repackage him as himself. This might have worked, if they ever taught him anything. They constantly told him how good he was, the proper verbiage should have been, how much potential he had. Jack was a good performer, though he never understood the business. How could he? He dedicated more time to working layaway at Wal- Mart telling the customers how big of a star he was. He was a typical West Virginia dumb hillbilly that had never been out of Beckley. He became a heat magnet in the dressing room, later he would become friend and follower of Kid Kash. He would just say the dumbest things to the worst people, at the most inopportune time. He would brag in the locker room to the boys about how much he was over. If he was over, it was only the promotion putting him over. Jack's true potential was never reached. He suffered a back injury that led to severe weight gain that took his boyish good looks. He failed due to his own causes. A huge ego, combined with a suede tough guy attitude would spell his demise in the sport. For years he was pushed down the throats of mostly young females at his own expense.

The second A.P.W. show was the beginning of one of the best angles that was ever done in West Virginia wrestling. Stevie Knight and Kerry Cabero had came over from England and toured with Brute Shooter, a local worker out of the Virginia's. Flex and I hit it off with them right off the bat and I got us booked with them as much as possible. They were real talent, and a breath of fresh air from the normal bunch of outlaw workers. I named them The British Knights, a complete rip off of the Blue Bloods and British Bulldogs. I put Jensai Rohnin with them and Brute Shooter as their mouth piece manager. They waged a foreign war against the local southern wrestlers.

The actual angle was between Flex and I, and Brute shooter's assortment of foreign monsters. We worked with The Knights several times. I always enjoyed their European style. Most of my matches in West Virginia were against talent of less experience. I always had to be careful to not outshine them, to keep the matches competitive. I had to be aware of their mistakes constantly, almost anticipating them, so I could be ready to cover them as they were occurring. This was not the case with Stevie and Kerry, they could work. I was able to relax and have fun with the match. Both teams understood how to do their job, and it showed in the product. Being close out of the ring helped a lot also, the matches were some of the best in West Virginia history.

The promotion A.P.W. suffered several set backs in their first month. Some of these set backs would personally bother me for years. It all began simply enough. I ran my bar again the week after the first A.P.W. shows. I wanted to advertise my show on the A.P.W. show. The same talent was booked to appear, and it was located only ten miles away from the weekly building. It made perfect sense to cross market it. Ward and Leonard did not want A.P.W.'s name to be associated with a bar. Ward was a former alcoholic and Leonard was a Christian. I tried to explain that it had nothing to do with personal demons, that it was simply another venue and should be advertised. They refused. I plugged it in my live interview. It was not much help. The show tanked and they forced me not to run it again.

The houses had been pathetic. I knew that running a weekly event in West Virginia at the time would be hard. They insisted on doing it their way. There were only twenty five people at most on any given week. The main reason was they didn't advertise. They thought that the wrestling business was all done by word of mouth. Even if the W.W.E. showed up in a town unannounced and presented their product, it would flop also. Advertisement is key in any business. W.W.E. is what it is due to the fact that they are a promotional machine in all areas. You could cut corners in any promotion in most areas, except the advertisement department. Nick Gulas would promote the Nashville area by walking around Nashville everyday putting up posters. He would walk holes in his shoes sometimes, cut out a new sole from a poster, place it in his shoe, and continue on. That is exactly what you have to do. When the circus comes to town every kid knows that it is there. There is a poster in every store and school. They are on every pole in town. That is what the wrestling business has to do. Children will then come home with visions of great possibilities in their heads, and beg their parents to take them to see the circus, or in this case wrestling. Mom and Dad will shell out the money, if for nothing else but to get junior to stop talking about it. There has to be an interest in the regards that something big is coming to town, and we can't miss it! Ward and Leonard never saw that. They said they don't have time to put up posters all day. It showed in the attendance at their shows. In return they did not have time to make money either.

The next thing was one of the stupidest things I have ever experienced. A.P.W. had not crowned any champions yet. Ward and Leonard had just seen that week, on W.C.W., a battle royal where the last two men remaining would have a match. They thought it was a great idea and innovative, despite the W.W.F. had done that years ago. This is how they wanted to crown their champion. They wanted two battle royals, with the last two wrestlers would meet, followed by the winners facing off for the A.P.W. title. They wanted the final match to between The War Machine and Anthony Perdue. This was confusing, but okay with me. The only catch is that they wanted it done in two weeks total, start to finish. It was impossible to make it all make sense, while fitting it all into two weeks. We finally compromised and did it in four. I still think it is too short. Remember I am running a marathon, not a sprint.

I had always envisioned one West Virginia champion, along with one West Virginia tag team champions. They had used this idea in Texas and Florida for years, but the idea never caught on here due to selfish promoters only seeing their ideas, not the big picture. Jim Hawkins promoted Oak Hill twice and was handing it over to me and A.P.W. to run. It was an agreement to separate the state into two territories. We drew a line from Huntington to Summersville, then over to the Virginia line. I had everything below Summersville, and he had everything above. On the first Oak Hill show I made me the first ever West Virginia Southern Regional Champion. The name was so long because that was my rib on everybody. They all hated the title. I would defend it on all the local events in the state, making it the first official West Virginia title since the seventies.

I had A.P.W. recognize it for a specific reason. Ward and Leonard resented it, never understood my plan. We would open the A.P.W. show two weeks in a row with a battle royal, which was a stupid idea. Battle royals are quick and boring; everyone just wants to get out of the thing. The correct idea was to do one battle royal a year, make it big and last a long time. Like the Royal Rumble concept. The semi-main event each week would be the last two from the battle royals. I would defend the West Virginia title in the main, carrying the show. I put Anthony over strong, as well as War Machine. Next, I defended my title against Anthony Perdue showing he could hang with me as a contender. He would eventually win the A.P.W. title and face me in a title vs. title match. Upon defeating me, and getting rid of the West Virginia title, he would be the undisputed champion, a long story to tell in a short time, but drawing money all the way and making a nobody into a legit champion.

Everything was going as planned until my match with Anthony Perdue for the West Virginia title. Anthony invited his friends to see his biggest match in his career, also his tenth match of his career. We both were baby face, but I was planned to slip into the heel role and be more aggressive. I wanted to make him the top baby in the company, just as Leonard had instructed. I would chop his chest and give him forearms taunting his people at ringside. I would give him several big moves, allowing him to kick out and gain strength. The fans would scream and I would just leer at them. I have always felt that chops and forearms are more realistic than several punches. Your opponent must be man enough to withstand the onslaught. The idea is building up tension until he finally unloads on me and begins a huge comeback. This is a professional sport. There is contact. It is not ballet! Men can take it; it is the way the sport is. I thought the match went well.

The night after the match Anthony's mom called Leonard and Ward complaining that I had beaten him up. Who did she think she was Judy Bagwell? Ward and Leonard were mad now. They had never seen a shoot, which this wasn't. They thought it was, and were very upset. Perdue's mommy was not even there that night. She had not even seen the match. Anthony had just gone home and literally cried about the match and she decided to do something about it. I had to explain my intentions to them, which by the way was none of their business. I was the booker and they were the money men. They hired me to a job, and they would not let me do it. I explained to them that if I wanted to shoot on Anthony Perdue it wouldn't take twenty minutes to do it. That a shoot is quick and I could have beaten him in the first minute legit, but instead I carried him for nineteen minutes longer.

We started the tag team tournament the following week. Thank God it was a normal eight team tournament. It was single elimination, and would take place over several weeks with no rush. Flex and I were scheduled to be put out in the first round, which was good because I was booked to face Anthony in the rematch the following week. The match did not take place though. Anthony's mommy wouldn't let him wrestle me ever again. Leonard and Ward agreed. That was a great business decision to cancel the rematch before your champion becomes the undisputed champion of the state. They just did business that way. In the tag tournament they booked the Batton Twins to come in, not the booker like it is usually done. They insisted that we face them in the opening round of the tournament. This was a great match and only had one problem; it was a Baby vs. Baby match, which didn't fit right then. So I explained that the Battons had to be heels. I told Leonard to explain it to them, even though their family lived just ten miles down the road, that putting the four of us together would make them heels, or we needed to pass on them until the time was right. I was thinking about their worth as a team and the company's ability to make money, and nothing else. Leonard never told the Twins anything I had said. When they arrived at the building they were hot. They refused to be heels that close to home. I understood, but it was Leonard's place to take care of it, not mine. I started to see the problems that would plague West Virginia until this very day start in that match. One of the Twins took Flex down and stretched him a little. It was no huge deal it just pissed me off that they tried it with the inexperienced one of us and not me. Flex is not a technical wrestler, but neither is Goldberg, both can draw money if used right. I had had enough with all the things I had been putting up with. I locked up with one of the Twins and went behind and took him down to the mat and said, "Grab your best hold!" This was old tricky statement, meaning that we were about to wrestle legit, a shoot! He grabbed a hold with me riding around to the advantage. I hooked a front sugar on him cranked it up, then released, and I stood up and said, "Quit fucking around!" The crowd thought we were working and didn't know the difference. They decided to work the rest of the match, it was good. I enjoyed the rest of the match with them.

I showed up for my match against Anthony Perdue on December 21st, 1998. I had not been made aware of the entire details about his mother at that point. I walked in and Ward was the only one there. He asked me if I had gotten his email. I have never been a fan of the internet and do not do my business on it. I do my business on the phone or in person; too many variables can happen with a person hiding behind a keyboard. He instructed me to go home and read it. He wouldn't tell me what it said. So, I drove home and read that I had been fired by email. That gutless bastard didn't even have the balls to tell me to my face. They discussed the Anthony Perdue situation and the Batton Twins fight and terminated my services. That was fine with me; I had been fired by men with more roots in this business than those two degenerate marks. I just wanted the respect of them firing me in person. What they didn't know was that I had them! I never let anyone see the book, when I am booking a territory. I kept all the angles written out ten weeks in advance under lock and key. Even the boys don't have a clue where their angles are going. I told them it was fine that I was fired, but I was taking the book with me. They didn't even know what the card was for that night. No one could tell them a thing. I had all the info and I was gone. I would always post the line up then take everyone aside separately and give them their instructions. I did this to protect my ass in this very case. It is the old school way of doing things. Also, if no one knows what you are doing they can't sabotage the angle, trying to get over more than you. It was plain job security. I had to be there to explain what was going on. They were lost. I used this to get a few weeks of pay after I actually got fired.

The decision to replace me with JD had been made. I did not mind. I figured that he would have to deal with their whacky ideas not me. We all decided that I would stay on to wrestle and not be a part of the office. They wanted my book still. They would not get it. I leveraged them into a compromise, JD and I would co-book. That night JD stepped aside and went with my booking. What ended up happening was, he went with my main event and my own match, and then he changed everything else.

I stole the Jack Hart angle from Dutch. I always loved the lovable loser gimmick. Barry Horowitz worked as Jack Hart in Florida. He never won a match. He lost so much that they kept a running tally, sort of an anti-Goldberg take. They would show the tally on the screen, 0 wins and 59 losses, and so forth. Then one day he cheats and lucks up and wins. Mikey Whipwreck did the same angle in E.C.W. as a baby face. Horowitz did a smaller run of the angle with Chris Candido in the W.W.F. later on. My guy, The Nomad, went searching for a win every week, but could not find one. I explained to him about the idea, and he realized that he had to loose for a long while for the angle to work. Then eventually the crowd would be behind him so much that he had to win, just for them. As soon as JD took over he had him win. It killed the entire thing.

After that no one in the wrestling business anywhere ever cared about The Nomad.

I was going to use the Coal Miner's Glove angle to turn on my friend Flex. You would think that in the heart of coal country that the Coal Miner's Glove would be a hot match. It was not. It was one of those trends that you have to be careful with. I made a real glove with real chains glued to it. This thing was a monster and legit. Every time I brought that thing out it killed the town. I used it three times before smartening up not to do it in West Virginia.

I had had trouble with one of the boys the entire time I was working with JD and also A.P.W. Joey Morton would turn out to be the final draw with A.P.W. Joey, who is a fine wrestler, was always accompanied by his girlfriend Carrie. She would always have to be in the locker room with him. She never let him out of her sight. She was short, fat, and loud. Joey had been trained by Danny Ray Nelson, who had been one of the original trainers of Jamie Nobel. That is before Jamie left West Virginia and trained with Dean Malenko foregoing his true ties to the Mountain State. When Carrie would come into the dressing room a lot of the boys would find a problem with her, but were too scared or inexperienced to do anything. I explained the situation twice to Joey and he said that he understood that only the boys could be back in the locker room, and said he would take care of it. On this particular night Bandi was back stage. The building was a bingo hall and a curtain separated the main floor from the locker room, which had plenty of room left to separate the music area from the changing area. Bandi was never in the back while the boys were changing. Carrie got mad at the fact that my girlfriend could be in the back and not her. She also just knew for sure Brandi was looking at Joey naked in the back, which was silly. Bandi was a wrestler and one of the boys. She had to be in the back because we had plans of using her and need her to be hidden. Brandi sat quietly at the monitor and watched the show. Carrie did not see it that way.

I went to the ring to do my "big" heel turn on the mic. I had just turned on my friend and beat him to a bloody pulp and was going to explain why to all the fans. I was about two sentences in to the interview, when Carrie came to ringside. She came right through the entrance way and up to the ring. She started heckling every word I was saying. I looked over at Leonard in the corner, he was laughing. He thought it was play time. I came up with every one liner I could remember from the Paul E. Dangerously/Missy Hyatt angle, just burning her right to her face. I spewed out everything from, "being able to see the stretch marks on her mouth", to "her servicing all of the boys at one time." She replied that she was going in the back to get Joey. I didn't care one single bit. She had just upstaged me, and that could hurt my worth, and possibility to make money. I belted out a couple more insults to regain my spot, and then followed her to the back.

I went straight up to Joey in the back. He was packing his gear, he was leaving. He didn't even want to defend her. I told him I had had enough and that he wasn't just going to leave. I instructed he had two choices: one, for us to go to the ring and we would settle it there like men. Or two, settle it right here and now. Either choice he made he was going to be on the wrong end of a ass kicking! He just kept saying that he understood, but he couldn't control her. He insisted that he was leaving. I began to cut a promo on his manhood for not wanting to face me. What happened next occurred real fast. Carrie comes from behind and spun me around and hit me in the face. Before I could do anything I hit her back out of reflex. As she was falling backward, like in those old Nestea commercials, Brandi grabs her by the hair and stops her from falling. Then as Carrie is bent over backwards, Brandi punches her face all the way till she hits the floor. Once on the floor she really laid in the punches and gave her the boots. Just as all of this is going on Joey tries to tackle me. I countered and hooked in the front sugar hold. All the boys rushed to break us apart. It only hurt Joey more. As they pulled on his body it only choked him out even more. Finally the Battons pulled the boys off us, and literally threw in a towel for Joey. I saw it and let go. I was old school that way. When I stood up, one of the Twins started in on Flex. Now me and Flex were in a fist fight with the Batton Twins over the match we had had. Finally it all stopped by the end of intermission and we all went back to work. Carrie called the police. She did not realize that she had started all of it and the police did nothing about it. I left. They shut down the show. A.P.W. was kicked out of the building. It was best for all parties involved. They relocated the show to Oak Hill at the Armory. It was a better draw. JD was lost for weeks. The company had to restart everything from scratch without me. I was fired and they took everyone else's side except mine. I was public enemy number one now. They were now promoting in my hometown every Tuesday. This bothered me. I had wrestled everywhere, but I had something to prove in my own home town. I now had two marks, turned promoters, running me out of my legacy. I had places I had to go. I left to work elsewhere. It always stayed with me.

Brandi had been working off and on for W.C.W. She had an ongoing feud with Miss Madness, who ended up being Molly Holly in the W.W.E. W.C.W. offices contacted her and offered her a full time contract. Her hero was Sherri Martel. She looked and works a lot like her. They wanted Brandi to replace Sherri and manage Harlem Heat. Brandi knew she had to decline the offer, we had found out that she was pregnant. It was hard for her to tell W.C.W. no, she did not want to have a baby. I did not believe in abortion. I was excited, because I would have a little buddy I could play with and call my own family.

The offers began to pour in for us. I received one call while Brandi was away on the road. I was showering one night. I usually took the phone in the bathroom with me, but this time I had forgotten it. My thoughts were, you never will know when you will get the "call". So I always tried to be prepared. When I got out of the shower I saw that I had a message. It was Bruce Pritchard. He asked me to call Titan Towers and ask for him. He had left for the day by the time I called the office. I was sure of how the process works. Out of sight, then you were out of mind, and they pass over to the next guy. He might have had a deal for me and I would have just missed it. I tried calling everyone I could think of to get a hold of him. Finally I called his brother Tom, from my SMW days. I explained my situation and Tom gave me his home number. Tom worked in the office at this point, and you would think he would have known what Bruce wanted. He didn't say. I called Bruce's house. I actually beat him there. That is how fast I was working. I left my most professional message and waited for the phone to ring. I just knew this was my shot at the big time. That all my hard work had paid off. He had to be offering me a contract, why else would he call? The phone rang. Bruce was on the other end. "Thanks for returning my call. We just wanted you to know that we appreciate receiving your tapes. Unfortunately, we don't have a spot for you right now. We will let you know if we do. Bye." Then he hung up! That was the entire conversation. I appreciate him calling, but could he have just left that on the machine? They like to do things in person, and professional. It was far from what I wanted, maybe it was so I would not send any more tapes. I always believe that the squeaky wheel gets the oil. So, I sent several matches, one tape at a time, for several weeks, one per week, for months. I was thorough. I wanted them to know the name Brian Logan. Now I knew they did.

I recommend this process to every young wrestler starting out. Each year Pro Wrestling Illustrated puts out a Guide to the Independents. It lists most companies and their addresses. I prepared a promo package consisting of 8x10 color photo, smaller pictures of different shot, and a tape/DVD, along with a resume. I mailed everyone in that magazine a pack for years. I got my name out there to where I was recognized by only my name. I would send out sixty to seventy at a time, a couple times a year. If you get just one booking from it, it would pay for the cost of the packs and the shipping.

Jim Cornette came though for me, once again, by getting me bookings for the W.W.F. I started making the TV tapings for Raw. The W.W.F., now W.W.E., is the most top notch promotion in the world of sports and entertainment. Anything can be said about Vince and his business dealings of the past. The bottom line is that it is a business company, which for me felt like a family. I was not anywhere close to being registered as a top talent, imagine the feeling that the Rock or Stone Cold had working there, they made little old me feel like a part of the big picture. It was an amazing feeling for me. I was on the door step of success. Vince, in contrast to W.C.W., puts the product first, not the pay check amount of his talent. In my opinion, that is the single reason for his success. The W.W.E.'s universal product is the focal point.

I was making TV's for them in Greensboro, NC, Richmond, VA, Knoxville, TN, and Louisville, KY. From the start of the new millennium. I was working there on a regular basis. My five hundredth match took place in Greensboro, NC on December 27th, 1999. It was a dark match, not filmed for TV, for the Raw show. I wrestled Ricky McDaniel's. He was billed as son of Native American legend Wahoo McDaniel's. In actuality he was just Wahoo's first student and took his name. That night Wahoo was in young Ricky's corner. It was my first of many milestones in my career. Most wrestlers currently never see five hundred matches. Many go on to have thousands. In the old days you had to have five hundred matches under your belt to be considered ready for doing business. I was no longer a green horn by any stretch of the imagination. I was a full fledged veteran. I had been told once by

Tito Santana that Vince would not even consider a talent till he had reached this mark. Due to changing times that statement would not be exactly true. It was important for me to have made it to that point.

The best part of the match was when I threw Ricky to the floor. I jumped out on to him and gave him the boots. When I turned around…Wham! Wahoo had given me his famous chop. We continued in the ring, and I had just worked with another legendary force in pro wrestling.

I did not know it at the time, but several of the A.P.W. boys were in the crowd that night. They had bought tickets to come see the show. They did not know I was booked. What a surprise it was for them to see me coming down the isle to wrestle for the W.W.F. I had at least one moral victory in the famous West Virginia wrestling war.

Blane DeSantes promoted the western Pennsylvania area. He had received one of my promo packages and noticed I was working opening matches for Vince. In March of 2000, he brought me into Pennsylvania Championship Wrestling. One of the towns he ran was the old TV building Vince used in Hamburg, PA in the seventies and eighties. I had grown up watching the building on TV.

Blane was a lawyer by trade, and was first class the entire way. His payouts were always great and reflected our talent. He put us up in nice hotels where all the expenses were paid. I forget the name of the hotel, but their mascot was a rubber ducky. They left several duckies in the rooms. I must have brought hundreds of these things home for my unborn son. Dylan must have had enough rubber duckies to last forever.

I would describe P.C.W. as the unofficial spring board to stardom. At one time or another Blane featured all, or most of W.C.W., W.W.F., and E.C.W.'s top talent. He had no TV show and ran only a limited area. He is the perfect example of quality, not quantity. His formula was to mix veterans like Bruno Sammartino, who made his last appearance for Blane, with rising young talent. He honored old school traditions and spiced things up with sports entertainment. He was a paradox of the changing times, and how to be successful and not go stagnant. I still think this is the formula for success on the Indies. Promoters usually go one way or the other. They never try both.

Blane put me in a group with Judd the Studd, Joey Mathews and Christian York. We were the Young Stallions. The name was a direct rip off of Paul Roma and Jim Powers, but when in Philly everything hot has to have the Stallion name in it from *Rocky*. The gimmick was that we were the new kids in wrestling, talented and very obnoxious. We had very low view points on tradition. This left Blane's group of traditional wrestlers like Jake the Ring Crew Guy and Cheetah Kid to feud with us. Then the veterans would get upset with us and want to face us also. We were the focal point of the entire promotion.

One such match was a eight person intergender match. On one side there was "Handsome" Jimmy Valiant, King Kong Bundy, Mea Young, and a manager they called Fireman. The other had Judd the Studd, Greg Valentine, Fabulous Moolah, and myself. I was among stars from my childhood. I loved this match; it was one of my favorites.

I won the P.C.W. Americas title in Hamburg, PA, defeating Alex Arion. I held the title the entire time I worked there. In fact, I was never beaten for that belt. I made several title defenses against Mike Modest, Jimmy Valiant, Rich Myers, and Frank Parker. I would later use this title as the background for the Blue Ridge Wrestling US title.

I had finally arrived as a name in our industry by the year 2000. I was busier than ever. I was working smaller shows in West Virginia. Then I started working for Harley Race in Missouri. I was all over the place Pennsylvania, Missouri, Tennessee, and the Virginias. Even the A.W.A. group in Indiana was running a lot. Then John Horton started back up in Mississippi. They all ran once or twice a month. They all wanted The Player. I was actually making real money now and being appreciated for my talent.

Brandi originally had gotten me booked in Missouri. Harley and I hit it off from the start. Brandi was in the ring wrestling Meleia Hosaka. Harley and I watched from behind the curtain. They were having a great match, but were doing it way too fast. Harley asked me what I thought of it. I replied, "Do you want the truth or do you want me to be politically correct?"

He said, "No, tell me what you really think, kid."

"I think they have a lot of talent, but its moving way too fast. No one can see the girls. Girls are to sell tits and ass. No one cares if they can work or not. We can't see the money, too much junk." I explained.

He appreciated my honesty and used me quite a lot from then on out. I don't know if he agreed with me, but he did like the fact that I was forth right with my opinion. Let me also explain what I meant. I am not a big fan of women's wrestling. Mostly because of my dealings with the women who do it. They are arrogant and not worth the trouble they cause. I do, however, realize the importance to the card. They draw money, and that's the bottom line. In the same breath, when was the last time a women's title main evented a pay per view? Never! They may be a huge feature act, but never a main event.

I do have respect for some of the women wrestlers. Girls like Brandi, whom I think was one of the best lady workers ever in our business but was over looked. Molly Holly, Trish Stratus, Jazz, and Victoria are some of the best athletes of all time, most recently Beth Pheonix and Nattie Neidhart. They are sweet nice people, who have broken the mold.

Harley flew me in to St. Louis. I was to meet Meng and The Disco Inferno at the airport. I arrived first around nine o'clock in the morning. Meng was the next to arrive at around ten or ten thirty. We had to wait for Disco's flight to arrive. Meng was hungry so we went to Ruby Tuesdays. I thought it was strange that Ruby Tuesdays was open so early. Meng who was self professed starving, walked in and just sat down. He ordered the salad bar and a Irish coffee hold the coffee. Just Irish if you know what I mean. He was starving, but only ordered a salad. He just wanted the liquor. That was fine with me. He just sat there drinking around two hours as we waited. I listened as he told me stories. I love Meng, he is a tremendous person. His real name is Tonga, formally King Tonga in the W.W.F. He is from Tonga, which makes him Samoan. I have one firm rule when it comes to Samoans, spend as much time as possible with them. They are truly special people.

Harley was another classic one of the boys. Everybody always talks about Harley's cooking. My first weekend there I went to dinner at Harley's house. He cooked all kinds of barbecue, tons of it. We ate like kings. The best thing was not the food, which was out of this world good. I got to sit on the porch with Meng while he talked to Harley while he cooked. Just the three of us. It was like Christmas for me. How many people can say that they did that?

Harley is in the top five greatest World's champions of all time. He is a legend and a Hall of Famer. A multi-time World's Champion who wrestled everywhere. He was a champion in every territory there was, including overseas and Japan. I consider myself lucky to know this great man.

On top of all these things that were good about Harley, he paid well too. All of the talent on his roster could work. He asked me at one point to move to Missouri full time and teach his school. I just couldn't at the time, but I would have loved to. Missouri just wasn't close to anywhere else that I worked.

Harley's wife, BJ, and step son, Johnny Gold, are special people. His wife, who helps him run his promotion, is just a sweetheart. She was just so good at taking care of us, like a mother. I hung out with her son Johnny Gold, who manages, while I was there. His daughter, Harley's granddaughter, was just the most adorable child. You just can't say enough about the Race family and organization. To sum it up, just a real class act all the way around.

In April of 2000, everything would get even better. I was booked in Indianapolis area for three days with the A.W.A. I called Cornette to pick up another day on the way up. Ohio Valley Wrestling taped TV on Wednesdays. He booked me for TV and on April 5th, 2000, I wrestled Flash Flannigan in my first O.V.W. match.

O.V.W., at the time, was a farm team for the W.W.F. I had talked to Jimmy while I was in Puerto Rico and he had told me about them moving from Connecticut back home to Louisville, and the office was putting him in charge of the developmental area along with Danny Davis. Danny was formally one half of the Nightmares from Memphis and Continental territories. Together they were going to create the talent that would be the current super stars of the W.W.E.

Jimmy took us aside before the match and told us, "Feel free to steal the show." This was Flash's gimmick. He always steals the show. We went out for seven minutes on TV and gave it everything we had. It impressed Jimmy and he brought me back the following week.

When I arrived the following week Jimmy and I had a meeting. It was more of a little talk. Jimmy has always been my unofficial mentor in the business. He never actually mentioned mentoring me, he just always helped me from day one. No matter what I needed, he was always there with advise. He has always looked over my career. He has gotten me booked for over half of the matches in my career. He sent me talent to use for my shows, and always had an opinion for me. I can not thank him enough. He is the single biggest influence in my career and contributor to my life. I think I remind him a lot of Bobby Eaton. Jimmy was one of the first characters I loved as a kid, and to grow into a man with him in my life has been priceless. I thank him so much for influencing both good and bad on my career. I would not have gotten to live my dream of being a pro wrestler with out his help. I am forever in his debt. Thank You, Jimmy!

Jimmy told me in our talk, that I would get a job if I changed my gimmick. I wanted the job, so I changed it. I had been thinking of doing that for a while, but I was too scared to reinvent myself. My hair had been long and blond for years. It was stringy and burnt from all the dying. He told me to cut it or fix it. Then he told me to get in shape. I was in ring shape, but for the W.W.F. that is different. W.W.F. wants professional athletes. He gave me a few months to make the changes. That night Brian Logan wrestled Mr. Black (Jack Black). Black destroyed Logan that night splashing him off the top rope several times. The Player was dead. Brian Logan was never seen again in O.V.W., and would forever transform everywhere else.

In Jefferson, IN, just across the river from Louisville, KY, Damian surfaced in a match of Scotty Saber. Damian attacked him and began a long feud on June 7th, 2000.

One week later on a live broadcast on the WB network The Pain Thrillers, Scotty Saber and BJ Pain, wrestled The Disciples of Synn. Synn, our manager, threw a fireball in the face of Saber and burnt him. Damian would face a young Randy Orton, in just his fifteenth match, later that night. I pinned Randy with a fireman's carry into a DDT, a move that Brock Lesnar would later make famous as the F5.

Three weeks from the night I had returned to O.V.W. the team of the Disciples of Synn debuted. Damian, my new persona, teamed with Wolfie D from Memphis TV. His new name was Slash. We were accompanied by our manager Synn, and Personal Preacher Judas. We defeated the Andretti Brothers and were instantly the hottest heel tag team in the territory.

Damian became my most successful character, also the hardest for me to get used to working. We were cast as demonic slaves of Synn. Synn was a dominatrix, with her patented whip and S & M clothing. Damian's origin was that he was the son of Beelzebub, the prodigal son of Satan himself. Which I found blastfoumous at first.

Slash was a serial killer, complete with is large dagger, and a slashed cut over his eye on his face. He was the leader in the ring of the team. His interviews featured off the wall remarks and actions. Once, in an interview promoting, an up and coming Garden's show, he cut his own head open with the knife on TV. This did not set well with O.V.W. officials. I always thought that we were to be like the Acolytes. In actuality there were no plans for us to copy their gimmick, we just had a lot of similarities. When our music first played, *Break Stuff* by Limp Bizcuit, people knew someone was going to get their ass kicked. We were going to beat up somebody. We might not win the match, but our opponents would be left lying in the ring each and every time. We featured a hard hitting brawling style, mixed with tag team perfection. There were continuous tags that led into double team moves. Wolfie and myself were very accomplished grapplers, but The Disciple chooses to fight. This was the point for us to get over. The announcers would ask, "The disciples can wrestle, why do they need to cheat?" That is what got us our heat, along with Synn's interaction. The crowd hated her obnoxious outfits, almost as much as the outrageous things she would say in our interviews.

On June 23rd, 2000, we won our first O.V.W. Southern tag team title. My second major Independent title, and my first tag team title. The Southern Tag title would eventually become the forth most prestigious tag team titles in the entire world. The Disciples beat the Pain Thrillers at the Louisville Garden's 30th Anniversary Show. We would hold that title about a month on our first reign.

During that first run as champions we faced several teams, while also feuding with the Pain Thrillers. Combinations of Chris Micheals, Trailer Park Trash, Rico Constantino, The Damaja, even Tracy Smothers and Steve Armstrong, The Young Pistols/Southern Boys.

We faced The Southern Boys in a series of matches that took place in Knoxville at the long time venue for wrestling, Chilhowie Park. We actually lost the Southern tag team titles twice in one week. Then won them back, and still were not the champions. Confused?

The Pain Thrillers beat us in Louisville, KY, for the Southern belts. We defended the titles in Knoxville, TN, against the Southern Boys on July 21st, 2000. Knoxville didn't air our TV program. We were still recognized as the champions there. The Southern boys defeated us in a phantom title change. Phantom meaning it never happened, except to the crowd in attendance in Knoxville that night. Then a week later, in a rematch against Smothers and Armstrong, we won our titles back. However, in Louisville, where the TV aired, no one knew of the change. When the TV aired in the territory the Pain Thrillers were the champions. This is how I held the Southern tag team title on five different occasions, but the record only shows four.

We finally faced the Thrillers in a rematch at the Louisville Gardens in August of 2000. The match was promoted as Titles vs. Synn's hair. If we did not beat them for the belts, Synn would shave her head in the middle of the ring. Her hair was safe. We won the titles for a third time. Synn made a open challenge after the match. It was accepted by the Big Show, Paul Weight. We faced off with him until Leviathan, known now as Bautista, hit the ring and began a feud with the Disciples and Big Show.

The angle set up for a six man tag on TV between Flash Flannigan, BJ Pain, and the Big Show vs. Leviathan, Wolfie, and me. It ended in a huge confrontation that set up for our street fight match at Night of the Demon, to be held at the Gardens.

Street fights were always wild affairs, and this would be no different. I used chairs, powder, trash cans, and even fans drinks to fight off the challenge of Flash and BJ. At one point the fight carried to the upper level of seats. They ended up throwing both of us off the upper level to the floor. Flash, ever stealing the show, jumped down on top of us to the amazement of the crowd.

The main event saw Leviathan facing off against Big Show. The two giants went head to head in a fierce confrontation. The fans loved the action until Wolfie and I interfered. We attacked Big Show, allowing Leviathan to take the advantage.

Facing the Big Show was no easy task. He is huge. TV makes him look smaller than he really is. His hand covers the width of my entire chest. It would almost kill me every time he laid in the chops in the corner. He was not stiff with them at all. However, the weight of his hands was tremendous, his hand weights as much as a person's leg.

I don't think Big Show ever really liked me. He lived with BJ while he was in Louisville. BJ hated working with Wolfie and I. He would mess up a spot, or try something stupid, and Wolfie and I would make him pay for it. Although Show was nice and professional, I think he held that against me. He was good business for me, and always treated as business. For doing that I respect him. I also appreciate him getting the Disciples over, with Leviathan. The Disciples sleighed a giant.

Brandi gave birth to Dylan Thomas on July 4th, 2000. Dylan was born in Beckley, WV. The delivery was hard on her. She was in labor twenty three hours. I don't know how she made it. I passed out from exhaustion about eight to ten hours in. Dylan was born healthy as could be. He is the greatest gift I have ever received. I want him to know how much his Daddy loves him. Once, Brandi and I were at a lamas class and the instructor asked the question about what we were most looking forward to or thinking about the births. Most of the soon to be fathers talked about changing diapers, or the long nights with out sleep. I answered, "I will have a little buddy to play with." I can't put into words how much I love Dylan. He was the first person that was my true blood on this Earth.

He was the first person to love me just for me. I loved him as I had loved nothing ever before or since.

I envisioned him loving me because I was his dad, not because I was a wrestler on TV, or because someone had bought another person and had to love it. It was just that simple. I wanted to be there for him to teach him right from wrong. To watch him succeed and fail in life, and help celebrate and comfort. I wanted to be his inspiration, as well as his friend. I wanted to see him grow, attend school. I wanted to attend sporting events and watch him play. If he wants to, he will grow into an incredible athlete. He has the genetics of two great athletes in his DNA. His genes are there for him to accomplish so much. He and I were to be linked as family together forever, no matter what happened along the way.

I was on the road constantly. I wanted to be home, but it is the life of a wrestler to be gone from home a lot. It takes a certain breed of person to do what we do. It also takes a understanding family to help with the burden of us being on the road. Brandi did not adjust to being a mother well. There were times when Dylan would cry and she would do nothing for him. I did as much as I could while I was home, but I just was not there often. What was I to do? I needed to work, but also I needed to take care of Dylan. Brandi suffered post partum depression. She had all the classic symptoms, moodiness, neglect of her child, and strong resentment of me. Then she began taking the Depo shot for birth control. The major side affects of which are mood swings. I was worried for her health, and the safety of my baby. I asked my parents if they could help watch him while I was gone. They ended up keeping him months at a time. I would be gone making a living, and Brandi would not want him. She never did. I was stuck. I couldn't hurt Dylan for anything in this world, but I also couldn't quit my job either, especially when that job was beginning to take off to new heights.

On the days I was home I spent as much time as I could with Dylan. Being around Brandi was unbearable, she blamed me for everything. She laid the blame on me from everything from her not working for W.C.W., to her credit card bills not getting paid, even though she had run them up before we even met. I was doing all I could, but it seemed that all I ever did was wrong. I was exhausted between the travel schedule, and also taking care of Dylan. I was starting to have trouble driving, I was always falling asleep. In the middle of all this I had to still work out and stay in shape. My own personal demons were mixed up in there too, to form an unholy cocktail. It was all too much. It was like I was on the bus, going a hundred miles an hour, strapped to a seat with no one driving the bus. The best I could hope for was to crash and die.

I was working full time for O.V.W. We did Tuesday house shows, and Wednesday TV tapings. I worked Tennessee and Kentucky on the weekends. Then in October of 2000, A.P.W. started booking me again. They had ousted JD, and a young performer named Brian Douglas took over the book. Brian, who's real last name is Pauley, was a young cruiser weight when I met him only a year earlier. Now he was in charge of the state. Most promoters described him as being "too small to use". He ousted a coup in A.P.W. and gained control. He was probably the best one for the job, but definitely not qualified to do it either.

As a performer he mixed cruiser weight moves with southern comedy. It was entertaining. As a booker, he wrote elaborate stories that were too short to tell, and way over the people's heads. I was brought in only to wrestle, not be in the office. It was fine with me, but he would frequently call me for ideas. He was burnt out himself, and claimed that if he left all the other boys would quit. He just wanted my ideas to keep him in power. I recognized that, and helped him anyway. I was booking the important angles through him. Only we knew of what help I was giving. If it worked he got the credit. If it was a bad idea it was my fault. I got all the heat from it. I just wanted paid.

The Disciples got booked on Smackdown in Indianapolis, IN, in November 2000. We had a conversation with Shane McMahon, who liked our gimmick, and discussed a full time spot. We did not wrestle that night, instead I was asked to help in a special angle on TV. Rikishi had just been revealed as the driver who hit and ran over "Stone Cold" Steve Austin. W.W.F. needed cops to arrest Rikishi. The O.V.W. boys were asked to be the cops. Wolfie was livid, and said we were too experienced to do that kind of stuff. He wanted the younger boys to do it, not us. He refused. I, on the other hand, wanted paid. So, I was a cop that arrested Rikishi on Smackdown. Rob Conway, Robbie D, and Flash Flannigan helped fill in the other roles. It was cool to be on W.W.F. TV and I got paid to take no bumps. It was good business experience.

The next night Wolfie and I worked for a new promotion in Evansville, IN, called Main Event

Championship Wrestling. This group had plans of a national company running everywhere. They ran the E.C.W. arena and used everyone under the sun, until the checks started bouncing and the government froze their assets. M.E.C.W. did not last very long. On this night the promoter brought food for a Thanksgiving dinner. Wolfie was hammered. He was so drunk he could barely stand. He managed to work a match. Then he went in the back and threw a complete fit. He told off everyone. Well, that is everyone except Moon Dog Rex, Gypsy Joe, Chris Champion, and myself. We would not have stood for that. The rest were fair game. Then he turned over the table, throwing all the food in the floor. Moon Dog Rex, Larry Lathem, picks up the turkey off the floor, and says, "Hell, Wolfie, don't do that. Let's eat this thing!" Then he did eat it.

Larry Lathem, Moon Dog Rex, died during the writing of this book. He was a friend and legend. He will be missed.

Wolfie did not stop there. He was booked in Memphis TV the following Saturday. He shows up drunk again, then he hides in a closet. He fell asleep, thinking it would only be a short nap. It turned out that the closet was the TV control room. They barely got him out in time to tape the live TV. Wolfie was fired.

The following Wednesday we were back at TV in O.V.W. The match was D.O.S. vs. Flash and BJ. It was billed as first blood and the looser gets whipped by Synn's whip. The match went just fine, the finish involved Flash and BJ turning on each other, and allowing us to win. We had an interview that night. Wolfie was once again shit faced drunk. He had this long crazy monologue, and the TV ran out of air time before he could finish. The cameras went to black in the middle of his interview. There is only so much time in each segment. If you have seven minutes, at seven minutes one second the commercial comes on. Wolfie was pissed and tore into the back cursing and throwing things. At the end he kicked the locker room door open, breaking it, and almost hitting Brock Lesnar with it. He was fired again, and I was now left without a partner. In a course of ten days Wolfie D was fired from every place he worked, and they were all top notch promotions anyone would die to work for. It was the biggest and quickest self destruction of a career I had ever seen.

Wolfie was my most successful partner. I enjoyed every night working with him. I have wrestled, half of my career, with many partners. We clicked as a tag team. After a while we could tell where each other was going in the ring and almost communicated telepathically. It was the continuity that makes up a great and successful team. We had the same heroes and influences growing up in the business. I only regret, for personal reasons, that we could not have been partners longer. I think that if he would not have self destructed, we could have done great business together. Maybe even as high as the World's Tag Team titles.

We always traveled together, ate together, and stayed together. In our off day we talked on the phone about where the team was going. We were a team in every sense of the word. That is the only way to do it and be a success. I was honored to be his partner. We were the original Disciples. It can't be imitated, or duplicated.

Wolfie was asked about me in his RF shoot video. He pretended to not know my last name, and called me kid. That was Wolfie, ego maniac, and a drug addict. He was my drug addict for a short time. All the Disciple fans remember the team, even if he does not remember me, them, or his mistakes.

About this time I started to develop Damian more. We made him into a real interesting character. On one interview, out of no where, I started hearing voices. I would smack at the voices, and also talk to them. It was innovative. Damian was the first schizophrenic pro wrestler. There had been people with alter egos, like Mankind and Dude Love. Damian actually heard voices talking to him. He was the one sole character haunted by demonic voices from the past. I later developed the good/bad side of Damian's voices, at the time, though, it was not brought out on O.V.W. TV. I always saw it as Damian wanted to be good, but the voices forced him to be evil. It was a inner struggle of good vs. evil we all share. Damian was a baby face at heart, but his voices led by Synn, would make him cheat and do bad things. I thought it was a interesting side, and made it less blasphemous. He was not a demon by nature, but by force. I would do a move, then talk to the voices, and shake my head "no" in protest. I would follow the self debate with furious angered attack on my opponent. Basically, Damian could wrestle, but the voices made him brawl. He was a paradox of unsurity. A oxymoron in itself, a man torn between right and wrong. We did a interview once to explain that as a child Damian had been locked in a closet, then abused. This was the cause of the voices. It was easy to be Damian with this story because I could relate my own issues to his.

I have never heard voices, but I have been locked in a room, abused, and have always wanted to do good but somehow mess things up in the end. Damian became a outlet for my problems. I was trying to turn negatives in my life, into positives.

A.P.W. held it's first one and only Brian Hildebrandt memorial show on November 24th, 2000. Brain Hildebrandt, referee Mark Curtis, passed away from cancer. About one year later A.P.W. did a show in his honor. At first they did not even want me to participate in the show at all. They thought there had been heat between Brian and me for some reason. They couldn't have been more wrong. What they misunderstood was that Brian made two business decisions that I disagreed with. I have always said I disagreed with them, and still do. Brian knew how I felt, it was just business. We disagreed on several things, but he was the type of person that didn't let things like that get in the way of friendships.

The first thing was real simple. When Sandy Scott moved in with him in S.M.W. it left a heavy financial burden on me and Anthony. Brian offered Sandy to stay for two reasons. It was good for his position in the office, and it saved the office money. Brian was concerned with the company. I did not want to pay more rent. So we disagreed. We had no words, no argument, I just got over it. It was no big deal.

The second was a tad bit more complex, but simple also. I had just left W.C.W. and Brian was on his sick leave from there as well. He started booking for Beau James's promotion. I called Beau for work and Beau told me to call Brian for the dates. I called Brian and he said he did not have a spot for me. I was pissed, and needed the work. He ended up making a spot for me later. It was no big deal. I got over it.

A.P.W. just liked starting controversy. They were afraid that Pam, Brian's wife, would not like me being there. I said for them to just call her and ask. They didn't, because they were afraid too. I had offered to get some of the old S.M.W. guys for the show. This would have been a huge help on the draw. Things like that take time to get done, most of the guys would have loved to do it. I would have had to go through the W.W.F.'s third party booking system, but I could have gotten the guys. They finally told me I was booked two days before. I could not get anyone on that short of a notice. I was not about to call anyone until I was officially in on the project. They still held it against me that I did not provide them any talent for the show. That is how they did business.

When Pam arrived that night she ran right up and hugged me. I was always like her little brother. She whispered in my ear, "Who are all these people I don't know a soul here." That's why they didn't call her. They were not afraid of her, they did not even know her. They just emailed her telling where the show was, and offered to pay her half the gate. So, she only showed up for the money.

I had a personal agenda that night. I have never shared it to any one until now. I liked Brian a lot. He was one of my brothers. I traveled with him countless times. When we traveled he played either a tape of old Elton John music, or a Bill Cosby tape. I would fall asleep instantly, it never failed. He refed all of my matches in Smoky Mountain. I wrestled him several times also, both as Mark Curtis and as the Ninja

Turtle. In my opinion he had the best dropkick I have ever seen. With his short stature he was still able to jump and kick me in the throat every time. It looked devastating. He always made sure that I had eaten on the road, and was always making sure I had enough food. He was a caring person towards his friends.

One night, while we were both in W.C.W, we went Christmas shopping after the TV tapings while we were in Florida. We would not be home until nearly Christmas, so we decided to just go have dinner, and do our shopping there. Shortly after that night he got real sick. I never saw him again after that night. I never got to say goodbye to him. I was never asked to be on any of his memorial shows. For me this night in Beckley was my way of saying goodbye to my friend. I wanted to do it in a way he would appreciate, so I went out there and had the best match I could have, just for him.

The match pitted the Urban Death Squad and The War Machine, A.P.W.'s top heels, against the home town boys Flex, Kid Apollo, and myself in the main event. The action started right away. The heels met us half way down the isle and we all fought around the building. Then we spilled into the ring to start the match. We out wrestled them for a bit, and then I hit the rope, as the War Machine pulled it down. I went crashing to the floor. When I got up Spider Crowley hit me with the bell. It busted my head wide open. The heels worked me over for a while. The blood covered my eyes. I could not see. I would feel the heels hitting me and I would just fall. I would get up, and get knocked right back down again. I remember looking up and it was like a scene from *Rocky* as he was getting battered by Apollo Creed. When I got hit blood and sweat would fly everywhere. The crowd ate it up. I made a tag, and my team mounted a comeback, ending in our victory. The three of us stood proud, in the ring alone, as our music played. As our hands were being raised, I walked away from the others to a corner of the ring. I looked at the stairs to the upper level, this was what I stared at in my first match in the Armory ever. I looked up and said, "That one was for you, Brian. I hope it was a good one, rest in peace brother." I wanted to cry, but I held it in. I said goodbye to my friend. I knew he was watching on from somewhere.

A week later we lucked into the biggest angle in A.P.W. history. I wrestled Chris Hambrick. I beat him by DQ when the Urban Death Squad hit the ring on me. They stretched me out and delivered several chair shots. They left me laying in the ring a bloody mess. I laid there forever. The fans bought it. They just knew I was injured. It was classic suspension of disbelief. Brandi, with Dylan in her arms, came to ringside to see if I was okay. She even thought I was hurt. People started really wondering the next week when I was not there. The third week I teamed with Nicole Starr to face Drake Tungsten and Brandi. People knew she was my girl, and now she was in a match against me. We reformed Brute Shooter's group earlier that night. It consisted of Drake, billed from Sweden, Brandi, and a Canadian Team of Brian Douglas and his partner Rocky Blankenship. Rocky had worked under a hood as the Canadian Grappler, we changed his name to Lance Erickson. The name I used in Music City for Bert Prentice.

I started feuding with the group. I also refused to attack Brandi during the bouts. The crowd understood that she and I were an item together. Next Brandi attacked me and caused me to loose a match. I followed that up by having an interview asking her to be a better person. The fans were tuned in directly to the soap opera. Once A.P.W. found out where I wanted to go with this they made me tone the entire thing down.

I wanted to do what I called the "Baby on a Pole" angle. I would keep doing interviews with Brandi, basically calling her a dead beat mother, without really saying it. She would do interviews with Dylan safely in her arms. The people knew about Dylan, and she would start dating Lance on the show. Each week we would reveal new twists about her stealing my identity. The thing about Lance's name would be first. He would then start wearing my tights that Brandi supposedly gave him. Next, he would hold Dylan in an interview while Brandi talks. Meanwhile, I wrestle everybody in the group but them. Finally we set a match me versus Lance, and the promotion would grant me any stipulation I wanted. I would ask for a baby on a pole match. We would put a rattle on top of a pole. This is where I really lost Ward and Leonard. Those idiot marks actually thought I would hang my only baby boy from a pole. Get real, you ignorant marks! Dylan was only going to be held by Brandi or Rocky at ring side a couple of times. He would have been completely safe. I would have never allowed him to be in danger. I would finally grab the rattle in the match and win custody of Dylan. I was Super Dad, the baby face, and the heels had real heat.

A.P.W. had so many problems with this angle. They thought it promoted child abuse. It does not. It gives a story every single person could relate to. They never understood good triumphs over evil in the end. They never grasped the concept of my ideas. It will only work if the baby face dad grabs the rattle to win in the end. If he doesn't, everything else seems cruel and pointless. It is designed to be an emotional roller coaster till the dad wins in the end. It has to be the dad chasing the rattle, if a woman tries the baby role it is cruelty to the weaker sex in the crowd's eyes. They can sympathize with the man having to endure. Society accepts the concept of bad women taking advantage over a good man, because she is a woman. If the tables are turned, people won't tolerate a bad man taking advantage over a good woman. This has to be a six month story. The details have to unfold each week. It can't be rushed. A.P.W. will hotshot a angle into a three match deal every time. I can honestly say that this would have drawn huge money. Brandi and I were half way into this angle when they canned it. We were happy, well at least on face value at home, as far as the public knew. We went to Wal-mart after the show one night. We were holding hands, when we came across a family that was regulars at the shows. The family started to cry when they saw us holding hands. They actually cried in public. They were happy to see us together, for the sake of Dylan. The fans had bought every second of our tale. That is real emotion, and suspension of disbelief. Their thoughts were wrestling is fake, but Brian Logan vs. Brandi Alexander over Dylan was real. That is what our business is about. Even though the Baby on a Pole match never matured, it led to a three year run with Lance Erickson. It is still today the top grossing angle in West Virginia history.

In O.V.W. The Disciple was beginning a different feud against, what would turn out to be, long term opponents in The Minnesota Stretching Crew, Shelton Benjamin and Brock Lesnar. I first wrestled them in the December of 2000. Brock was the 2000 N.C.A.A.(National Collegiate Athletic Association) Champion. He was fresh out of college at Minnesota State. Shelton was his roommate in college, and coach of the team. Shelton had a impressive career at Minnesota State as well. We started a feud that would span both Brock and Shelton's stay at O.V.W. We faced them in one manner or another every night; we might as well have been married to those two guys. Brock Lesnar went on to be considered the most legitimate fighter of the modern era by winning the W.W.E. Undisputed Championship, I.W.G.P.(International Wrestling Grand Prix) championship, as well as the U.F.C.(Ultimate Fighting Championship) title. Shelton would find glory as a W.W.E. super star and holder of many titles as well.

BJ turned on Flash and became the newest member of the Disciples. The two had a Last Man Standing match, akin to a Texas Death Match, where the Southern tag team titles would go to the winner. The winner would keep the belts, and choose a new partner. BJ won and choose me to be his partner, instantly making him a Disciple of Synn. This would be my fourth tag team title reign. BJ dropped his first initials and went by the name Pain. The new incarnation was formed, The Disciples of Synn, Pain and Damian.

BJ is a good fellow. He has a good heart, and is a gifted athlete. Wolfie and I hated to work with him. He always wanted to do complicated spots that he was not capable of doing. We broke his neck in a match by dropping him on his head during a double team move, due to his not cooperating in the match. BJ and I never gelled as a team. We had continuity, but were not a team. He was not dedicated to the success of the Disciples. He never went out with the boys, and we never traveled together. I only saw him at the buildings. I had several conversations about being more of a team, but he wanted sole success. He was all about himself. We would set a pace in a match, I would tag him in, and he would do some seven stage spot and totally screw up the flow of the entire thing. We had both good and bad matches. Sometimes we were on our game, others we weren't. It would depend on which BJ would show up.

The O.V.W. talent began to work dark matches regularly for the W.W.F. I faced the Mean Street Posse in Charlotte, N.C. In Georgia I wrestled in front of forty thousand people at the Georgia Dome. I was booked against Brian Christopher and Steve Blackman with a new partner that would come to O.V.W. later, Seven. He became the Vampire Kevin Thorn in years to come. W.W.F. paired us together, and left BJ out on the bigger events.

In the middle of the feud with the Crew, we faced a special challenge that would be one of my biggest matches ever. Christmas Chaos at the Louisville Gardens, was scheduled in Mid December of 2000. However, a blizzard postponed the event until January 31st, 2001. The Disciples of Synn faced W.W.F. super stars The Hardy Boyz, Matt and Jeff. The match we had was one of the best matches I have ever competed in. I had known the Hardys forever, but had never wrestled them. I was starting to be in great shape, how could I not wrestling every night of the week. When I got in the ring with Team Extreme, Matt, Jeff, and Lita; it was almost effortless. They are that good. Both BJ and Synn were on their game that night. It was a classic for O.V.W. and a milestone for me. I love being around the Hardy Boys they are just great guys and true pros. In my opinion Jeff is the next generation's Shawn Micheals. I have proclaimed this for years to people riding the roads with me. Jeff just recently won the W.W.E. championship.

I had worked for Kenny McCoy's N.P.W. (National Pro Wrestling) since mid- 2000. Kenny, who wrestles as Chris Draven, is just a top notch person. The promotion in eastern Kentucky, now called N.W.A. Bluegrass is just a great place to work. Kenny, who is in the cars sales business by trade, always took great care of me. He paid well and on time. He even paid me when he had to cancel a show. That is unheard of these days. He would always book me in the main events with top named stars. At Christmas I would receive bonuses. I received a pair of red wrestling boots, that became Damian's, and a leather coat with the company logo on it. Kenny and his family are tremendous people. He was trained by Jimmy Valiant.

I had four main opponents in N.P.W. Buddy Landell was a Southern legend. The only problem Buddy has is bad luck. The Nature Boy was scheduled to win the N.W.A. World's title in the eighties. He was going to beat the real "Nature Boy" Ric Flair. He began pre-celebrating, got self medicated, and forgot to show up for the match. One version of this story says that when Dusty Rhodes called him to tell him he would win, Buddy didn't believe it was him, so he hung up on Dusty. Another time W.W.F. needed someone to put Ahmed Johnson over on TV. Johnson was the then I-C champion. Rumor has it that Dean Douglas, Shane, was asked and refused. Buddy walking by hears the conversation, and volunteers to do the job. The match went great. W.W.F. officials were so happy, they offered Buddy a job. Shortly after this Buddy was in New York for a W.W.F. show, he walks out of his hotel and falls off the curb, shattering his leg into pieces. W.W.F. had to release him. Buddy couldn't win. If it was not for bad luck, he would have no luck at all. I loved wrestling Buddy, I dominated most of the matches. He is an interesting, fun, and whacky character.

In February of 2001, I wrestled Terry "Bam Bam" Gordy. I was a huge Fabulous Freebirds fan growing up. Who wasn't? I watched World Class Championship wrestling from Texas religiously. The Birds were main event talent there for years. When I found out I was booked against Gordy I began doing my homework. I have always been a proponent of viewing video tapes. A lot of guys now a days show up to work a star, but don't understand their style. They don't have a clue how to work with them. A person wouldn't wrestle Lou Thesz, the same was they would Andre the Giant, or Kurt Angle the same way you would Big Show. One must know his opponent. Do we go to war against Iraq without knowing what weapons they have? Well yes, we did do that, but you get my point. How can one expect to get his moves in the match, and the star's, all the while making the match flow properly. You can't, and you wouldn't try if you were a real competitor. I found a real good deal on ebay for World Class tapes, I snatched them up, and studied nine, eight hour World Class TV tapes for the match.

Terry suffered an overdose in Japan years ago. I remember this vividly, because one of his first matches back was in Knoxville, TN. He faced the Dirty White Boy for the Smoky MT. title. Terry was not quite himself then. DWB carried him. Terry's heath improved, but it was never the same again. When I met Terry in the ring I was confident that I knew what he used to do, and what he could do now. I loved the match, it is one of my favorites. He milked the oriental spike, while I pounded on him. He hit me with his clothesline. It was classic Gordy. Rocky took him aside before the match and told Terry that I had studied for the match. Before the match Terry explained privately about his heath and asked if I could call the match and make him look good. I joke by saying, "I'll take care of you kid", as I patted him on the back. He smiled and off to the ring we went. That was one of the greatest honors I had ever had, to be asked and given the reigns by such a legend. Working with him, and just being around him, was a present from the wrestling Gods. Four or five months later, I was scheduled for a rematch against him. Terry never made it. He passed away less than a week before the match.

Kenny had to find a replacement for Gordy on the fair shows. We had several booked that week. In Inez, KY, Kenny got "Wild Fire" Tommy Rich. Tommy was the youngest N.W.A. World's champion. He is a legend. He is also an asshole. He knows he is a legend, and still lives in the late seventies and early eighties when he was champion, on top of the wrestling world. He did not understand that times had changed, and his business had changed as well. Sometimes though, the more they change, the more they stay the same.

Tommy had been involved in questionable dealings in the past, like the time he and Doug Gilbert stole Richard Arpin's cash box after a show one night. Arpin had to get the police to track them down. Tommy was classic for getting naive promoters who would pay him before he performed, and would leave without doing so. Occasionally Tommy demanded double pay, and promoters would actually pay him twice for working once. He claimed one was a fee for appearing, the second was to wrestle.

This was the case in Inez, Ky. I tried to smarten Kenny up to Tommy's tricks. Kenny being the good person he is paid him extra. I also insisted that I put Tommy over. I knew he would throw a huge fit if asked to do a job to what he considered a nobody. I was Kenny's champion, and he did not want anyone to beat his champion. The idea was the right one, but Tommy did not see it that way. In his mind he was still the N.W.A. World's champion and was not lying down for a regional champion, especially one he did not even know. After Kenny told Tommy what he wanted, Tommy threw a fit. Finally we reached a compromise. It would be a double count out, outside of the ring. I would roll back in after the bell and proclaim the victory. This hurt no one involved in eyes of the fans. Tommy began drinking, and soon was belligerent. The match went real well, which shows how talented Tommy actually was. We stumbled to the floor for the count out, Tommy started complaining. The bell rang and I rolled myself back into the ring. Tommy wouldn't even roll me in himself. The announcer announces me as the winner by count out. That made no sense, but was Kenny's idea. Tommy was hot, and thought I pulled a fast one on him. I just wanted a good match, and to get paid. Tommy however, conjured up a huge conspiracy against the former champion. He takes the mic and starts running me down to all the people. He talked about my talent, and the promoters like Cornette that I worked for claiming that we were all below him. I, in a working way, attacked him and we brawled to the back. I changed and showered before I went to talk to him. He started in on me again. I explained that I knew who he was, and how much of a honor it was to wrestle him. He couldn't have cared less. I went on to explain that the promoter called the finish and I had nothing to do with it. He still blamed me. I stood there for five minutes as he yelled right into my face about it. I told him what I thought about it, "Look here, I respect you! I know you are a former World's champion. I had a finish that put you over, but nobody wanted to do it. Regardless, that was then and this is now. If you want to yell at me, I will kick your N.W.A. former champion ass!" I then suggested that he go sell Polaroids. He did.

After facing several local N.P.W. talent Kenny brought in Steve Corino. "The King of Old School" was a former N.W.A. World's champion himself. He actually took the E.C.W. job I was offered, changed his looks, and basically stole my gimmick. That was fine with me, I like Steve. Steve is a politically correct suck ass, but it works for him. I do business differently, and it works for me. Steve had just lost his N.W.A. title in Japan, then it was held up in England, or it would have been my first World's title match. Before I found out about him losing the title, I joked about beating him legit. I knew I could take him, but it was only a joke. That would have been bad business, so I never really considered it. Steve and I had a real easy match. He is a great person, once he lets his political guard down.

O.V.W. was running all the time. Tuesday spot towns, Wednesday TV, bar shows on weekends, and when we weren't doing those we worked dark matches for the W.W.F. We wrestled Brock and Shelton every night. On the TV we would face enhancement talent, but ended up brawling with the Stretching Crew.

At the Bluegrass Brawl, in Louisville at the Gardens, we faced The Crew in a match where the stipulation was if we lost we left town, and if they lost referee Robert Brisco would get whipped by Synn. We dropped the Southern tag team belts to them later, and eventually won them back. Finally it concluded on Smackdown, in the W.W.F., this, by far, was the biggest match of my career, up until that point.

We made W.W.F. and O.V.W. history that night. The match took place on May 15th, 2001. It was the first time that the O.V.W. Southern Tag Team Title was defended at a W.W.F. event, and the first title change of a developmental title on the W.W.F. show. This is something that I was a part of that can never be taken away from me. I made wrestling history, and that is a real accomplishment.

The match was The Disciples vs. The Stretching Crew. I trained harder than I ever had prior to that match. When I arrived that night I was in the top shape of my life. I was lean, cut, and ready for the task at hand. I was mentally prepared and knew this match was the opportunity to be brought on the Smackdown roster. The TV matches leading up to this night were some of our best. We had momentum on our side as well. Both teams were ready.

Our music played, which was cool that our O.V.W. music was used on the W.W.F. show. I had been given music before there, but it was just generic music they used for opening matches. This time they played the actual Disciple music. When that first note of *Break Stuff* by Limp Bizcuit played, the crowd knew it was us. They were in a frenzy. They anticipated our arrival and the match. When the match began we were precise on all of our moves and forgot nothing. It was a physical contest and the crowd enjoyed it. The match was a huge success.

We continued to feud with the Crew up till Brock got called up to full time. Brock became the youngest, at the time, to ever be W.W.E. Undisputed Champion. Randy Orton of course became the youngest World's champion, knocking off Tommy Rich's spot from the N.W.A. In my opinion Brock is a hell of a nice guy. He is one of the top amateur competitors of all time, and as I stated earlier the most legit fighter in the world today, bar none. The night he beat the Rock for his first W.W.E. title, I stood a little taller. Danny Davis and Jim Cornette did the actual training outside the shows of Brock. I wrestled him in ninety present of his first matches developing the next big thing. I was the on the job in ring trainer. I was so proud that I could have a small part in such a large career. He is a legend in the making, if he is not already one. It was a privilege to compete with him.

In Brock's absence we briefly feuded with Bolan Services. Kenny Bolan, King B, led his men on an onslaught of Synn's virtues, or lack thereof. They did a parody of the Disciples in an interview. It was classic! Mr. Black, was a fat Levitation, Bolan dressed up as Synn, Rob Conway impersonated BJ, and John Cena portrayed me. The funniest thing was that Cena was so good; he did the Damian character, as well as I did. I was the original.

I really enjoyed wrestling Bolan Services. We entered into a small feud with Rico Constantino and Cena, who was called Prototype then. These guys learned their craft and made a way for themselves. Rico was over forty, but looked twenty, former American Gladiator. Who had a short run doing the Adrian Street gimmick in the W.W.E. It is no wonder that Cena became a main event star so quick. He is truly the total package. He can talk. His body is in phenomenal condition, and on top of that he can wrestle. He is a prototype.

After Bolan Services we were scheduled to face Eric and Kurt Angle at the next Garden's show. It was billed as "The Last Dance". It would be the last Louisville Garden's show ever. Our opponents were going to be a huge stepping stone in my career. Wrestling Kurt Angle, who is our generation's Lou Thesz, would raise my level of worth considerably.

The Disciples shut Eric Angle's arm up in a car door to ignite the feud. Eric needed triceps surgery, and this allowed the story to flow in his absence. In the time leading up to the match we feuded with Ron "H2O" Waterman. He took up the cause till the Angles would return and seek revenge. The week prior to the big match, Kurt wrestled Shane McMahon in a street fight at King of the Ring on PPV. Kurt suffered a broken neck. The clip is shown almost every week in some form on W.W.E. TV and DVD. Shane attempts to over the top belly to belly suplex Angle through a piece of glass. The glass doesn't break and Angle falls on his neck to the floor. Angle was not able to compete in our match due to the injury. O.V.W. substituted Waterman and Bobby Eaton instead. The match was not as high profile as originally planned with the substitution. It was a good match. I always liked working with Ron, and Bobby is phenomenal. I was told by Synn that our pay off for the Angles match was to be around four hundred and fifty dollars. I did not think it would be that high, but expected a good pay day from the match. Due to the substitution I received one hundred and fifty dollars. This prompts the question, "What is the difference between Kurt Angle and Bobby Eaton? The answer, about three hundred dollars!"

Ron Waterman was a former U.F.C. winner. He was a real tough man. A legit fighter. His personality was gentle as could be. He is a born again Christian, who is as tame as a field mouse. In the ring he could hurt you. He was no one to mess with. Every time he hit me he left a mark on my face. For months I went around with black eyes and torked elbows. I would joke with him telling him he hit too soft, like a girl. The truth was he was killing me, but I did not let him know that. At least it looked great on TV. He was good to be around for the boys. He probably never realized it, but he was a good influence in a mostly corrupt business, with his clean living and lifestyle. Ron now performs with a Christian weightlifting team that travels nationally teaching the word of God.

In July of 2001, I decided to leave A.P.W. They were constricting my work more and more every week. It was hard to go from the bright lights of the W.W.F. back to the bugtussel of West Virginia independents. A.P.W. did not allow me to do interviews or even go near a mic. They couldn't control what I said and censored me for it. The fans knew I was Damian, and the turn from Logan to Damian had begun. They wanted to sabotage him as well. I would not let that happen to Damian, so I left. JD had opened up again, trying to run opposition to A.P.W. I went with his group A.S.W. (All Star Wrestling). I chased Scotty Mckeever for his A.S.W. United States title. We had classic bouts. We had street fights, chain match, two out of three falls, and others. Our biggest match, and one that is still talked about in West Virginia wrestling lore, is the one hour war. We wrestled to a one hour time limit draw for the United States title on July 29th, 2001, at the Princeton Rec. Center in Princeton, WV. A one hour draw is unheard of these days. Most competitors can't go fifteen minutes, much less sixty. I was always a good wrestler in the longer matches. I have great in ring stamina. Sure, you will have an Iron Man match in the W.W.E. every now and then, but it is not common practice. On the Independent circuit it is art form long forgotten. Wrestling for one hour is hard. It is like wrestling six matches of today's standard in a row with no rest. We pulled it off; the fans were into it and on their feet at the end. After the match I sat in the shower on a folding chair under the cool water for about another hour.

Things at home were terrible. I would invent reasons to stay on the road sometimes just to get away from Brandi. We always fought. She wanted to go visit her friend Patti, Brittany Brown. Patti was running four shows to steal back all her equipment from Mike Sparta. Against my will I went. The deal was that we would get our money from her before we worked. I would wrestle Flex each night, and we would stay at Patti's. Mike was living back in the house, but we were reassured that everything was different. At first they were.

The first issue we had was the scheduling. Brandi flew up to Massachusetts. I couldn't, I had other dates to fill. My travel schedule went like this. August 16th Blue Well, WV; August 17th Uxbridge, Mass; August 18th Waterbury, Conn.; August 22nd Jeffersonville, IN; August 23rd Blue Well, WV; August 24th back to Massachusetts; August 25th Cape Cod, Mass.; August 29th back to Jeffersonville, IN; August 30th back to Blue Well. It was impossible to make them all. I drove to every event, I did not fly. I somehow made every single one of the shows. I drove, wrestled, and then drove again. I was off for two days then back on for fourteen straight in September. Dylan had to stay with my parents the entire time. I hated it; I had to have help. I could not take care of him while I was gone. Brandi wouldn't.

Mike was nice for the first two dates. Then he ran into problems, then so did I. Virgil was booked on the next two cards. Nobody wanted to work Virgil. Mike took me aside and asked me if I would. He was professional about it, probably the first and last time in his life, so I said I would do it.

The first night I worked with Virgil we got to the building late. We drove from West Virginia the night before, had left right after the match, and arrived just before the next. When I got there I got my envelop and the money was wrong. It was half of what I was suppose to have. Brandi, without my knowing, had made the agreement to get half before and half that night back at Mike's. Mike and Patti did not want the boys knowing that we got paid in full when they had got a pay cut. That did not make sense, I never show my pay envelop to anyone. It is none of their business, plus there can be heat if the boys don't agree with what they think you are worth. I suspected we were being taken advantage of. I yelled across the room to Flex, who had traveled the entire trip with me, to take his boots off the money was wrong. Our money was wrong we weren't wrestling, it was that simple. The entire locker room heard. At that point, I was so tired I did not care if we worked or not. I would have just rather gone to eat across the street as work, because I was so hungry. Brandi and Patti both tried to talk to me. It was simple, pay me my money and I would work, if not I was going to go get something to eat. If I left, there was no one to work Virgil. So, I got my money, and I wrestled Virgil. It was typical Virgil all hype, and no talent. He super starred it up, and then would not do anything in the ring. It was short. Then I went to eat.

The second night to make up for the inconvenience, Mike wanted me to go over Virgil. It was the Tommy Rich Thing all over again. I did not care who won, I just wanted paid. I tried to tell Mike the same thing I told Kenny McCoy. Finally, I convinced him to let me put Virgil over. I would hit Virgil with a chain and pin him, the ref would find the chain, and as I was arguing with the ref, Virgil would roll me up and pin me. We never made it that far. Virgil decides to give me a wrestling lesson in the back before the match. He began telling me how to work. While I am no Lou Thesz, I am, on my worst day, a better wrestler than Virgil ever was. After he was done I went over to the women's dressing room to tell Brandi to talk to Patti about it. She didn't. I came back to tell Patti myself, that as the promoter it was her job to tell Virgil that I did not just start the wrestling business yesterday. At one point in the lesson, Virgil puts me in the floor in front of all the boys and explains the mechanics of a rear chin lock. Dylan, a child at the time, could put on a rear chin lock. So could I. You learn that move on day one of wrestling school. I had taken all I could of the matter. If Virgil wouldn't respect me, then I would make him respect me in the ring. I went and informed the promoter that tonight's match would be legit.

When we locked up I took Virgil straight into the corner and chopped him in his throat twice. He asked, "Are you shooting on me?"

"No, I don't know enough to shoot on you." I responded.

I then grabbed a headlock and worked the first spot that put him over. I wanted to get him comfortable, in case someone smartened him up. I cut him off for the heat, and shot him in to the ropes. I called for a power slam. Virgil stopped in mid ring before he ever got to the other side. I went to kick him, real slow so he would grab it. He did. When he ducked to grab my leg, I snatched him in the front sugar hold. I cranked it for a couple of seconds, enough to leave him scatter brained. Then I went behind him, and delivered hard forearm shots to his head. When he turned around I shot the double leg and took him down, hooking the sugar again. The crowd, who had realized it was a shoot, booed. I stood up, and so did he. Virgil begged me to work with him. I then yawned so all could see, and fell straight on my back. Virgil and the crowd were stunned. "Pin me! Pin me, Super Star! Pin me!" I yelled. Then I got straight up and left the arena. Virgil caught up with me and apologized. In my mind it was way too late. We had not been fully paid yet, so Flex, Brandi, and I went back to Providence, RI, to Patti's house where we had been staying.

When we arrived back at Patti's, we phoned her and told her we wanted all of our money, or else. I had been taken by her once, but never twice. She refused to settle. Some things in her house got broken, and Patti called the police from Cape Cod. When they arrived Brandi confessed to breaking the items. The police called Patti twice asking if she wanted to press charges. Patti answered no both times. The police called her back a third time and talked her into pressing charges. Once their talk was over Patti wanted to press charges. They, however, wanted to arrest me. Brandi had already told them she did it. We had a key and there was no breaking or entering, things just got broken. I was still being arrested. When I arrived at the station the police finger printed me and gave me a court date. Then just let me go. The officer explained to me to just leave and go home. They went on to tell me that things like this were no big deal in Rhode Island. We left that night and I have never gone back to Providence.

When we got home Brandi blamed me for the entire incident. She could care less about the disrespect to me, or the sham her friend orchestrated. The internet picked up the story, and by the time they were done I had done fifty two thousand dollars damage to her belongings. The entire apartment complex was not worth that much. It also tried accusing me of trying to kill her dog. I love dogs more than people. I have always had dogs. Anyone who really knows me, knows I would never hurt a dog. I replied with my own account on the O.V.W. website. Still Brandi placed blame of her loss of Patti's friendship on me. I don't think a real friend would have done that to another friend in the first place. We never got our money, she didn't care about that either. When her credit card bills weren't paid, that was my fault too. This all put more tension and strain on the relationship.

When I left A.P.W. for A.S.W. it officially started what was known as the West Virginia Wrestling War. I admit I was the large cause of it, but I was fed up with the way Leonard and Ward did things. A.P.W. refused to let their talent work anywhere else. It was ridiculous. It was not like they were two huge companies like W.W.F. and W.C.W. It was two independent marks running dead towns, in a state that was struggling. Animosity grew between JD and Leonard. The first blow in the war was scored by me. My buddy, the Cuban Assassin, was the A.P.W. champion. So, I booked him against me. It was for bragging rights. I made sure that the A.S.W. and U.S. title came out on top. Ritchie caught a lot of heat for that. They ended up firing him, so he started to work for us.

In October of 2001, The Disciples wrestled the Stretching Crew for a spot on Raw. The winners would face Bolan Services team of Rico and Proto for their Southern Tag team titles. We lost. The Crew got the job. I started realizing my hopes for a full time spot with the W.W.E. was fleeting. A few weeks later we faced the Crew again, on TV, in a six man, their partner was Val Venis. Shawn Morley is a heck of an athlete. The match was a O.V.W. classic. It was around this time O.V.W. felt the affect of the end of the Monday Night Wars and the W.C.W. buyout by Vince. We were receiving a lot of talent to O.V.W. Guys like Lash Lareaux, Jason Jett (my old friend EZ Money), Kanyon, and others were brought into O.V.W. My last W.W.F. appearance, now officially changed to W.W.E., was in Louisville, KY, at Freedom Hall, on October 29th 2001. I didn't even wrestle that night. There were so many wrestlers there I couldn't even get a match. They had seen me many times before, and were not sold on me. Now there were younger athletes, in better shape, ready and eager. I enjoyed being there, the boys were always family. I have not been back to a W.W.E. show since. All good things must come to an end. Things in my private life were also coming to an end. I could not live with Brandi anymore. I had talked with Cornette and he offered me a office job. He wanted me to promote the spot towns in Kentucky for O.V.W. It was a way to make money and be a part of the O.V.W. family. The catch was that I needed to live in Louisville. Brandi refused to move. I had to turn down the job. Eventually Super Nova from E.C.W. took the job and parlayed it in to a creative development office position with the W.W.E. for a short time. With all that had happened, and

Brandi's "new" personality, I just had to leave. It was the single hardest decision I have ever made. I could not bear to leave Dylan. I wanted to be with him more than anyone on the face of the earth. For his sake, at the time, I needed to be in a stable home. I tried to spend as much time as I could with him, and went to visit him often. Still, to this day, I love him with everything in me.

Dylan, your father thinks about you every single moment of each day. I love you right now, and have always loved you every second from the day I met you. I would do anything to help you and spend time with you. I never left you. I only did what I thought I had to, to make life livable for all of us. I hope one day you will forgive me for not being present all this time. I only left that home, not my little buddy!

During the writing of this book Brandi became pregnant again. This time Kid Apollo, Waylon Payne, was the father to be. They had a little girl, I am told. I wish them all luck.

When I moved out I moved to Princeton, WV. I took over running A.S.W. JD decided to call it quits once again. He left me in charge of all the shows, as he always does. The deal was for him to pay all the bills of the company, while I sent him the profits. He never did. Eventually A.S.W. shut down due to unpaid bills.

The last program I worked with O.V.W. was with Shelton Benjamin and new partner Red Dog. Red Dog came from E.C.W. and went on to be Rodney Mack in the W.W.E. He was a character that resembled the Junkyard Dog. I was a huge fan of the JYD so our matches went real smooth. The intensity was not the same without Brock, but were classic in their own right.

My most memorable bout took place in January 2002. It was a Double Dog Collar match in Jeffersonville, IN, on O.V.W. TV. I had had several chain matches in West Virginia. In fact, most of my angles in West Virginia ended in chain matches. Growing up chain matches were never my favorite to watch. I had seen first hand the Dirty White Boy in several. I had several with Scotty McKeever, and learned the psychology of them real well. I have probably had more chain matches than any of the other specialty matches. I have been lucky to have never lost one of this type of match. The Double Chain pitted the D.O.S. with Synn against Red Dog and Shelton. Red Dog always carried a chain around his neck on the way to the ring, we used it against him. The match is simple, each person has a collar around his neck, and two by two in this case, a chain is attacked to each of them. Then, anything goes in the match. BJ was connected to Red Dog, and I to Shelton. It was a wild affair. I was lacerated early. Blood was everywhere. It was so bad I had to hold on to the top rope because I could not see. I fought by feel the entire match. Eventually we gained the victory in true heel fashion. I unhooked my collar, and hit Shelton with a steel chair and gained the pin. BJ and I were both covered in blood. I had never bled so much. I needed stitches, but refused to go to the hospital. When I worked the following night I bled profusely again. I ended up at the hospital, but the wound was so old they could not do anything about it, except stop the bleeding. After twelve hours you can't treat a cut. They wrapped my head like a mummy, then I was off to the next town.

Nydia, from *Tough Enough*, was added to the fold as we continued our feud. She became enemies with Synn. We worked six man tags out of the addition of her. The most memorable of which was featured at Six Flags Kentucky Kingdom, in Louisville. We got good press off the show, Bill Apter featured pictures of us in Pro Wrestling Illustrated. Finally, after years in the business, my first picture appeared in a magazine. It was featured in a story about Shelton. I take it any way I can get.

Our feud with them was short lived. We faced various opponents over then next few months. David Flair, Nick Densemore (Eugene), Mark Jindrack, and Bautista to name a few. BJ quit over his long drawn out neck injury, which Wolfie and I had caused a year earlier. Seven was now my new partner. We had good continuity from the times we teamed in the W.W.E. We had just not been a team very long.

Six Flags was scheduled in the Summer of 2002. I was so exhausted and burnt out from the business I made a terrible mistake. I had been on the road for eight and a half years straight, no rest and no let up. This mistake cost me my job in O.V.W. I was late getting to the show that night. I went to talk to Synn about it. She was having a bad day, and we butted heads about it. Then BJ entered the conversation, and I told him what I thought about his attitude and athletic ability. We all argued right in front of all the boys. It was bad business, and wrong on my part. Cornette was pissed and, well, he should have been. He and I then had our first and last argument. I was unemployed. Cornette and I quickly reconciled, and nothing was ever mentioned about it again.

I returned months later to team with BJ versus the New Disciples Seven and Bain, Tyson Tomko. It was a street fight. I had hoped for a feud like the Midnight Express vs. Original Midnight Express. It never came to be. I was pinned and passed the tag team torch to Seven and Bain. It was the last time I ever worked for O.V.W.

Working in O.V.W. was a blessing. I had been on top there for three years. That is one hell of a run! I got to work with every top name star in the industry today. It was the best company I have ever worked for. The guys of O.V.W. will always be in my memories, and remain my friends. It was a pleasure to a part of a great organization. The big push was over.

Chapter 9: Blue Ridge Promotions

I moved to Princeton, WV, in late 2001. I began seeing Lisa Thomas around Christmas of that year. We moved in with each other shortly after that. She had three children of her own from a previous marriage, Laken, Blake, and Brooke. Being a step parent is a hard job. It is a lot of work. I took example from what Glen, Kane, did with Crystal's daughters. So, I tried to embrace the challenge. I went from being a super hero in the ring to them, to being a new father figure at home. They viewed me as a replacement for their dad. I never tried to replace their father, just take care of them. He had a drug addition problem, and was not there at all for them. All I wanted to do was be there for them. I had no experience with children, other than Dylan. He was a baby. I now had older children to deal with. I would have to learn on the job with them.

Flex and I, who self medicated ourselves often, made a decision not to see each other anymore. We thought it was best for my career and his life. The toxic twins needed to move on so they could survive. Flex went to Florida for Christmas and did not come back.

He was my best friend, a true brother. The boys in the business were frat brothers. Flex was like my real brother. I never had any siblings, Jeremy was as close as I ever got.

Brandi had grown ever more tired of being a mom. She wanted to wrestle full time again. Full time to her was just on weekends. We decided that Dylan would live with me for a couple of months. She told me, "I can't take him anymore!" I was more than happy to take Dylan with me.

All of Lisa's children loved Dylan. They were all close. Lisa had no problem helping me with Dylan. I moved all the kids, hers and mine, and her brother into a house I rented in Princeton. We were a makeshift family. I thought I was content with life more than ever.

I went back to work for A.P.W. June 1st, 2002. This time they were called Mid Atlantic Wrestling. A.P.W. promoted Oak Hill under the new banner. Brian Douglas had new ideas about how to run towns. Over the years we had discussed a third company starting up and taking over the state. We discussed strategies of putting both A.P.W. and A.S.W. out of business. A.S.W. had already gone under, but I continued to run shows there with no affiliations. Douglas was running a few towns on his own that A.P.W. had ignored.

A short time later I received a call from Douglas; and a second confirming from Rocky. A.P.W. was folding. Leonard was run off shortly after. His ideas did not mix with the others, and they out lasted him. Ward was sole owner, and running out of money fast. He was ready to sell. I saw the opportunity and I took it. The West Virginia Wrestling war was over. I had won!

I bought out A.P.W. I bought all the equipment, and took over all the towns. I changed the name to Blue Ridge Wrestling Promotions (BRW). All of a sudden, the talent from both shows was united. The fans were the ones that really won. Life does truly imitate art. This was shortly after W.W.E. purchased W.C.W. I never pretend that the two worlds are anywhere near each other, as I have already stated. They are universes apart. The similarities between the struggles of the companies in comparison are interesting. The feuds, that months before were internet gossip, were now being played out in the ring for real.

We ran Oak Hill every Tuesday, which eventually changed to Thursday and Princeton every Sunday. We also had revolving spot shows that included Harlan, Beckley, Ghent, Pax, and Naomi. We stayed busy. That was the name of the game. Work as often as you can, and make as much money possible. These two things some people had problems with.

Several of the A.P.W. regulars were not used to traveling. They complained all the time they were on the road. Some would no show, or show late regularly. I was running a serious company, so I fired them. Others were not happy with the roll they were now playing. Jack Miller who was an A.P.W. star was now my opening match. There were definite changes.

I funded the company in a new unusual way. It made perfect sense to me, but was a different approach to finding financial backing. I had collected wrestling dolls and action figures my entire life, since I was a boy. I had almost every one available, both American and foreign, up till 2002. I had my private collection, which was open. I still have that collection nearly six hundred strong. I had a set of non opened ones. I sold the set of non opened ones on E-Bay. One of the first things I did was make a former student of mine a Lieutenant. He was a twenty percent partner. He took all the time to sell all of our stuff. If not for him, I would have never been able to start. He sold the entire set, individually, for around ten thousand dollars. This gave us the funds to run the company.

Eric, who wrestles as the Rebel and manages as Eric St. Clair, is one of my best friends. He was also my best student. He is not a natural athlete. In fact he is no athlete at all, his heart and desire, along with his love for our sport more than made up for his lack of genetics. He is fully capable of competing on the same level as more legit athletes. His charisma and drive made him an asset in the ring. He is the only student to do exactly what I asked him to do.

When he first started training he was struggling to keep up. I took him aside, and explained his limitations. I told him to go home and do free standing squats every day. They would help him increase his wind in the ring. He improved from pathetic, to holding his own against life long athletes like Flex and Ron Ray.

Eric's character, The Rebel, is Dusty Rhodes's Midnight Rider gimmick. The difference is The Rebel is covered in Confederate flags. He was a huge baby face for B.R.W. The fans ate up the southern pride stuff. He was complete with his Hank Williams Jr. ring music, *The South is Gonna Rise Again*.

Eric St.Clair, his evil managing alter-ego is J.J. Dillon. He would give these great old school promos that were natural heat seekers. I feuded with his stable of men, with him by their side for a long time. We did all the classic J.J. spots. We even competed in bull rope matches. These are akin to the chain matches, except substitute a rope and cow bell for the chain. For a non athlete, Eric drew money with that bull rope match. He had several over his career. All of them were excellent.

Eric is a person second to none. He is the most honest person I have ever met. How he ended up in a profession that is surrounded by beer drinking thugs, immoral crooks, and roust about individuals is beyond me. Eric will avoid confrontation at all cost. Traveling with me was an experience for him. He would never hurt anyone for any reason. Earlier in his career promoters like JD and Ward took advantage of him. This was one of the main reasons I wanted him a part of my office. Also along with his desire to be in the wrestling business, and his knowledge of the West Virginia Indy scene. He deserved some recognition. Unlike the Anthony Perdues and Jack Millers, Eric paid his dues, the hard way. He wrestled night in and night out, he earned it. Eric, however, is the type of person who could be late for Wrestlemania if he was driving. He only drives the speed limit, whether we were late or not. It drove me insane. Eric never drank, or smoked, and never caroused with women. He even married his high school sweetheart. He is a true gem in a coalfield. He was a great business partner. I want to thank him tremendously for his dedication and loyalty to me. I am honored to call him a friend.

One of my first feuds in B.R.W. was with Brad Ricter, Brad Thomas. Ricter was Brian Douglas's brother-in-law. That in no way got him his spot; in fact it may have held him back. Brad earned it on talent. He only had four matches when I started working a program with him. Brad has since came into his own, traveling with Ricky Morton to places that were "sold out".

I called in favors, and in true Jerry Lawler like fashion, I beat every one of them. Jim Cornette sent Leviathan, Dave Bautista, down to challenge for the U.S. title. Friends of mine like John Nobel and Shawn Casey all tried too. Locals like Elishia O'Mally and Jamie Boland attempted to win the belt, but failed.

When I faced Ricter in a non-title bout in our first ever encounter, he beat me. Setting up the feud. We worked several time limit draws. Taped Fist Matches were next. Finally we met in a Texas Death match. He eventually won the U.S. title from me. He successfully defended his B.R.W. U.S. title till April of 2003. He lost it to "Southern Comfort" Chris Vega. Vega would be the last U.S. champion. Ricter and I were scheduled to meet in a Coal Miner's Glove match, it never occurred. The curse of the Coal Miner's Glove in West Virginia struck again.

Blue Ridge was running strong, and we were working four nights a week. We tried to help the community also. Eric set up a charity event at the Glenwood 4-H camp in Princeton, WV. The 4-H camp hosts a camp for Down's syndrome kids every year. So we had a show for them and a dance afterwards. They all loved it, and I did too. It is one of my all time favorite shows to work. We also did benefits for the Children's Miracle Network through Wal-Mart in Beckley. Things were going well for B.R.W.

On August 2nd, 2002, we promoted our first thousand dollar house. That was unheard of in West Virginia at the time. This fortified us as a company, and my beliefs that you can draw money in this state. It was at Marsh Fork High School in Naomi, WV. The school was trying raise money for a lawyer fee they had acquired fighting consolidation by the school board. It was so successful they signed a contract for two more shows, after those two events they agreed to sign for a once a month deal for the period of one year. For the first time real business was being done in West Virginia wrestling. A real territory was forming, all with out the use of TV.

My goal was to make B.R.W. a cross between the Memphis territory and Stu Hart's Stampede territory. The first six months to a year would establish our area and fan base, which we were doing. In January I planed to start filming angles on video. I wanted the boys to learn to work TV style matches and practice interviews. I wanted to market the live shows on video and sell on the internet and at live events. I then was aiming for TV production in June of 2003. This would give me a year to line up TV production. We were right on schedule.

One of the most interesting combinations was our Mid Appalachian division. It was molded after Stampede's World's Mid Heavyweight title, which was the pre-cursor to most of the cruiser weight titles in Japan and the states alike. I also combined the idea that TNA used in the X division of no weight class, just style. All of this was told through stories from Memphis style booking.

The first champion was Spider Crowley. He was formerly one-half of the Urban Death Squad. He feuded with Brian Douglas for the title. They both exhibited what it took to get the title over. They both competed in series of matches that switched the title to Douglas. The switch occurred in a belt on a pole match. I love the "on a pole" matches. The two never shared my vision of the division. I just wanted to establish the title, so I could put it on the up and coming Kid Apollo.

Kid Apollo, whose real name is Waylon Payne, was a true cruiser weight. Waylon Payne, what a gimmick name to have as a real name. He was a natural at the sport, and one of my students as well. He only trained four times before a promoter stuck him in the ring, but to his credit he was a natural. If he would have spent more time learning, he would have been a real competitor. He was of the Kid Kash school of thought that flips make the man. He was an exceptional high flier, but can't wrestle a bit. He doesn't know a wrist lock, from a wrist watch. It always held his talent back. Plus he has Brandi guiding his career.

Our weekly town in Oak Hill, WV, needed spicing up. Over the years they had seen everything. I called in several favors to freshen it up. I called Tracy Smothers and brought him in to work with Rocky, Lance Erickson. I was building him through Tracy, so we could continue our feud. Tracy was more than happy to help out. When you have a veteran who is willing to put over a green horn it helps out tremendously. As I stated earlier, by sighting trends I was able to book Tracy at a great price, and he was happy to get the work. We had him for two months straight every show.

I called in a favor to Cornette when we ran Athens, WV, at Concord College. Eric set up the deal and we did the show there in September three years running. Jimmy loaned me talent like Red Dog, David Flair, and Nick Densemore. Combined with Tracy this was a great crew of real professionals. The local guys who couldn't hold their own weight got very jealous. That is business.

I brought in former O.V.W. talent Flash Flannigan and Shawn Casey with manager Phil Phare. They added more talent to the cards. I paired these three for a combination of matches that lit up the area. The fans loved seeing talent they had never seen before.

Brian Douglas got married in late 2002. While he was away on his honeymoon, Eric and I took over booking from him full time. Till then Douglas and Eric shared the book. I would have the final say on every decision. During Douglas's time away we experienced a two hundred and fifty percent increase in profit. We doubled our money and then some. This did not sit well with Douglas. There were less people by number at the show, due to us cutting out the fee tickets that were being given away. Leonard and Brian always gave out fifty or more free tickets. At some points there were half as many people in attendance. They were all paid and spending money while they were there as well. It helped that this was the Clinton years when the economy was in an upswing, and the national debt was low, with the Untied States holding a reserve. All important business trends to know. For the first time in the modern era, wrestling in West Virginia was a business, not just for fun. We were wrestlers, not just playing wrestling.

Due to certain events that were beyond control, Blue Ridge Wrestling Promotions had its last event on September 26th, 2002. It did not reach my expectations. I did prove that my plans would work, and were possible.

The timing just was not right. We made a few mistakes, but a blueprint was there. I had discovered a formula that worked. I proved that a successful territory could be ran in West Virginia. The question would turn out to be, would local government allow this to happen?

Chapter 10: A Shot in the Night

Due to pressure from my family and Brandi, I started seeing a psychologist again. I sought treatment at the New River Family Heath Center in Scarboro, WV. I saw Dr. Sara Peltnic, and then later, counselor Sara Ramono. Dr. Peltnic prescribed medications for depression. I saw Sara Ramono on a weekly basis for counseling. Dr. Peltnic helped me with my panic attacks. They were the main reason I sought treatment. Anytime I had one she was just a phone call away. She would always return my call with in five minutes to help with my issue. Due to the fact of the Health Center's lack of money to provide her service, she moved on to practice out of state. They refused to offer her a correct amount of money for her services and mobility to advance in the company.

Sara Ramono was the best person I have ever seen with in the heath care industry. We talked and were able to work on any problems I had. She was down to earth and treated people like people. She told me once, "I am working with people here, not building cheese sandwiches." My appointment time had expired, but she wanted to help me, instead of just ushering me off, and herding in another client, just to be able to bill for the hour. She treated their problems in the same manner. She was interested in helping people, not just making the center a profit. So many times heath care providers get in such a hurry of assembly line treatment. They forget the human aspect of care. People are always debating what is wrong with society today. I will sum it up without debate. People do not treat other people like they are human beings any more. They worry too much about their own self. That is okay, but not if you are in the business to provide service to help people with a better way of life. Unfortunately, it is like that in every professional business today. That is what is wrong with the world. The human element is gone.

I made tremendous progress with Ms. Ramono. I worked though some long term issues. She finally said we should take a couple of months break on my care. She wanted me to apply what we had discussed to my life. I did. When I returned two months later I found out she was gone also. They did not offer her a job after her grants were up. She was working on grant money, and if they would have offered her a job, she would have stayed. They didn't and she moved to Colorado. The Health Center never even told her patients. They just showed up one day with a new counselor, and had to start treatment from scratch.

After Dr. Peltnic left I was given Deborah Mooney. She was one of my original choices when I first sought care. She was employed by a different facility. She told me that she would not provide me care, so I ended up at New River Health Center. Dr. Mooney switched her employer and was given my case. She switched all of my medication first thing. Typically when a patient switches doctors, the new doctor will switch the meds from the previous doctor. I guess it is a superiority thing. She put me on 200mg. of Zoloft and 800 mg. Topamax.

I later found out, through other doctors and nurses, that 800mg. of Topamax was illegal to prescribe. The most the law will allow is 600mg. It is prescribed to be taken over the course of the day. Typically 200mg. three times a day; this is still an extremely high dose. Most people only take 200mg. for the entire day. There were many times I would run out of Zoloft and only take the Topamax. Dr. Mooney said that it was okay to take them separate. I later consulted with Dr. Sheila Wender of Spring Haven Heath Systems in Princeton, WV. Dr. Wender explained to me that Topamax is a mood stabilizer. If it is taken by itself it would cause manic bi polar side effects.

I was real sleepy and felt that the medication was doping me up. I told Dr. Mooney this. She Said, "Just play with it. Take it all at once in the morning, or at night. See what time is best." I was not a doctor, how would I know what is best? It was her job to regulate the meds. Isn't that what they go to school for? Why was I always running out of Zoloft before the Topamax? The answer was simple, I was being over prescribed. I was so doped up that once I passed out driving to a town, and totaled my car. I told her that I felt the medicine caused me to pass out, she instructed me to keep taking them.

I was also given a new counselor, Mary Powell. This did not last long. Every time you receive a new doctor, you have to start at the beginning. It would take several months of billable sessions to just get back to where I was at in treatment. I asked her to read the chart so that we could just pick up from where I was currently at. Mary Powell replied, "I don't read charts! I don't have time to. How could I see patients, if I spent all day reading charts?" My question is how she could treat patients without reading their charts and history. Is she that good of a healer, that she can treat patients by intuition? I was not comfortable with a doctor that didn't have time to check out my medical history.

The ironic factor in this is that my dad and uncle, Paul Lively, founded the New River Health Center. It was one of the hospitals that Patch Adams set up. He was the doctor that was played by Robin Williams in the movie, *Patch Adams*. It was designed to provide quality health care to people who were not of typical health standards. They provided service without discrimination of insurance, race, or financial back ground. In my opinion, they failed miserably! I made formal complaints to my uncle, who is the head of the board of directors, for years about my case. I also met with numerous board members filing complaints. Nothing was ever done.

On June 14th, 2002, my life forever changed. It started a chain reaction of events that almost ended my life. I had felt very ancy the previous week. I was taking my 800mg. of Topamax religiously. I was taking it all at once in the morning, as prescribed by Dr. Mooney. Lisa and Laken, her daughter, had argued earlier in the day. Things were odd between Lisa and me, even though nothing had happened yet. All the children started arguing. Laken had a book that one of the other two had colored in, she was upset. I went to sort the situation out. The children argued over who did it, and settled on that Blake was the culprit. I suspected that Brook, the youngest, had done it, but they settled on that Blake had done it. So I punished Blake. I spanked him three times on his butt. I had never spanked anyone before, nor will I again. I used the same method that I saw his mother and other family members use. I was aggravated, but in no way did I hurt Blake. Lisa flipped out and called the police. I was arrested. I feel that the Topamax had a large influence on my decision to spank him. Lisa and I split up for a week or so over it.

For a short fleeting moment I had it all. It was only over a period of two months or so. Dylan was with me, I was with Lisa, and happy we had three children I loved very much, my traveling was shortened and I was working with in a hundred miles of the house every night, and I was making a decent living. I had a promotion that was about to prove what I had been saying for years. I had no idea that it was all about to end.

I returned to Oak Hill to stay with my parents. Dylan went to Brandi, but only for one night. She still did not want him. She brought him back to me. Once she heard all the rumors from the wrestling world she flipped out. She told me, "You made a clown out of me in front of all our friends. I will get you! I will make sure you pay!" Two days later she shows up to get Dylan. I needed his medical card so that I could get him his shots later that week. She refused to give it to me. My parents and I tried to explain the importance of him receiving his booster shots. She did not care, and did not want him to have them. Then she assaulted my mom. She pushed her, bad back and all, into the stove. She hit her back on the handle of the oven. Next she threw my mom onto the couch in a suplex type throw. As she left she threw poor Dylan head first into the car, and drove off with no car seat. He was only two. The neighbors watched as she sped off throwing gravel everywhere. Brandi went to the Holiday Inn and called the police. She told them that I had beaten her. They arrested me. I was found not guilty by the magistrate court. However, she did not let me see Dylan again. It was over one hundred and forty days later before I would see him again. The Family Court in Fayette county had ordered me visitation. She went into contempt for over one hundred days. Nothing was ever done about that. Dylan had spent every day with his daddy, and now was not allowed to see him for over five months, and he had to live with a stranger.

I hired Clint Gallagher IV to legally represent me. He was a former family law master in Fayette County. My parents insisted on him. I paid him seven thousand dollars up front. He wrote one letter and attended court one time. In that hearing he said nothing. Not one single word was spoken by him. At the end he finally spoke up and said, "What about supervised visitation?" Those were the only words he ever spoke on my behalf. I was against the supervised visitation. She was the one in contempt. He guaranteed me that it would all be okay in the long run. The following week he quit. He offered to refund my money. All I received was one check for thirty five hundred dollars. It was marked "partial payment". I asked for an itemized statement of charges, he refused to give one to me. I was out half of my money and my lawyer. I was also stuck with supervised visitations. Gallagher was later diagnosed with brain cancer. I had mentioned this to my family the day we left court. I told them what had happened, and about the glowing green spot on his head. I knew something was wrong, but there was nothing I could do. It was too late. Clint Gallagher IV died of brain cancer. His estate never paid me the rest of my money, or provided a statement of charges.

Lisa and I had patched things up. She realized that I had not beaten Blake, or so she claimed. Her story would switch many times. She understood that my erratic behavior was due to the Topamax. She had lost our house in Princeton when I stopped paying the rent. That, too, had played a factor in her reconciliation, even though at the time I was blind to that. I had just paid the last payment of five hundred dollars for the rent, and Lisa had no proof of where the money went. We all moved in with my parents in their three bedroom townhouse until we could regroup. All seven of us lived in the small apartment. It was a struggle to be back around my parents. We were living like Mexicans in that place. Lisa and I slept in the floor. Mom and Dad slept in their room. The children slept in my old room, two in the bed and one in the floor.

Lisa and I went to Kroger for bread on September 4th, 2002. Kroger employs an off duty Oak Hill City Police officer as security. His job is to make sure no one parks in the fire lane, except when loading groceries. I pulled the car up to get Lisa. He told me I could not park there. I explained that Lisa was coming out the door. He made me park the car. He actually made me pull back into the spot I came from and re-park the car. Then he instructed me to pull out of the slot, move back to the exact place I just was, and pick her up. I did as he asked and people began to complain. They claimed I was running all over the parking lot causing a nuisance. I told the people to take it up with the cop. A lady went to get him. While she was inside her husband started cursing me. He reached into his pocket, I thought for a knife. I started calling for help from the officer. When the officer came out I began telling him about the guy. He grabbed me and threw me on top of my car. He grabbed for his gun and unsnapped it, then took hold of the handle. I was scared. I had been harassed and followed by the Oak Hill Police for years. I thought the cop was going to shoot me. So did Lisa, who saved the whole thing. I just reacted, jumped up, and got in the car. I drove away as fast as I could. I told my Dad, like I had for years, about the Police and their harassment. He, once again, thought it was no big deal. I insisted it was. It would take three weeks, but it turned out to be a huge deal.

On September 26th, 2002, B.R.W. promoted its last show in Oak Hill, WV. The main event was Lance Erickson and I inside a steel cage. It was for the M.S.W.A. (Mid South Wrestling Association) championship. It was the main title recognized by A.P.W. The plan was to unify the A.P.W. title later on with the B.R.W. title. This was also the big blow off of the three year feud of me and Rocky. This was one of the biggest cards B.R.W. ever promoted. It was to end all the feuds of the first six months of work.

During the intermission Brian Douglas comes up to me and gives me a paper with the name and number of a woman interested in doing a fund raiser. I hollered the information across the room to Eric Lester. The entire locker room heard me tell him about her.

Lance and I go to the ring and start the cage match. The crowd was very much on the edge of their seat. The house that night was above average. They were anticipating the big pay off from the feud. After five minutes or so one lady starts heckling us. She became very belligerent towards us. We tried to ignore her, but she became worse by each second. I signaled to Lisa, who was watching the match, to throw her out. Lisa had to get help from the Armory's security to try to throw this woman out. She would not leave. The match continued on. She became so bad that the crowd was watching her not us. Then all of a sudden she climbs over three rows of chairs and charges the ring. Eric was Lance's manager, and was hand cuffed to the cage. It was part of the angle to avoid his interference. She causes a bigger scene by yelling at him. Then she hit him. In all fairness to this story, some people claim she never hit him. I thought she did. That was exactly what I was thinking at the time. Eric was helpless. The cuffs would not let him be very mobile. He was a sitting target. Next she went towards the announcer's table. I expected her to attack Jim Hawkins, a lawyer, next, or worse say something on the live p.a. system. I watched as my promotion disintegrated before my very own eyes. I started screaming for Lisa and the security to get her. The cage door opened next. All I could see to do was throw her out myself. I exited the cage. I was covered in blood, and slipped in my own juice. My blood went everywhere. I tried to grab the woman; instead I gave her a weak clothes line. She fell to the ground selling the blow. It would have been a perfect work if planned, but it wasn't. The locker room erupted. The division between my boys and Douglas's was clear now. It was a full scale riot. I finally got the woman outside. I'm not really sure how. Things tried to settle down, but it was not working. Somebody then calls the police.

When the officers arrive Corporal Edwards and Brian Goins step right over the woman lying in the doorway and came straight to me. As soon as they entered into the building they asked for me. I could hear them from the locker room. When they found me, I was still bleeding from the match. I offered the tape to them to show what the woman had done. They were not interested. They asked me to come with them. I asked if I was under arrest. They said, "No". Then I asked why I had to go with them, if I was not under arrest. They responded with, "Because we told you to!" They mentioned nothing about warrants or anything, just to go with them. I was still in my tights and bleeding profusely. I told them I would change my clothes, clean up the blood off my face, and then I would come to the station. They said that I had to come with them right then. I asked to change clothes, they refused. I asked if I could stop the bleeding, they said no to that as well. I begged them to let me stop the bleeding. They said it would be okay if I went to the bathroom to clean it up. They tried to follow me inside, this made me extremely nervous. There was only one door and it was a small room. I got the impression, when they extended their clubs, that if I went in there I wasn't coming out. So, I stopped and asked why I had to go with them if I was not under arrest. They wouldn't answer me. They got out their cuffs to go with the batons. When I saw this I panicked. I did not trust them, due to the past and, recently, at Kroger. Who had ever heard of the police not arresting someone, but forcing them to come with them? I started having a panic attack. Lisa came over to tell them about my condition, and while she was telling them about my panic attacks Corporal Edwards maced me. They drug me outside and beat my head into the car's trunk. He did it at least thirty times, I stopped counting at thirty. A paramedic came over to look at the cut on my head that was now flowing blood with no end. The officer sent her away, saying that the blood in wrestling is not real. They cuffed me and took me to the station. I was never read my rights, and was not under arrest. When I arrived at the station they served warrants from September 4th, at Kroger. I had wrestled every Thursday night before this in Oak Hill. Why did they pick that night to finally serve me? They knew I was there; why not serve me as soon as the warrants were taken out? They never mentioned the riot, or the fan. Was it not the reason they were called there in the first place? They served the warrants, but I never saw them. Usually you can go to the Magistrate and post bond and leave. They refused to send me to the Magistrate, it was a city matter. I was still covered in blood and had an open wound. I needed stitches at this point. I was forced to put my head in a trash can. I was forced to lead forward. For a head injury one should tilt the head backwards and up. Forwards and gravity would force the wound to bleed out. I was not allowed bond, and Corporal Edwards took me to regional Jail. They held me overnight. On the way to the jail, about twenty miles in to the ride, Corporal

Edwards proceeds to tell me, "Oak Hill police will not stand for you! If you don't quit messing with Oak Hill Police, and quit wrestling then you will wind up in the hospital or worse!" He repeated that several times before adding, "If you do not quit wrestling you will end up seriously hurt or killed!" It was not advice, it was a threat.

When I arrived at the jail I explained to the nurse what had happened and the threats. She got the Oak Hill City officer to leave. She could see how badly I had been beaten by them. I had marks all over my body. The water main that night at the jail had busted. They had no water to clean out my cut, or wash the blood off. I spent eight hours in the drunk tank just bleeding on myself and ten other guys. My blood would not clot well due to the type of gash and all the medicine I was on. I was taken to the city court the next day and was allowed to bond out, and go home.

If someone runs on stage at a Rolling Stones concert and hits Mick Jagger is it his fault? If a fan jumps out on the field at Yankee Stadium, is it George Steinbrenner responsible? I think it is the individual who leaves their seat at the event, who is responsible. Less than a week later I was arrested for assault on the fan. This time I was taken to the Magistrate's office. Why not the city? Why did I not go to the Magistrate's office the first time? I was then re-arrested two other times, for a total of three times for the same crime. Why? I wish I could answer all these questions I have asked, or even one. I have no answers, it is still a mystery. I was told that the police did not have to read people their rights anymore, that they were understood.

On the Kroger incident I was charged with reckless driving, and fined five hundred dollars.

On December 11th, the next step of a Bizzaro puzzle occurred. I was seeing Dylan on my visitations. Three weeks before Thanksgiving I talked with the owner of the day care center, A Place to Grow, in Oak Hill, about Brandi going in contempt again, either at Thanksgiving or Christmas. She would travel back to Connecticut to visit her family each year on one of these holidays. There was no possible way for her to visit home and still make my visitation days. I saw Dylan every Tuesday and Thursday. Even if she flew to Connecticut she could only stay for a day or two at most. I knew she would stay longer. She went into contempt again at the end of November. She wrote me a note, which no contact was allowed outside of using lawyers. She told me Dylan was missing two visits. I showed up for the visits and signed in anyway, just for the record that I was there. On December 11th I talked with the owner again about the contempt. It was her duty, as well as mine, to report the contempt of a court order. She never recalled the violation or our talk. I had told her to replay the video tape from the cameras that day. They were conveniently lost. It was like I was on the wrong end of a bad lifetime movie. I showed her the note, and she argued over it's authenticity. I decided to leave. I could not accomplish a thing; the woman either would or would not help me. Dad and Paul came to pick me up. As we were leaving Dad slipped and fell on the ice. There was a terrible snow storm that week. A stranger in a car jumped out and grabbed me. He thought I had hit Dad, instead of him falling. I had not; he just fell on the slippery ice. The stranger grabbed a hold of my coat with all his might. He started leading me towards the road. I asked him, "Please sir, let go of me." I asked him three or four times then said, "Sir, if you do not let go of me I will defend myself!" He did not let go. I swept one arm away, and then hit him. I had to, or I would have been run over by a car passing by. I did not want his hands on me. I never touched him, only to make him let go. I was arrested again for assault on him.

Lisa and I got married on February 14th 2003. I thought, at the time, I was deeply in love with her. I was closer to her than anyone, at that time. I thought she was different from the other girls I was with, and was deeply committed to the relationship. I put all my old ways behind me, I no longer wanted to go out and party. Other women did not matter to me anymore either. I wanted to grow old with her. I was so blind to her and what was going on around me at that time.

I was indited for spanking Blake. I was told by my new layer, Public Defender, Andrew Maier of Mercer County, that I would get probation guaranteed. So I pled down to a battery charge. The pre-sentencing report was filled with lies. First was that Brian Douglas owned M.S.W.A. and had fired me for being too violent in the incident at the Armory. He never owned the company, I did. How could I fire myself? Second was that I had committed several crimes while I was in W.C.W. They would not state what the crimes were, because there was none, but used them against me. I was also accused of things that other people had done, that I was not even involved in. You have a constitutional right to face your accusers. At the trial I was not given any information as to the origins of these statements, even though they were admissible as evidence. They claimed the information just appeared one day. They also used gossip from the internet as facts against me. At the sentencing trial my lawyer, Andrew Maier, hands me a file and says, "Here you can do this better than me." I had to try to explain every aspect of the case. I was not a lawyer. I provided paper proof of my discrepancies in the case. I presented building contracts, pay stubs, event programs with names I used, all supporting my case. They could care less. I presented thirteen letters on my behalf, one of which was Lisa's. If I would have gone to trial I could have beaten the case. I was trying to spare my family any more hassle. They also used the Armory events as facts before I was ever set a trial date for the incident. I was sentenced to sixty days in jail at Southern Regional, a maximum security facility. Following that I got three years of probation. It would have placed me on probation till 2006. I was in jail with a guy who had sewn his child's hands together with a needle and thread. He pled guilty and received thirty days, six months after that he was back with his child. He received no probation either. Lisa was the one who supplied the court with their information I would find out later. She was playing both ends against the middle.

Jail was tough. I could not stand to be confined in the small room. The food was so bad, and they were over populated. I slept on the dirty floor. They, of course, changed all my medications. I was given Depicote. It made me so drunk I could not get out of the floor for three days straight. I stopped taking the drug before it killed me. I could not move to even eat. They would give the meds when they wanted, even if you were prescribed them. I saw people freak out and go literally crazy from either not getting their meds or getting the wrong ones. If you were left off the meds list for a day, you did not get any. If a person needed medicine to sustain life, they would die if not given their meds. I saw this every day.

Lisa visited me in jail. My Dad came the first time to visit, then never came back again. Mom never came at all. I would call them from jail and explain how we all needed to be a family once this was over. They agreed at the moment, but it was a lie.

Lisa told me while I was in jail that she was pregnant. I thought this was hard to believe, because she had had her tubes tied. Also, we had not been together since our wedding night, which was months before. I was happy about the news, but could not believe the tale. After being released from jail I was so happy to be home. It was the old "Don't know what you got till it is gone" theory towards my family. Things had changed; I was shown more than ever by everyone. Lisa acted different, and the kids had completely changed.

Laken, who was a straight A student was now failing out. I actually got a call from her teacher who claimed she had not turned in her home work for all of 2003. Laken had told her teacher stuff like it had fallen in a mud puddle, or she lost it, and even the dog ate it. These were the actual excuses she used. I could not believe it. I thought the teacher had exaggerated it at first. She told me Laken actually used these excuses.

Blake never wanted to stay home. He was always staying with friends. He became mouthy towards adults. He was disobedient with his mother, as well as me. He was having trouble in school also. He had always had a hard time, but this was worse.

Brooke was the only one who seemed to be unaffected. Other than being separated from her siblings, she was fine. On some occasions they would play with her, but for the most part they had turned on her. She never seemed to mind. She went on about her own business.

I was no longer allowed to be a part of the children's problems. Laken, who seemed to hate all men, always ran her mouth to the adults, even about little things like asking her to pick up her clothes. I asked her to clean her room, and repeated it twice, over a three day period. Still she would not do it. I told her to clean it up or she would be grounded. She replied, "You had better ask Mommy for permission before you do that, you're not allowed to ground me."

Lisa never disciplined the children. They ran wild. The house was filthy with clothes and food strung everywhere. Anytime something would happen, I could not tell them right from wrong. There was a hole in the floor from a rotted board that the land lord had not fixed. I asked the children not to run and to be careful. Brooke, who was six at the time, went to get scissors. She ran back down the hall, hit the hole, and fell down. She skidded down the hallway hitting our door. I tried to tell her about being careful. Lisa threw a fit. I was worried Brooke might have been hurt by the scissors, or the fall. It did not matter to Lisa.

Blake was always to be in the house at dark. One night he did not come home. I got real worried. Lisa was fine, at first, after a couple of hours she got worried too. I had started searching the neighborhood for him after he was forty five minutes late. I walked the entire neighborhood looking and shouting his name for two hours. We finally found him at some little girl's house. I explained to him how worried I was, and how hurt he could have been. He did not care about either. I asked him, "What if a drunken person hurt you". He replied, "They will just go to jail." The children thought they were untouchable. I went on to explain that they probably would, but he would still be hurt. He answered back, "I don't care." Things like that happened everyday.

Lisa started acting real funny, stranger than she normally acted. She would scream out at me at the top of her lungs, and then claim she never did it. She would be sitting rocking her body, then begin hitting herself. She would leave bruises on her legs.

She suffered a miscariage, a tubular pregnancy, conveniently in her sixteenth week. There was no proof of her ever being pregnant. There was also no proof of a miscarriage either. I asked to go to the doctor with her, or even speak with him so I would know what was going on. She avoided the issue. I never got any information. She had faked the pregnancy the entire time.

She would start fights and accuse me of things. One time she called 911 for no reason. She reported her children were in danger. I was watching TV when I found out she had called. I left after that. I was scared for my probation being violated. She was trying to get rid of me. Two days later she served a restraining order, and then dropped it a week later. I moved out, fourteen days later she wanted to make up. She had lost another one of our houses and could not pay the rent.

Child Protective Services started getting on our case. They had reopened the Mercer County report. The one I had already done the jail time for, and paid my debt to society. Kim Bolt tells us that we were not allowed to be married by law. She told us that the state of West Virginia would not allow us to continue to be married. If we wanted to stay married we had to take her marriage counseling class. I agreed to jump though her hoops for the sake of our family. Lisa refused! She claimed she feared loosing the children. She rented a house less than one hundred feet from my parents place. We could be together and still keep CPS happy. I took several meetings with CPS and it's management. I did not have a leg to stand on with them; I was the one they were complaining about. Without Lisa it was impossible. I did find out that Laken and Blake were the ones that called CPS and complained about me. It was all orchestrated lies from Lisa.

Things were starting to get to me. I had not seen Dylan since December 11th 2002. It was now August 2003. I was doing all I could to convince CPS of my situation. Lisa was little to no help. The kids did not care either. I tried to explain that if we were a family, we had better act like one. Brooke was the only one to understand. She truly loved me, and I her. I wish I could have just had Dylan and Brooke as my own, on my own. Their lives would have turned out different. Brooke was tuned in more than anyone; she wanted us to be a family more than any of us.

My career was over like a light bulb being turned out. After September's Armory incident I was black balled. The internet was full of accusations of my guilt, long before I was tried. I had been trying to do business with the N.W.A., but Richard Arpin, the then president, and West Virginia promotor. He urged the other N.W.A. members to do the same.

Richard Arpin is now retired from the wrestling business after loosing his family and home to his own drug abuse problems.

No one would return my phone calls. Kenny McCoy of N.W.A. Bluegrass had to stop contact to continue with the N.W.A. Eric Lester, Terry Rahn, and Jim Cornette were the only ones who would talk to me. Cornette could not help me with W.W.E. until this all had settled down. My run with him was over. I could not conduct business anymore. My life was shattered. I was afraid to go out in public. On March 17th, 2003, I was found guilty on the charges of beating the stranger at the day care center, but was only ordered to pay a fine. I was told that day by the Judge, Prosecutor, and my lawyer that I was not ever allowed to defend myself in any situation. They came right out and blatantly said that if someone was to beat me, just simply take the beating. If I was injured or threatened with a weapon, just take it. I was scared I would be killed. I also took Corporal Edward's threat very seriously. I reported it, but no one seemed to care. All of this came to a head in August.

August 10th was a Sunday night. I started a conversation with my family that proved to be deadly. I was scheduled in court on the following Tuesday about the Armory incident. I talked with Mom, Dad, and Lisa. I voiced all of my concerns. I talked about court, wrestling, and everything that was bothering me. We talked for over three hours. While some of the conversation was heated at times, it was a conversation, not an argument. We all had our opinions about the Dylan situation, court, police, and how the lawyers had treated me. At one point my dad called me a failure in the wrestling business. I tried to explain to the contrary. This talk was my last effort to heal my family. Dad zoned out for about ten minutes. I thought he was having a seizure. He had already suffered a stroke. He gets up from his chair and walks upstairs. I thought to go to bed. Mom rushes over and starts yelling in my face about Dylan. I asked her to calm down, and to back up. Dad returns down the stairs, and starts firing a gun. Lisa runs and hides for a moment, then runs up to get the children from their room upstairs, finally out the door. I push Mom to safety, out of the way. In doing so I turned my back to Dad. He shot me in my back. Had I not pushed her down it would have been my Mom's back that was shot. I was then shot in the arm and chest. I tried to run, but couldn't, my leg gave out on me. I stared up at Dad poised over me holding the gun, a .38. I begged him not to kill me! He looked me straight in the eye, and then pulled the trigger again. It was by reflex, from all those chair shots over the years, I put my hand up and turned my head. The bullet went into my arm instead of my head. He had fired all six bullets, three had hit me. He began pistol whipping me with the butt of the gun. He split my head open. I could have taken the gun away and saved myself. I focused on what I had been told by the court Judge and others about defending myself. I choose to take my chances with surviving. I never touched anyone. I took all the blows without defending myself once. Dad went back upstairs. I was a bloody mess. I tried to call 911. Mom forced me to get off the phone. She hung the phone up. Then she called 911 back. I crawled down the hall. Dad returned. He had reloaded. He shot again hitting me in the throat. I raced despite the great pain to the door. It was locked. Mom had locked the door on me. When Lisa left, Mom locked the door behind her. It was a bolt lock that could only be locked from the inside. Dad, who was now just a foot away, shot me point plank in the back of the head. The bullet bounced off. I got the door open and ran outside. The shots continued, but I took no more. I started screaming for help, and that my father was trying to kill me. I walked a block with no help. Lisa had came back in the car. I went to her for help. She sped off in the car almost running me over. I screamed for help, as I walked up the street like a bloody zombie until the ambulance found me. I was still walking when they stopped.

    I was taken to Plateau Medical Center in Oak Hill first. Then I was taken to Charleston Area Medical Center, in Charleston. They wanted to medivac me in the helicopter, but there was too much fog that night. I was put in an ambulance and driven forty minutes to CAMC.

    My doctor was an intern named Dr. Elmore. He was great. He never left me the whole time, unless he had to. He kept me calm and treated me accordingly. He had a great bedside manner that doesn't occur today. They ran several tests on me, they x-rayed and called for specialists. I knew I was going to die. There were times over the years, because of depression, I thought of suicide. I felt I was ready to die prior to this night. I just wanted relief from my problems. I was stuck in a hole, in one way or another, my entire life. What I needed was a change, not to die.

When I was faced with my own mortality, I quickly decided I wanted to live. I love Dylan and think about him everyday. I had ill feelings about my birth parents. I have abandonment issues. I had dealt with them daily. Issues I discovered on my own, with out doctors advise. I do not hate them; I just try to understand my biological parents' decisions. I only hope that when Dylan is older, he can come to understand that I never left him. That I am still here waiting to have a relationship with him. I did all I could to see him. I will be here for him until the day I die, if ever he wants to see me, for whatever reason.

After thinking about these issues, while laying on a gurney not knowing my future, I decided I wanted to live. If I gave up, I would not be giving up on me. I would be giving up on God and his purpose for me, as well as Dylan. If I would have died I would have hurt them, no one else. I wanted to live!

I was scared that if I fell asleep I would not wake up. I was awake in all, before and after the shooting, for around thirty six hours. I was almost delirious from exhaustion. My right leg was in tremendous pain. At the time I thought I had been shot in the leg. It was diagnosed later that one of the bullets had been lodged in my back against one of the nerves in my spine. The pain was the signal to the nerve endings that the injury had occurred. That meant that basically my leg was dying. It hurt so much that at one point I told them seriously to cut the leg off. Thank God they did not have to. I thought about Kerry Von Erich and his leg. Eventually they treated the pain with morphine and it became tolerable. I was admitted to a room and awaited the test results and the specialist's opinions.

Lisa had arrived after three hours from the time I was admitted, and was the only one I allowed in to see me. I was put under security because I did not know who would come in and try to kill me. I was worried dad would come back to finish me off. The hospital was good about security. Even my lawyer, at the time, was not allowed in. This was the safest I had felt in years. Too bad I had nine holes in my body at the time. The specialist doctors came in the next evening. It was a long worrisome wait. I had five staples in my left leg from a cut from a piece of flying glass. I had seven staples in my head from blows from the butt of the gun, a flush hole in the back of my head. One bullet went in my upper chest and came out my right arm; another straight through the back of my right arm. My left arm had two holes where the bullet had gone straight through. The shot in my neck went in one side and out the other. It missed my jugular on both side by a centimeter. The last was lodged against a nerve in my back, close to the spinal chord. I should have been dead. My doctor had seen less kill people. People talk about miracles, or divine intervention, I am an example of that. I should be dead now. There should be no book written. For some reason I was alive. The bullet in the back of my head should have pierced my brain. My jugular should have been opened, killing me instantly. Neither occurred, I did not even have one broken bone. The shots in my arm all hit meat. In it's self is a miracle. The left arm wound is right on top of the bone. I don't know how it did not shatter my arm. The nerve in my back is the nerve right above the one that controls all body functions from the waist down. If it would have hit that nerve, I would have been a paraplegic. They only injury I have is that my right leg is dead, without feeling, from the hip to the knee. I still have excruciating pain in my back. It is a true miracle I can even walk. From what it could have possibly been, I feel lucky that was all I was injured. The doctors left the bullet in my back. They were scared to operate; worried the operation would cause more damage than good. I was relieved that I did not have to have surgery. While I was lucky injury wise, person luck was still the same.

Lisa stayed with me until she realized that I was not going to die. When she found out I was going to live, she left to go get the kids. She freaked out again. I begged her not to go. She just suddenly got up and left. She promised after she got the kids she would come back. She never did. She just left me lying there.

The hospital released me on Tuesday, August 12th. My court date was continued, postponed indefinitely. My uncle, Paul, picked me up at the hospital after they threatened to send me to a homeless shelter. They wanted me to leave earlier; I begged them to let me stay until he got there. Paul picked me up and took me to their house.

I have not said much about my Aunt Kathleen, Kat for short, and Uncle Paul. They were there for me more than any other family member. They always tried to help me whenever they could. They had no children, but they always said I was like their own. This was mostly while I was a child. The older I got, the more I was let to slip away. Sides in our family had been drawn over the years. I knew where most people stood on things that had happened over the years. I would soon find out where they stood. They took me in when I had no one. They let me live with them until I could get back on my feet, literally. I could not have rebounded with out them. I appreciate them for all they have done for me over the years. With that said, I found out what they really thought as time progressed. My Aunt blamed me for getting shot. She stood in her kitchen and told me it was my fault. She said I asked for it. She also said that she thought I would kill my Dad. I can't kill anyone or anything. I don't have it in me. I am still that scared little boy deep down. For years I claimed I was treated different for being adopted. They said I was wrong. They also thought I was crazy. I had all their professional help, but things kept happening. They only had parts of stories, and heard what they wanted.

Brooke's birthday was in September. Lisa called me for money, as usual. She had no money for presents or a party. It broke my heart to think that little baby would not have a birthday, so many of my birthdays were ruined for me. While on the outside my birthdays were okay for everyone involved. On the inside, it was not fun, and hurt me more and more each year. I did not want Brooke to experience that. I had no money, by this point. It was all gone. Lisa had spent every dime I had ever made. All I was a man trying to heal. I went to Kat and Paul to talk about her birthday. They acted like I was speaking Japanese. They were no help. I borrowed the money from a long time friend, Tabitha. She had dated Lisa's brother, and we had become close over the years. She loved the kids as much as I and she also knew better than I did how evil Lisa was. Brooke had her birthday. I was not allowed to stay.

I dropped off the presents and cake, and then was forced to leave.

There was a dispute the next day about Dylan having a coat. Kat and Paul rushed to the opportunity to buy him a coat. I questioned them about it. It was not the fact that Dylan needed the coat. He would have a coat, I would see to that. A day earlier they were no help to Brooke's birthday. They would have let her go without. When asked about it Kat replied, "Shouldn't you take care of blood first?" That was what was exactly wrong with my life! No, you should not take care of blood first. Those four children were all my kids. Dylan by birth, and I was stepfather of the others. They should be treated equally. How could someone line up four kids, and choose to give one something first over the others while they suffer? You can't, and shouldn't. They should all be treated the same regardless of blood. I love them all.

I had been treated differently my whole life by my family. Until then, they claimed it was me. I saw every single member of my family betray me one by one. Now, they too, had let it out. Blood came first; it always had, from that little fire engine, until now. I was not blood, so I was looked down on.

My Mom sided with Dad. She had left him eight years earlier, now she wanted to stand by her man while her boy was left to almost die. I was blamed by her for the shooting, even though it was me that pushed her to safety. She refuses to see me now. She claims she can't handle it. She denies locking the door, even though there was only one way to lock it.

My Dad was brought in for questioning by the Oak Hill Police. They released him two hours later.

He claimed self defense. I never touched him to provoke him that night. My uncle had kept my Dad's guns ever since my Mom tried to commit suicide with them. After years of them not being in the house, he suddenly, just before that night, got them back. Paul claims he does not remember when. He forgets a lot of stuff. I did not make a statement the night of the shooting to the police because I was scared of them, and what my Dad might do in retaliation. Oak Hill Police never arrested him. Brian Goins was one of the officers. The shots took place almost a year later from when Corporal Edwards claimed I would be killed if I did not quit wrestling. My Dad's last words before the shooting to me was, "You love Jim Cornette more than me, why don't you get him to be your father. You are a failure in the wrestling business. I lost ninety five thousand dollars of my severance from work. You failed me!" The news and newspapers both headlined, Pro Wrestler mauls Mother, and Father shoots in self defense.

The week after Brooke's birthday, Lisa told me she had slept with Rocky, Lance Erickson. She claimed only once, I suspected longer. Tabitha had filled me in on Lisa spiking my food with arsenic and talking about killing me. It was rumored by her close friend, Lisa Kinsler, that she had bragged about taking out an insurance policy on me just before I was shot. I was the only one surprised by this. I filed for divorce on November 4th, 2003.

I went back six weeks after being shot to Plateau Medical Center to have my staples removed. I had a paper from CAMC to go to my local hospital to have them removed. The staples were starting to get infected. Plateau Medical Center refused to see me. They threw me out.

I went to continue my care at New River Heath Center. They also terminated and refused my care. Mary Powell and Dr. Ahmed would not treat me on the grounds of my trust issue with people. How could I not have trust issues after living this story? I have been beaten, locked up, betrayed, stolen from, and shot all in one year's time. Who wouldn't? They quit on me, I made formal complaints, and wrote numerous letters. I had meetings with board members, still no care. Paul Lively and the management of New River Health Center violated HIPPA laws in regards to my file. He is still the CEO there and receives free health care for my Aunt. He sacrificed me for free health care.

None of my friends or family members ever called or came to see me after the shooting. The boys did not return my phone calls. I received only one card in the mail, after the shooting. It was from a long time wrestling fan.

As I look back over the pages of this story and reflect it has been a long curvy winding road. Much like the highways I traveled in my career it has many turns and stops. When I look back at it, it is as if I am standing on the top rope looking down on my prone career. My career lies in center ring as I look down. Not just my career, but my life.

My early life was troubled. I was put in an environment that was familiar with violence. I was left with a feeling of not belonging. When it came time to adjust to life's choices, it was an unsettling decision. I was put places I didn't care to be.

I choose to be a man. To fight for my right to be who I wanted to be. By choosing this, I embraced my dreams. As a free spirit I was challenged by what life offered. I embraced these things in joy. I learned from them, profiting and losing.

I became who I was. A profound statement, but not an easy task. I lived life. I met heroes and villains, I saw right and wrong. I shared time with people who were very special and unique each in their own way. People I am forever grateful to and some I will never forget.

I have loved, lost, and returned to love again and again. I have shattered my heart, but found ways to mend. The times I have spent have been irreplaceable. The places I have gone are unforgettable.

I realize my goals, only to sprout new dreams. I have received gifts from heaven, but have surely felt hell. I have surrendered, but only to suffice myself.

I captured it all. In return, I surrendered it. My rights, liberties, and pursuit of all happiness stolen from me, not allowed to be a human, only to live like a beast.

I have conquered death, only by surrender to God. I have lived. No one can steal that from me. I can be broken, but not destroyed. I can loose, but still win. I can succeed in spite of failure. I have been slowed, but will not stop.

I embrace the future, hoping not for the past, remembering most, and learning from all. How would I like to be remembered? Simply as a wrestler.

What is next for me? Where will Brian Logan travel next? I am reminded of an old story of three wrestlers in the locker room playing poker. These wrestlers are playing cards when the promoter rushes in, and explains that the world is ending. The first wrestler jumps up and says he is going to the church to pray. The second wrestler jumps from his seat, and says he is going to get a case of whisky and go to the whore house and wait for Armageddon. As the two wrestlers are leaving, they look back at the third wrestler who is sitting there looking at his cards. They ask him what he is going to do. He looks up from the hand that he had been dealt, and says, "I shall finish the game!" So, what will Brian Logan do? I too shall finish the game.

I started writing this book after I was shot. I feared my life at anytime could be taken from me. I wanted to write an American novel, but the tale turned out to be my own. On February 3rd, 1992, I first put pen to paper. I would write notes and kept a journal. Seventeen years later I had a book written. I also wanted Dylan to know who his father is. I have not seen him since December 11th 2002. I hope one day he will read these pages and want to know his father. I finished the last paragraph, the one you had just read on September 30th 2003. I thought that my story was done. I even came up with at catchy title, Mediocre on the Mat, Pro Wrestling's Main Event Wrestler; you have never heard of and never will. Much to my surprise my story was not over, or mediocre. Not even close. So the bulk of my book was written, but my final chapters had yet to be lived. So now I continue, into what has been a wonderful surprise to experience.

Chapter 11: Religion

I'm not going to preach to anyone. I'm not like that. I had an unusual take on life, and experienced certain things. I did not suddenly find religion. It was not lost. I am also not a Bible thumper now because I have lived. I do want to share my opinion on religion.

Religion has always been a part of my life from the time I was a little boy I attended church with my Grandfather. It was a part of my life though high school, and all the way through life until I was laying on that gurney in the hospital. One way or another it was a part of me.

I have done some wild things. I have sinned more than most. There was no reason for me to survive the shooting, not with the life I had lived. Women, drugs, booze, and anger filled my life. I was not spared in my moment of death because I was a great person. I came from little, and did what I had to do to get away from my situation. I did anything I could to make it in my profession. I had lived a full life doing things people only dream about. Me included. Some were right and some were wrong.

On that night I prayed from the time I was put in the ambulance until the next morning. I begged God for life. I remembered everything I had ever done, good and bad. I did not like myself, others did not either. After six hours of straight praying, I was allowed to live. This book should not have been written. I should be dead. I was spared. I was given a clean slate. Not just spiritually, but in life here, in the natural. All my obstacles were cleared from me. All my troubles, that have haunted me for years, some how left. All my doubts reassured. I was saved! I was allowed to live. There is not one reason why I should have lived, but I did. The doctors did not understand. They couldn't have. They had nothing to do with it. My Dad didn't end the problems, he couldn't either. He also did not have the power to destroy me.

All these things are this way for a reason. A reason I did not know. I do recognize it exists. I know where it is from, the Lord above. It was His choice I remain living. Most things in my life occurred when I had to be exactly where I was at that given minute, or they would not have happened. I experienced life the way I did for one simple reason, I was supposed to. It was God's greater plan. I have been taught, led to succeed and fail, and saved by One. God. Physically and spiritually He has saved me.

The first verse of the Bible I ever memorized and learned would describe it perfectly. 1 John 5:12.

Chapter 12: Jailbird

Apparently indefinitely in Fayette County is around sixty days. My trial was postponed indefinitely due to my injuries. Sixty days from then, on December 16th, 2003, I was in court answering the Unlawful Assault charges. Just before entering the court room my lawyer informed me that if I wanted to receive the plea-bargain deal, that I had already signed, I would have to give her twelve thousand dollars cash. I flat out did not have it. I told her that she had already taken twelve thousand. She wanted another twelve in cash this time.

The court proceedings began and Judge Charles Vickers, a man my Dad helped get elected years earlier, presided. He shuffled though the particulars. My plea deal was for me to receive one year home confinement. Uncle Paul had finally agreed to allow this to be served at his house, after first refusing completely, a fact that he still denies. The Woman was in the court to testify against me. When asked how she felt, on the record, she stated "Justice would not be served if he did not spend every second of the maximum penalty."

The prosecution made its recommendation for home confinement. The Judge then looked at me and held up an empty folder. "Mr. Kees, I have no doubt you are injured. I can see the pain on your face and your inability to walk well. However, I do not have one single piece of evidence before me that proves you are hurt. Plea denied! One to Five in the State Penitentiary!" He hit the gavel and the bailiff grabbed me. I dropped the cane I was using to help me walk. I was ushered immediately into a side room, cuffed, and thrown into a chair. An hour later I was in The Southern Regional Jail, awaiting transfer to State Prison.

The law in West Virginia is that a felon sentenced to Penitentiary must be placed in Penitentiary with in one hundred and twenty days. Due to over crowdedness they will keep an inmate for as long as they wish. I was still not fully healed. There was such a lack of space that once again I was made to sleep on the floor. I did not matter as to the extent of my injuries from being shot. I was flat out told that I had not been shot. Once I proved that I had, they simply told me, "If we took care of everyone who had been shot, or stabbed, then we would have no resources, or time, to do anything else. Just get over it." Sound familiar?

I pursued the medical help as much as they would let me. I was placed in the medical pod and allowed my cane, but only for a week before they said it was too dangerous for me to have. I was then brought to general population. After being moved pod by pod every three days, I was finally shipped out to a second regional jail. This time in Barboursville, WV. The brand new Western Regional Jail Facility. It replaced the old Cable County Jail.

Tabitha, whom I was now seeing, was right there for support. We had plans of being together after I served my sentence. We connected so deeply. We were friends and then lovers. I felt I could trust her. The only one I could trust. I gave her power of attorney, and I officially did not exist as a person. Legally or otherwise. She worked night and day trying to get the Judge to hear a Motion for Reconsideration of Sentence. None was to be heard. I literally thought that at any moment, just like on TV that they would let me out and finally come to their senses. Tabi met with lawyer after lawyer. It was all the same. They all had to do business with the jail system, so they did not want to get involved. She met with one lawyer in Charleston, a black man whom I will leave nameless, who said that if she would give him ten thousand dollars cash, I could be out the following Friday. We did not have it, and my family would not pool together to help. In their minds I got what I deserved.

Tabi came to visit every other day, driving three and half hours from Princeton to Barboursville. All the same time working full time at Princeton Hospital, and catching flack from her parents for supporting me. She was a trooper and did all she could. Time and loneliness took its toll on both of us. Finally on July 25th, 2004, Tabi wrote me a letter telling me how I was on my own and that she had started seeing another man. This was difficult on not only personal fronts, but she was my power of attorney. Only she could make legal decisions for me. She was handling my only source of income, a lawsuit I had filed in a previous car accident. I stood to receive a settlement that would now go straight to her.

I would call my family often. One day I asked my uncle why he did not look into why Dad had shot me. He replied, "People get shot everyday and I don't feel the need to look into it." Another statement he denied ever saying. I hung up the phone and went to my cell and sat on the floor and cried. I was truly alone in life for the first time ever. I had never felt anything like I did that day. I was stuck in prison, no way out. I had no real contact with anyone outside and no chance for support on the inside of any kind. I had fallen into the abyss.

Tabi allowed me to call her once a week and I longed for those days. For fifteen minutes, once a week, I would get some peace. In reality it just made things worse. She would let me write her letters, but she rarely responded. Before, we would talk everyday and write everyday to each other. Our correspondence filled up several note books. I could hold her hand once a month at a contact visit. Then, overnight after seven months, it was changed to a casual friendship, just as it was in the beginning.

Doing time is hard thing for anyone. Some are life long cons that are institutionalized and are more at home within the rules and regulations of the system; while most are petty offenders that have just been caught up in a happenstance occurrence, or one bad decision. The jail system is a business to make money. If you think it is to rehabilitate an evil person, you are sadly mistaken. The state pays fifty five dollars a day, per inmate to each Regional Jail. It costs about thirty cents to actually pay for that inmate, with only four cents going towards a meal three times a day. The jail system sells inmates food, clothing, and paper. That is the sole reason it is so hard to get out of the system. You become a market commodity for the state. You are a slave to be sold.

I met several people in jail, some good and some bad. I was surrounded by murders, rapist, and arsonist. All at the same time of being surrounded by drug addicts, mentally impaired people, and victims.

One guy we called Minute Made, known for being able to roll an entire poke of Bugle tobacco in one minute, had been in and out of jail on misdemeanors all his life. He was schizophrenic and heard voices. His mom became ill and they couldn't afford the bills, so he burned the house down and got her the insurance to send her to a nursing home. She had to press the charges against him, so she could collect the insurance. She is fine now living in a home in Huntington. He is doing a life sentence.

Another guy Frailey, a small nerdy man was dating this huge Amazon woman three times his size. He broke off the relationship and she began to stalk him. He had a good job as a Xerox repairman. She would follow him to work, and at home. She came in his house and attacked him twice. He filed charges and got the proper retraining orders. The authorities laughed it out of court. On the final time she attacked him he blew her head off with a shot gun. There is no self defense in West Virginia, so he is now doing life.

Other stories are not so ambigulent. Alfie Grey, know around biker bars in Beckley as Pork Chop, killed his stripper wife in a jealous rage. I was friends with him and we talked a lot. However, I was stunned when he showed me a picture of his once living wife and I had realized I had been with her years earlier at the bar, Heart Breakers, in Beckley. He is serving a life sentence.

Another inmate claimed that his wife was beating their seven year old son. The court wouldn't do any thing about it. He had my lawyer, that's a huge coincidence. One day he shoots the kid with a shot gun killing the boy and turns the shot gun on himself blowing his chin off. He lived and is now serving a life sentence. That is if they haven't killed him yet in prison for murdering a child.

A inmate who's last name is Tabor from Mercer County was a seventeen year old kid. He and his friends snorted some oxycottins and drank Jack Daniels. They decided to rob an ATM. They kidnapped an old man and the machine and took it back to a friend's house. They couldn't get the machine open and began beating the old man. Tabor watched stoned out of his gord as his friends beat and sexually assaulted this poor man. In the end, when they were caught, the friends testified against Tabor and received immunity. Tabor got seventeen years to life. He was seventeen years old when he started serving his sentence. He never touched the old man, he just watched.

The jails were filthy. WRJ was a brand new facility and was still dirty. We were the first inmates there. For a couple of weeks it ran smoothly as the guards from the old Cable County Jail didn't know how a Regional Jail had to be run. They smartened up quickly. The food was uneatable again, but I had to eat it to survive. I rarely left the pod. It was so much a hassle, and I avoided any disruption to my schedule.

I would walk around the pod for hours in a circle. Then, at night, I would be exhausted and read till I fell asleep. I read the Bible everyday and became close with Christ. I also read stories about a cowboy named *Longarm,* and *The Complete Works of Sherlock Holmes.* When I was done with Sir Author Conan Doyle's tales it was as if I lost a great friend. For fifteen hundred and four pages I was not alone. I rarely thought of Professional Wrestling. The business was dead to me, as I was to it.

I spent every second of 2004 incarcerated. Playing cards, reading, and walking miles of laps. Eventually I would get my own cell. I had the occasional weekender, who stops in to serve his DUI weekend, which slept in my floor. I was slowly loosing my sanity and becoming institutionalized. I would eat my food so fast, as to not have it stolen, and would sleep my days away. It was boring routine.

Several people would recognize me as a wrestler. Some of the guards would know someone in the business, or had seen me wrestle. Same went for the inmates. A well know drug dealer from Detroit called Puff would be housed in my pod. Puff was head of the Detroit/Huntington connection that is responsible for all of the drug crime in Huntington area. Puff had finally been arrested for a parole violation and was waiting to be indited for a kidnapping charge. He was put in my pod for a special reason. Everyone was scared of him and they wanted me to bring him down a notch. One guard said, "He will stay in this pod until somebody slams him to the concrete." I told Puff about their idea and that we should be friends. He did not see it that way. Puff was around five nine, and buff. He had a great look for a pro wrestler. His ego was that of a hard man living a hard life. I had no beef with him, even though I could have easily taken him. Puff felt the need to establish his turf and assembled a gang inside the pod. He announced that someone would die by morning and that he would kill them right in the spot where I ate breakfast. I knew he wouldn't kill me, but it was an intense situation. By nightfall one inmate was beaten badly. Just before lockdown a second was thrown down the stairs. Morning came and I went to eat breakfast. Nothing happened. Later a guard moved him to another pod. I had made it clear that I got paid to fight. Pay me and I would; don't pay me and I wouldn't. It was that simple.

Puff would later ask me for my help months down the road. Any infraction in jail house rules constituted a write up. That write up would affect your parole. It also could land you in solitary confinement. They have Kangaroo Court. Where the guards try you like a court system on the complaint of a fellow guard. It was not a matter of guilt or not, but how guilty. I was often asked to be a jail house lawyer and defend the inmates against the guards. I was intelligent, and knew the handbook backwards and forward and was some what respected. I was able to get small sentences like lockdown in their cells, or no outside recreation times, which were mild punishments, compared to lengthily stays in solitude. So I defended Puff and got him lock down in his cell for thirty days for him getting caught with contraband. He was very happy and he called me Sir the rest of my stay.

I always tried to help. I never fought. Mostly because if I would lay one hand on someone, they would be proven right that I was violent. I helped inmates learn to read, I counseled them on issues and decisions. I also arranged to have over two hundred books from the outside be donated to the jail library. I did anything I could to look like a decent person. I helped my good friend, Lucas, to read and discern his legal papers, and wrote a letter to his lawyer; he was released on home confinement for my findings. I also began to write novels. I wrote several short stories and one novel I plan to one day publish.

One year later I was eligible for parole. Just being eligible doesn't mean that you will see the board, even though it is the law. You have to have a DOC (Department of Corrections) number before seeing the Parole Board. You have to go through receiving at prison before you get a number. There has to be room at a prison to go through receiving. It takes a month to go though receiving, get you number, and be housed in a Penitentiary. Once in Penitentiary, you have to be seen by the board, which goes on first come, first cased served basis.

I was moved to Mt. Olive State Prison in December 2004. I became violently ill from a stomach virus that was circulating around; of course they denied we were all sick. I finally had good food, but could not eat any of it. I was locked down twenty three hours a day for three weeks so they could protect everyone. They had to see how violent we were.

Finally in January 2005, I was moved to St. Mary's Correctional Facility. Medium security State Prison. St. Mary's use to be an old hospital. I had wrestled only a few miles down the road before. St. Mary's is a place where you are to be rehabilitated; they offer classes for GED, and also put everyone to work. They pay you, seven cents a day. I never worked in jail. Some can work time off, but when you are a felon it doesn't count on your time. I saw working as slave labor for the state. You're doing their job for them. I refused. They didn't make you, but they insisted that it would look better for you that you did.

I was scheduled to see the parole board in April. I found out that Christine Love, Senator Shirley Love's daughter, was on the parole board. Shirley Love was one of the boys. I managed to get a hold of him through outside contact, and explained my case. I went before the board and they granted me parole. Shirley asked me not to ever tell of his involvement in my case. He claimed that he would not be able to help anyone if they knew. He is retired now and I feel it should be stated. My home plan was approved, and I only had one stipulation by the board, that I was to seek anger management. A class that the system was required to provide, but never did, even after I request in writing several times. St. Mary's even suggested I stay and not be paroled, so that they could begin to provide the class just for me. They didn't want to loose that money generated from the state.

On May 15th, 2005, I was released from prison. I was picked up by my Uncle Paul and taken back to his house to start a new beginning.

Chapter 13: Reaching My Apex

When you have been locked up like an animal, your first taste of freedom is like becoming a child again. I could smell the air outdoors. In the spring air, I could detect life again. I dreamt of sitting on the back porch and listening to music. The first thing I did was sat and smoked a cigar, which made me violently ill. I didn't care. I listened to Lynard Skynard's *Simple Man*, and *Forth of July*, By Shooter Jennings. I had had no peace and/or quiet for fifteen months. I had peace, but I could hear every sway of the passing time. I could pick up all the sounds that I was not used to hearing, sounds like passing cars, mowing of grass, and life being lived.

I met with my parole officer and he laid down the rules. They consisted of: report regularly and be sure to pay them their forty dollars fee each month. At first I had a curfew of nine o'clock, but I had nowhere to go. I was instructed not to handle guns and knives, which was not even an issue. I would have three years on paper as part of my sentence, but should be released from parole within one year with no problems, I was told. I also had to attend Anger Management classes.

The original plan that I provided was that I would attend school. I was going to study psychology. I applied at Mount State University, a local college in Beckley. I was accepted, but financial aide said I had an outstanding bill from classes I had taken while in Atlanta years ago. Until I had paid them off, which was around two thousand dollars, I was not eligible to receive any loans. So, school quickly was not an option.

I wondered in to Alter Ego for a tattoo the following week. I wanted to get Dylan's name put on my arm, along with a picture of Jesus. While in jail I had read an article about the artist in the "new faces" column. Oak Hill had never had a tattoo shop or anything else along those lines. I met Kate. We discussed the tattoo, and I asked her out. We had breakfast the following day. Over the course of the next few weeks we would become close and begin dating.

I just wanted to live. Wrestling was the farthest from my mind. I read the occasional books about it, but it was stories of the business that were long past. I spent my days hanging out at the tattoo shop. I would go to Riley's Restaurant, that was owned by new found friends at the time, Robert and Shaundra Sizemore, everyday at eleven and hang out between the restaurant and shop. I started working out again. I had a great time entering back into society. New people and a new routine consumed my hours. At night I would watch old horror movies. I would find that I would have the passion for film, and the masters of slasher films just as much as I enjoyed the wrestling business. It took me three months of this before I realized I had to actually do something with my life.

I petitioned the court to legally change my name to Brian Thomas Logan. I went back before Judge Hatcher. I explained that I wanted to distance myself far away from the Kees family. He agreed that, for business purposes, that it was a good idea. He ruled in my favor, for once, and I was officially Brian Logan.

The settlement I had waited on from the car accident had paid off while I was in jail. Tabi had taken care of it all, and true to her word she saved every penny for me. She delivered the money to me the first week I was out. I had hoped to heal our relationship, but it just was not meant to be. She understood how much I needed the money for my new life. I was so amazed at how she did not take one bit of it. All the other women in my life had stolen something in one way or another from me. We parted ways and I had money in the bank.

I quickly realized that the only job I knew, and was capable of doing was professional wrestling. The parole board had suddenly come up with a new rule about how I could not wrestle in the state of West Virginia. At first Officer Webb, no relation, allowed me to travel to Kentucky to wrestle as long as he did not hear of any problems. I worked the Kentucky fair circuit that spring. Promoters being a never changing animal, the tour did not last long.

The only choice I had was to promote shows in West Virginia. Off and on, I had jotted down notes of things that I had learned, or ideas that I had. I studied those notes and devised a plan. I first noticed a building for rent when Kate had decided to open her own tattoo shop, and quit working for someone else. While looking at the location I noticed it had twenty foot high ceilings. It was the only building in town like it. The Armory had been sold to the Methodist Church and I was banned from running it. So, I assembled a staff that consisted of Shane Mathews, Terry Rahn, and Chris Vega. They all thought I was crazy to try it. During our first meeting, I received a phone call from the landlord of the building, and she was willing to rent to me, and more importantly, willing to let me remodel. I paid the first six months rent in advance on the years lease. I had a venue. I then began to knock down walls, paint, cut holes in existing walls, and panel in wood styled brick. I painted the walls black, and on the right side I glued paneling to the wall to look like it was made of brick. I then hung flags around the entire main room to give it that Mid Atlantic studio look.

All this time Kate and I were pretty serious. She obtained a business loan and opened her own tattoo shop just down the block from my location. For a time we were all quite the little mover and shakers around town, Robert and Shaundra owning a business, and Kate and I each with one. In the case of me and Kate it was a mutual thing. She helped me and I her.

I assembled a crew and on June 15th, 2005, Apex Wrestling and Entertainment was born. I did all this without a formal office from a little booth in Riley's Restaurant. I ran every Tuesday night. I used people that I did not burn a bridge with, which left very few. Word got around, and the wrestling business in West Virginia was about to change.

On July 17th, 2005, I crowned my first championship, the Shooting Star title. It was my brain child from the World's Middle weight title from Calgary, and my Appalachian Championship. It was a title for Shooting Stars, talent who would be up and comers in our area. A title that, I explained in mid ring, would show case a hard hitting, fast paces, entertaining style; no matter the weight class. Terry Rahn, as Dice Del Ray defeated Shane Mathews in the finals of the tournament. A week later Shane would defeat him, and the following week Dice would win it back. I did this to start the tradition, if a fan missed attending a show one week; they would possibly miss something big happening.

I made a deal with the local cable access channel, The Gorge Channel to air our TV show each week on Saturday mornings at eleven o'clock. It was the perfect time slot. It cost me one hundred dollars a week for TV, and went into fourteen thousand homes. Robert Sizemore had been running the production and sound for me. When I told him that we tape our first episodes of TV on the first Saturday in November, and go on air the first week of December he was astounded. He was shocked because we had no cameras or a way to edit the footage. I took the if you build it, it will come theory. I totally gambled and put the cart before the horse. Hell, I did not even have a cart, much less a horse.

While we were scrambling to find equipment I gathered other venues for spot towns. I tried a new concept in West Virginia, but one that made Vince who he is today. I had each town sign venue contracts for twelve dates a year, and it had a clause in the contract that no other sports entertainment could be at that venue. I amassed eight spot towns a month. Sabine, Mullens, Summersville, Princeton were just some of the towns we ran regularly. I now had guaranteed in writing a TV studio, Spot towns, and a TV spot. Next sponsors would come.

Kate was the first to join of course because it only made good sense to advertise the shop on TV. Second, a friend by the name of Jessie Mann, who was apprenticing at the shop, set up a meeting with The Beckley Home Show, a local manufactured home sales lot. His mother was in charge, and she signed a deal for a year to be our official sponsor. The TV was paid for before it ever went on air. Kate's sponsorship, a tax write off, paid for the TV cameras and editing equipment. I even set up an official booking office in the loft over top the tattoo shop. I did all of this in two months time, all the time running live shows.

The next piece of the puzzle was to guarantee me loyal workers to run my ship. I pitched another idea that made Vince famous. Guaranteed money if they signed a contract with me for me to be their booking agent. The agreement was with me personally, and did not matter what company they worked for. I gained exclusive rights to book, and use their images. I owned them once they signed. Like contacts at a gym, it rolled over every six months. I still have the contracts I never released guys from that technically today I still own their likeness. Sorry guys, just business.

In the beginning I signed, Shane Mathews, Chris Vega, Bret Taylor, Dice Del Ray, and Jason Kincaid. Later I signed Phil Anderson, who became Mr. Black, Danny Boyd and Bill Bitner, who were Professor Danger and The Death Falcon Zero. Before too long, my old friends Flex and The Cuban Assassin came back to work with me. Finally, I had new friends like

Cody Mathues and Jeff Waldridge coming in from Kentucky. I had quite a crew of contact talent to start with. Along with that I made a deal with XMCW (Extreme Maximum Championship Wrestling) to use Allen Lynch, Wes Lynch, Team G.A.Y. and Devin Davis. I had a territory!

Just because I had the horses, did not mean they would let me into the race. The race being the "real" wrestling world. I was missing legitimacy. So, I contacted Dale Gagner, known then as Dale Gagne, to become sanctioned by the American Wrestling Association. They were trying the concept made famous by the N.W.A. and selling franchises to little territories. Dale and I talked once and he sold me the rights for the entire state of West Virginia. I had made West Virginia an official territory for the first time in wrestling history. Dave Meltzer even acknowledged its existence as part of the wrestling world. Magazines would eventually cover the area. I had made the bastard son of the wrestling world, finally, legitimate.

My last piece of the puzzle was when I contacted Jim Cornette about becoming the commissioner. I met him in Pikeville, KY, where he was doing an appearance and he agreed to shoot some commercials and interviews. He agreed to be the commissioner via tape to be aired on TV. He never had to be there, and the people actually thought he owned the company.

On December 4th, 2005, twenty eight years after WOAY went off air, AWA APEX aired its first episode led by me doing commentary, and taking Shirley Love's old spot. Jim Cornette magically at the helm and Jason Kincaid wrestled Allen Lynch in the first match, of the first episode, of modern TV in West Virginia. Allen won.

Jason would become the greatest star in West Virginia history, surpassing both Jene Madrid and myself. Apex would run one hundred and thirty five shows over the next year, including TV. All the talent would finally realize what the "real" wrestling business was like. The talent would fall in line with other A.W.A. territories like C.W.F. out of the Carolina's, Brew City Wrestling out of Milwaukee, and WSW out of Connecticut. As much as the wrestling world tried to keep me down, they could not. I was born to lead West Virginia, hard as it was, to the wrestling world. I had done that, but I needed to resurrect my own career. That would be a harder thing to do with the all seeing eye of the state over my shoulder.

Chapter 14: Conquering the World

Every single person ever on the Apex roster, as well as every single person I ever met, played a roll in me realizing my dream. God, in his infinite ways, always looking after me also is to be given total credit. I did not accomplish anything without God or the Apex crew that helped me get back on track.

Along the way several angles in Apex helped forge stepping stones to opportunity. I wish to tell you about each one individually.

The first big angle that Apex had was Team Gorgeous and Young versus the Cuban Commandos. Shane Storm and Jerry Lynch were booked as filler talent. Two struggling guys underneath that were extremely forgettable. One night J.C. comes to me and tells me that they were struggling and that they had a gay gimmick. I hated the idea. He explained that they held hands and pranced around. It was pure comedy. I did not need comedy. Gay gimmicks don't usually get over because the guys are not really homosexuals and people can tell that. I said they could do it if they kissed. He agreed. So the following week Team Gorgeous and

Young, a.k.a. Team G.A.Y. was born. They had done the gimmick before, but never like this. They held hands hugged and even kissed no tongue though. (Thank God!) I thought for sure they would be heels. I could not have ever been more wrong. The crowd in Oak Hill ate it up. They loved them, and thought they were hilarious. I needed a strong heal to beat the little fairies down. Enter Cuban Assassin. Ritchie was well known in town, and as a villain. They hated him and loved G.A.Y. If they liked Cuban, they knew he was fighting a bunch of sissy boys. On TV I gave clever names to their moves. Their finisher was called "Over the Rainbow" a combination rolling suplex and press. JC would do a splash and cover and I would say, "Fairy press in the corner, and a precarious pin attempt." We never called them queer, homos, or actually gay. We referred to them as alternative lifestyles, and sissy. The gay and lesbian organization GLAD sent me a email once. It stated, "Team G.A.Y. has set our people back one hundred years, but it is the funniest thing we have ever seen. In the end they become champions. Keep it up." They were the underdogs. Cuban, the entire angle each week would go on TV stating that in Cuba men were men and women were women, and that he could not understand them. He had Devin Davis and later Gunny Simms as his Commando partners. They feuded for thirty weeks on top over the Apex tag team titles. Twenty six weeks of that feud Apex sold out the Apex arena. Cuban bought a car with the money he made from the angle. They had street fights, Cuban strap matches, singles, tag, and brawls. It was the glue that allowed me to get creative with the rest of the card.

The Parole office, who had now switched my handling over to Officer Scott Rhodes, a angry fat military reject, decreed that I could promote wrestling, train guys in the ring, produce television, commentate on air, but could not sell tickets to watch or tape me physically involved in a pro wrestling event. This was not in official writing, just told to me as a rule from Scott Rhodes. Rhodes, at times, was cool and civil to me, but other times wound up like a cheap watch. I could not wrestle or even get involved, so I needed someone to take my place and guild the company as its top draw. Phil Anderson was a four hundred and fifty pound luchador. He moved with grace, but too much and often. I had seen how Cornette used Jack Black as part of Bolan Services in OVW and I created my own. Dressed in a suit like Bubba Rodgers, I added a new diminution to the character. I love Quinton Tarantino, and in *Reservoir Dogs* the guys were named by colors and wore black suits. I supplied the *Kill Bill* theme music and had Mr. Black defeat everyone in the Apex heavy weight title tournament in under a minute. He became champion in one night beating four guys, and only wrestled for five minutes total. On top of that he never left his feet. I stole the Goldberg idea of playing the music and Black's song played the entire minute he faced his foes. I had installed lights that could be controlled from the back of the studio. When Mr. Black came to the ring the arena went dark, strobe lights flickered and Kill Bill theme echoed. Mr. Black would step in the ring and the lights would rise back up. Total gimmick and total show, but Mr. Black was over. Just before he gave his Black Attack slam, he would shout, "Scrape'em Up!" The crowd began to shout it back at him. Mr. Black was undefeated for two and a half years. He was Heavyweight champion the entire time. He defended the title no less than ten times a month, while never taking a bump. He was believable as a giant. He beat the entire roster, talent from other companies, stars like Henry Godwin and Tracy Smothers, all in the same way. We even put up five thousand dollars to anyone who could beat him. In two and a half years, the greatest run in West Virginia sports history, no one ever came close to beating him. His undefeated streak was longer than any College Football team, basketball, or baseball team run in West Virginia history, even if they were all combined. I had created my version of Andre the Giant. The best thing was Phil understood how important he was to me, and to Apex. All the boys liked him and were happy to lose to him. I can not thank him enough for carrying the ball once I gave it to him. He ran it the entire way.

In Team G.A.Y. and the Cuban I had the money match, and in Mr. Black I had the big attraction; but I needed the meat and potatoes of the card. The work horses that kept the fans coming back to each and every show. Guys like Jason Kincaid, Allan and Wes Lynch, Death Falcon Zero, Flex, Scotty McKeever, and Bret Taylor were those guys. They all fought over the A.W.A. Shooting Star title, so named because it was the only one of its kind. The division was so competitive because of those men. I used Scufflin' Hillbilly, Jessie Ortega, and Noah Lott as contenders to the thrown. It was Flex and Allen Lynch who really set the division apart.

Flex had moved back from Florida just to do my TV. He just showed up one day. His wife Angie, in no uncertain tones, told me that I had one year to make him a star. I did all I could. We turned him into Jessie Ventura. Sunglasses and capes, along with mix matched clashing head bands. What he lacked in ring skills he made up for in charisma. Flex had good matches with Allen. Classic wrestling matches with Scott McKeever and Cuban. He also had hard hitting brawls with Jessie Ortega. He was my second big attraction, as the girls loved to pay money to see him.

Allen Lynch is a fabulous wrestler, but the worst business man I have ever seen. He cares too much about people's opinions, than putting money in his pocket. He and his wife, Sara, agreed to sell me XMCW for two thousand dollars. It included the name, video footage, venues rights to his towns, and his ring. It was a smart buy. I agreed to use his guys for six months before firing them. Sara loved the idea and wanted out of the business. Allen agreed also, that is right up until the last moment. He backed out to save his precious back yarders club. The heat over this issue stands to this day. I still try to do business with Allen, but he refuses to do business with me. His loss. I would expect nothing less from a total back yard mark. Hey Allen, at least being king of the back yarders still allows you to be a king instead of a popper.

Jason Kincaid was the Golden Goose. I saw it from moment one. I tried to protect his character. Oak Hill's nickname is the "Pride of the Plateau." So, naturally, Oak Hill's favorite son became "The Pride of the Plateau" Jason Kincaid. This was long before he was "The Gift" and started owning people. Jason held the Shooting Star title, and three Apex tag team titles. His greatest accomplishment was his feud with

"Krazy K" Kirby Mack for the A.W.A. World's light weight championship. They had seven matches, each of which did a sell out and made Jason appear to have won the title, with Kirby managing to hang onto the belt somehow. We billed him as the uncrowned Light Weight champion of the World.

I had my army primed. Like Germany I planed to swipe across the A.W.A. building my empire. I was not doing this out of malice, but out of hunger to be back where I once was, and should have never been taken from. Destiny was on the horizon.

Dale Gagne was impressed by me and the way I did business. He made me the A.W.A. Talent Coordinator. A position I created upon request to help book and handle talent among the thirty territories Dale had. I was in charge of finding the best talent in the A.W.A., developing and making sure they were booked regularly somewhere within the system. This position also made me the booker of the conglomerate "Super Shows" ran by Dale himself.

I was working eighteen hour days, everyday. I worked as Talent Coordinator, Executive Producer and Director for Apex TV, booker for West Virginia, and ran the training school, postered the towns, and anything else that came up like editing TV, taking phone calls, and making copies. I had to eventually hire two separate assistants. I was a fully functional office unto myself. We did everything Vince McMahon and the W.W.E. does, except on a much smaller scale. I ate, slept, dreamed, and practiced wrestling. I loved it. Some of the people around me did not as much care for my attitude, which was grouchy and strict. I wanted optimal performances from everyone, because I knew how close we were.

I scheduled September to Dismember along with Danny Boyd at West Virginia State University. It was the biggest event in West Virginia wrestling history up until that time. It was also the biggest production yet, as I worked with State's film program to produce the DVD of the show. I brought in Dale from Minnesota, and the several of the top stars from around the A.W.A. I originally thought I would be off parole and scheduled myself a match against the then World's Champion Ric Converse. The parole office would not put in for my early release, they always had excuses. Reasons like the office lost paper work, or give them two more months, and that I had not paid them enough money. I never missed a money payment, and that's why they would not put in for release. They wanted my money. So the title match went to Flex.

Danny Boyd is an acclaimed film maker who decided late in life to become a pro wrestler. I wanted to get into the film business and he the wrestling business. It was a perfect match, at first. Danny knows film, no arguing at that. He taught me everything I know about the film industry. He knows nothing about wrestling. He would fight you the entire way when you tried to get him to do something.

Bill Bitner, The Death Falcon Zero, was trained by Bobby Blaze and had formed a tag team with Danny Boyd. While it opened numerous doors for him, wrestling wise it held him back. DFZ would go on to hold the Apex Heavyweight title as well as many others as a single. Bill authored two books, *Death Falcon Zero vs. The Zombie Slug Lords,* and *M is for Murder.* He has also stared in five independent films with the most famous being *Johnny Boy*. Bill is one of my closest friends and without him this book would not be possible.

Professor Danger, Danny Boyd, and The DFZ headlined September to Dismember against the Apex tag team champions Mr. Black and Scufflin' Hillbilly. Where they won the tag team titles in a hardcore wrestling match. Also on the card was Midnight Express vs. Ricky Landell and Bret Taylor, Xciris and Jason Kincaid challenging Kirby Mack for the Light Weight title. Flex had a tremendous contest with Converse for the World's title, and the night showed Gagne that I was capable of big business.

Everything was going perfectly as planned into the year 2007. I just could not get released from parole. They would not loosen their grip. It was starting to take its toll on me. I was grouchy and short with people. Kate was starting to wonder if the wrestling was worth it. It wasn't losing money, it just wasn't making any. We seemed to break even each month. She felt that she was paying out too much, but after all her commercials aired every week. She had asked me to live with her and expected me to pay some of the bills. I should have, but when we stated this whole thing she knew the long road that laid a head. Our relationship started to get strained. The business always seemed to kill off a good love life. The rest of the boys too felt slack from their home lives, as their wives began to complain too.

At one point, the entire company agreed to turn the other way as I wrestled one match in Sabine, WV in full body suit as the Executioner against Flex. I could have gone to jail, but I needed to get out there and work. No one saw me in the locker room. I got dressed in a separate dressing room. The boys didn't even watch the match, that way if any of them were asked they could say they had not seen it. It was a way for everyone to tell me to lighten up. I just felt that all my hard work and Oak Hill was taking it all away from me again. I was so tired of history repeating itself again and again. I had wised up, but I was still trapped in the treadmill.

Flex defeated the Executioner. Allen Lynch and I split for good. I received a heating bill for two thousand dollars. The whole block was being heated from the control in my studio. I had no idea. The landlord had broken up a larger building into smaller pieces and the heat was controlled by my building. I decided it was time to settle this ride down. I closed the studio and went off air.

In the months that followed I promoted sparse shows. Just enough to keep my ties with the A.W.A. Most of my guys went to work for Leonard Simms who had resurfaced and gained TV one month after I began mine. Although he was never competition to me. He was third rate in a two horse race. Now, he had my talent and I needed to move on. I struggled again. Just sitting around doing nothing. I tried working at the tattoo shop, but it just was not my thing. I even tried working in the bar business. I knew one thing, and that is pro wrestling. For fifteen years that's all I had ever known.

In September of 2007 my parole ran out. They could no longer hold me back. I had done every second of every minute on that sentence. Just as the woman had said. So, in return I proclaim justice was served. I booked myself a flight, and the first day I was free I went to Hawaii to wrestle. I got off parole at midnight and at six thirty a.m. I boarded a plane to Honolulu, HI. On September 15, 2007, I wrestled again, with no strings attached. Not a bad way to return.

I traveled to several A.W.A. territories to work, first to Connecticut for World Star Wrestling, where I won the company title after two appearances on September 22, 2007. Next I went to Milwaukee, WI. The A.W.A. had been a smart move. They were waiting, as was I, for me to return to wrestle. All of a sudden, I was flying from major city to major city to wrestle. I had a career. I found out one special thing. While I was persecuted in West Virginia, in other states I was a legend. I was the guy who hit a fan. You Tube and the internet had made me a household name. I quickly incorporated the stick of "beating women" in to the act. Combined with the full sleeves of tattoos, I now sported; I was a new marketable commodity in the wrestling business. What's old is new.

There was one major reason for my success at this time. During the months just prior to being released, while I was in the bar business I met the love of my life. My wife, Ashley. We had known each other since high school, but never really talked. She knew me as Brian, not as the wrestler. She did know what business I was in, and watched my TV show. She was a lost soul too. We began spending time with each other. She believed in me. She allowed me to be me. She supported my dreams, hopes, and understood my defeats. She truly loves me. I prayed, as she did, for a partner. She is my best friend, and biggest supporter. I love her with all I have in me. She understands I have to be gone several days every month, and also the money involved. All she wants is to be apart of my life. I can do no wrong in her eyes, even though I do plenty wrong. She stands by my side. I attribute my ultimate success to her support. I am free and clear to do business the way I want without her saying one bad thing about it. Her parents, Brenda and Steve, are behind me as well, and are family and friends. With that, I have achieved happiness, security, and accomplished my highest dreams in life. Ashley you are my wife, my friend, my soul mate. I could not live without you. I love you!

I was confident and ready to make my return to wrestling in West Virginia, but I had to do it big. I rented the Fayetteville Memorial Building in Fayetteville, WV on September 17th, 2007, and promoted Thanksgiving Thunder '07. I had put on the posters Brian Logan returns to wrestle first time in five years, will he be arrested? I also booked Jim Cornette and Baby Doll to draw attention. I used radio ads and a marketing team to get the word out.

My opponent would be none other than the undefeated A.W.A. Phenom and Apex Champion Mr. Black. Jim Cornette would be at ringside in his corner, and Baby Doll was my manager. I defeated Mr. Black and took the coveted title from him ending his streak. Big Phil's job was complete. He had done as I asked. He carried the torch, and then passed it back to me.

As soon as the word got out around the south, old friends came calling. Beau James and Tony Givens were now in charge in Tennessee. Tony was running Championship Wrestling and allowing Beau to cling on to his heels with S.S.W. I was brought back in as a mystery man under a hood. I was billed as the Disciple, but with the new tights, different build, and tattoos no one knew who I was. Eventually I was unmasked and started a huge feud with Tony Givens that would ignite the entire state of Tennessee. In the months that followed I would become the top draw and most hated wrestler in East Tennessee.

Tony Givens has the best wrestling mind in independent wrestling. He remembered all I had done to help him as he was breaking in. Some things I don't even remember. He has made me a part of his family. He is a tremendous performer on the lines of the best of any I have ever fought. With his real life brother Ricky, who works as Chris Richards, I feel we are as close as blood brothers. I would take a bullet for Tony and Ricky (Joan Fonda too), and walk though the fires of hell to help them. With Tony all hopped up and hyper sometimes it's like walking though hell, but it is all worth it.

Ricky is my road partner. He, Joan and June Fonda, and I have rambled though many a state in a state that should have not been rambled in. Ricky who is six foot six and three hundred and fifteen pounds is the exact opposite of Tony in so many ways. He is C.W.A.'s chief instigator, checker, and beer taster. He hopes to out drink the legendary stories of Andre the Giant, even though I hold the Tri Cities Beer Drinking Championship with a win at Dave Robert's house over him. I have never traveled with a more fun person. We will be friends until the day we die, and the other one whores out himself to do a benefit show for the other one.

Robbie Cassidy, on the other hand, is the biggest prick I have ever met. I'm just kidding, but he does owe me money. Robbie is the essential wrestler of the

C.W.A. He has been the backbone and the go to guy in the company. He is main event the entire way. He is flashy, charismatic, and entertaining. Somebody really showed this kid how to wrestle. He is top notch in my book. This is my book, so I give him the Brian Logan seal of approval in the main event spot.

Rob Knight is the ref/commissioner, and doubles as the best wing man in the business. His generosity astounds me. He has taken his friends on trips to the Bahamas and even bought them cars. I don't think I have ever met such an unselfish person in our industry. I am so glad he has allowed me to be his friend.

C.W.A. has lots of great talent. It is by far the best group around. Every week stars like Chase Owens and Ashley Hope, John Hawkins, Nick Hammons, Honkytonk Matt, Cole Layton King, Cody Ices, Alyx Winters, and Bryan Wayne captivate audiences and draw real money to the East Tennessee towns. Wayne Atkins can also been seen flying through the air, or in some rat's car at the shows each night. Keith Knox might be with him, or might not, you can never tell. Bottom line is that I would put these guys up against T.N.A. and Ring of Honor any night. If I had the marketing for them, as Vince does, I put up against the W.W.E. also. No matter what arena, which area, or state of the industry everyone on the roster at Championship Wrestling is a true pro in every sense.

I defeated Chris Thorn on April 4th 2008, to become the C.W.A. TV champion. I was now holding three belts at once. I was WSW champion in Connecticut, Apex champion in West Virginia, and TV champion in Tennessee. I was regularly flying to Hawaii to compete, and had done all of this within eight months of restarting my career. I lobbied that I was the hottest heel in the independent wrestling, and I was. Dale Gagne booked a match for me to wrestle for the World's title. It was my first World's title match. To make things sweeter, it was to be held in Fayetteville, WV. Essentially in my own home town.

After sixteen years, the night I had dreamt about was finally here. I found a secluded place on the stage at the Memorial Building where I could get dressed. Just on the other side of the curtain I could hear the fans cheering the match in the ring. I could see the other wrestlers talking and joking around. I laced up my boots real tight. That scared little boy had finally become a man. I put my tights on. I was ready to face Larry Zybisco and Ricky Landell in a three way dance for the American Wrestling Association World's Heavy Weight Championship.

I walked outside for air. I was so nervous. I was the old pro, but you would think that tonight was day one. I was calmed by thoughts of Ashley, the fact that we had just bought our new house and land, and it was already paid in full. In a few short minutes I would not be the same person. Not because of the belt or title, but because I would have reached my goals. I was a success. That was no small feat. I had went though hell. By the grace of God I had survived.

My music played and I went to the ring. My family was in the stands, Ashley and her parents, Brenda and Steve, Kat and Paul. All the boys looked on from behind the curtain and from the balcony. The bell rang and it began. "Oh, God I'm blown up already," I thought. If I was to die tonight, I'm going out champion. I worked the shine with vigorous fire. Then they settled me down for the heat. Finally it was time Zybisco hit me with a stiff reverse kick in the stomach as if to say, "So, you think you're good enough to be World champion." Zybisco sends Landell flying to the floor. I beat him to the corner and went for my super kick, just as I had done thousands of times before. He hesitated and I missed. As he turned back in to me I cradled him as stiff and as hard as I ever had. There was no way he was going to kick out. One, Two, Three! Tears swelled in my eyes. The announcer, one of my students, Sam Ramsey, announced, "Winner and new A.W.A. World's Heavy Weight champion, The Disciple, Brian Logan!" The ref, Monty, handed me the belt. I raised it over my head thanking God in my prayers, and thinking about Dylan. I pointed to Big Phil running the camera on the second level as the belt was being strapped around my waist. All the boys rushed in to congratulate me. Then I was handed the mic.

I told the people "Don't ever stop believing in yourself and your dreams, because they really do come true." I had done it. Sixteen long years and I was now the best wrestler in the entire world. That's the big one! I had a home, a wife, and a wonderful dog named Jasmine. A company I could work for my whole life. Like Clark Griswold at the end of Christmas Vacation, I took a small breath and exhaled relief after the match in the back. I did it.

In the months to come I would regularly defend the title for Mike Howerton's Mountaineer Wrestling Association, part of the A.W.A., as well as in Tennessee and Kentucky. Dale Gagne would later be sued by W.W.E. for trademark infringement, thus making the

World's Title property of Championship Wrestling Alliance in Tennessee. It is still defended there today.

After winning the World's title I proclaimed that I was the only Wrestling World's Champion. There were entertainment champions, action champions, ultimate champions, and traditional champions, but I was the only wrestling champion, the last of dying breed. I challenged Triple H, Kurt Angle, Brock Lesnar, Jeff Hardy, and Blue Demon Jr. to a straight up shoot. I also challenged anyone in the world to a straight shoot. It can be viewed on You tube. No one accepted the challenge. At one point, during my first reign as champion, I had held victories over every world champion there was at that time, at one time or another during my career. In the words of Gino Hernandez and Dr. Tom Pritchard, "I am Your Champion!"

Brian Logan Fun Facts

1. Brian Logan started out with Smoky Mountain Wrestling on December 6th, 1993 in Jefferson, NC

2. Brian Logan has held 21 different championships in Pro Wrestling

1- SMW TV title
2- SSW tag team title
3- Mid South US tag team title
4- MSWA title
5- MDW/ACCW title
6- Appalachia Wrestling Alliance title
7- AWA TV title (Indiana)
8- WV So Regional title
9- OVW So tag team title 5 times
10- PCW Americas title
11- All Star Wrestling US title
12- NWA Bluegrass title
13- NCW tag team title
14- NSW Tenn. title
15- NSW title
16- APW/MSWA title (Oak Hill)
17- AWA WSW title
18- AWA Apex title
19- AWA MWA title
20- CW TV title
21- AWA World's title

3. Brian Logan has wrestled in over 1000 professional wrestling matches all before the age of 35.

4. Brian Logan has wrestled in Puerto Rico, WCW, OVW, and WWE all in the same year.

5. Brian Logan's female fans are known as the Playerettes

6. Brian Logan wrestled Chris Jericho's first match in the US

7. Brian Logan's picture can be found in Chris Jericho's autobiography

8. Brian Logan carries the number 207, from a hotel room door, in his bag every town he wrestles in.

9. Brian Logan's favorite restaurant on the road is Applebee's

10. Brian Logan has only used two songs as ring music in his career Hot Stuff by Donna Summer, and Break Stuff by Limp Bizcuit

COMING SOON FROM BRIAN LOGAN —THE CONGREGATION

A FICTIONAL NOVEL BASED ON THE BOOK OF REVOLATION

Feel Free to email Brian Logan at awatalentcord@hotmail.com
Also check him out on www.facebook.com
Email address for facebook: awatalentcord@yahoo.com
Or each week on www.championshipwrestlingtv.com
Or you can contact him at:
P.O. Box 586
Summersville, WV 26651

Printed in Great Britain
by Amazon